About the Author

Carol Harris is the founder of Management Magic, an independent consultancy based in the UK specialising in the development of people and organisations. She runs in-house and open courses on a wide range of business and personal skills.

Carol is the author of *The Elements of NLP, NLP: New Perspectives* and *Think Yourself Slim* (Element Books), co-author of *How to Be Your Own Management Consultant* (Kogan Page) and has produced the *Success in Mind* series of audiotapes on personal effectiveness.

Carol is Chair of the Association for Neuro-Linguistic Programming and Editor of the Association's magazine *Rapport*. She has a degree in Sociology and is a Fellow of the Institute of Management Consultancy and the Institute of Personnel and Development.

Carol can be contacted at PO Box 47, Welshpool, Powys, SY21 7NX, Wales, UK.

NETWORKING FOR SUCCESS

The NLP Approach to a Key Business and Social Skill

Carol Harris

Oak Tree Press
Dublin

Oak Tree Press
Merrion Building
Lower Merrion Street
Dublin 2, Ireland
http://www.oaktreepress.com

A catalogue record of this book is
available from the British Library.

ISBN 1 86076 161 5

Printed in the Republic of Ireland by Colour Books Ltd.

Contents

Acknowledgements

When I was a child, my parents had what they called "open house" every Friday evening. This meant that anyone they knew, and any friend of anyone they knew, was welcome to drop in for a chat and a cup of tea. The evenings usually went on until the small hours of the morning and you never knew whether there would be two people or twenty; a quiet discussion or a provocative and histrionic display. My father revelled in these sessions, my mother endured them and I generally sat under the stairs, observing at a distance (not that I wasn't encouraged to attend; I simply preferred to be on my own).

Many of the people who came to the Friday evenings formed, and maintained, long-lasting friendships and associations and, 50 years on, they are still remembered with affection.

This was my first introduction to networking and this book is dedicated to the memory of my father who regarded (almost) everyone on the planet as fair game!

Preface

Networking has become a vital skill in today's world. As communities expand, borders become more fluid and the pace of change accelerates, skills that enable people to survive and prosper are increasingly valued and sought after.

I will explain the term "networking" in some detail later in the book but, put simply, it encompasses all those skills and processes that assist and support interactions between people. People often like to give labels to concepts and ideas; these labels help to categorise and explain. However, labelling can often limit one's understanding and responses. The label "networking" might imply that it is a discrete set of techniques, applicable in a limited range of situations, but I believe that the skills of networking can be found in all social situations and that most people possess networking skills already.

This book is designed to give you an understanding of what networking is, explain its techniques and approaches, and show how you can transfer networking skills from normal, everyday situations, to particular contexts in both your business and social life.

I hope that the book will provide you with ideas to enhance your own networking skills and that, in turn, you may wish to pass on some of these skills to others. One thing is certain: used effectively, networking can widen your social circle, improve your information base, give you access to valuable business contacts and raise your own image and profile.

I wish you every success in applying the principles and practices contained in the book.

Introduction

When we look back at history, each decade can be remembered, in part, by particular events or activities that mark it out. The 1990s may well be recalled as the decade of networking.

You may have heard the word "networking" and thought it was either simply a popular buzzword or a term used by technical buffs to describe linking up with others through the use of telephone lines and computers. The reality, however, is that networking offers powerful ways of using relationships to enhance your success.

Many people use formalised organisational processes to achieve results, but networking adds another dimension — the personal one. It can enable you to cross apparent boundaries and barriers, and can help you create and use personal and professional contacts in ways that work. This book will show you how.

How my own Interest in Networking Developed

You may be familiar with the idea of "team roles" in business. The main principle is that an effective team is made up of individuals possessing various complementary skills and abilities. There are tests for these attributes and when I did one, the Belbin team role test, many years ago, it showed my personal strengths were in the "Shaper" area (pushing things forward and making them happen) and the "Plant" area (having ideas and being creative). I did not score highly on most of the other areas, although I did have a few points in the "Completer-Finisher" role, which accounts for the fact that I do actually get things done. (It also accounts for my fussiness over such things as typing mistakes and poor grammar!)

Ten years later, when I repeated the test, another quality came out quite highly: the "Resource Investigator". This is the networking role — a person who is good at making contacts with others and exploring opportunities. So, over the years, I had developed skills in networking. Not surprising, as this period coincided with me setting up and running my own business — a time when I had to make the most of contacts and opportunities or I would not have survived financially. This was all reflected in my new test scores.

So, I know that networking can be learned and used to good effect. I hope this book will enable you to benefit from other people's experience so that you can apply new insights and techniques to your own activities, becoming more successful and getting the results you want.

A Brief Definition of Networking

It may be useful to have a working definition of networking. I will be going into more detail about what is involved in networking in later chapters but, for now, I would like to suggest the following as a guide:

> *"The creation, development and use of personal contacts*
> *for mutual benefit or for the benefit of others."*

Networking can involve promoting, maintaining and optimising interactions between people and also involves both parties benefiting from the interchange — networking can help everybody enhance their success. If you adopt this definition, it presupposes that you have some responsibility for the creation of networking opportunities and that, as you do so, you consider both your own needs and those of the people with whom you come into contact.

The Concepts Used in this Book

The book uses two concepts which may be familiar to some readers, but are possibly new to others; these are Neuro-Linguistic Programming (NLP) and Accelerated Learning (AL). Both these fields of study are used increasingly as ways of enhancing learning, performance and personal wellbeing, and I would like to explain them, briefly, here. If you wish to pursue either of these topics further, you will find useful references in the Bibliography.

Neuro-Linguistic Programming

NLP as a discipline was founded in the early 1970s and incorporated ideas, some of them centuries old, from many fields of study. The birthplace of NLP was California. The term NLP covers three elements: *Neuro* (how we use our minds), *Linguistic* (how we communicate our experience of the world) and *Programming* (the patterns we follow in our everyday life).

NLP's developers (originally Richard Bandler, John Grinder, Leslie Cameron Bandler, Judith DeLozier, Robert Dilts and David Gordon) became fascinated by how people function and especially by how effective people achieve their results. Bandler and Grinder, in particular, studied some notable people of their time and found it was possible to elicit patterns in their behaviour, their language and their thoughts and feelings, patterns that could be replicated by others to obtain similar results.

This process of pattern replication, often referred to as modelling, is the foundation of NLP and is what enables people to enhance their skills by copying what excellent performers do. NLP is now used widely in business, education, health, personal development and many other fields. Some of NLP's business applications include sales, negotiating, presenting, teambuilding, customer care and time management. Later in the book, I will be suggesting ways in which you can use the role-modelling process to help you copy the skills of excellent networkers.

As well as pattern replication, NLP offers ways of helping people to change unrewarding patterns into rewarding ones. For example, changing negative thinking into positive; changing unresourceful states into resourceful ones; changing limiting beliefs into empowering ones; and changing unproductive behaviour into success achievement. I will be showing you how this works and how it can help your networking in the chapters that follow.

Accelerated Learning

Accelerated Learning owed much of its development to the concept of "Suggestopaedia", a language teaching method developed by a Bulgarian doctor and psychiatrist, Georgi Lozanov, in the 1960s. The principles of Accelerated Learning overlap with NLP and it focuses particularly on matching teaching and training to people's individual learning processes.

Accelerated Learning identifies a number of major patterns which affect how people learn and shows how development can be drastically improved through using these patterns as a basis for personal enhancement. Seven patterns were identified by Dr Howard Gardner, a Harvard researcher who based some of his work on identifiable differences in brain functioning. Since his original work, Gardner has added a further category, and a possible second one, to the initial seven. I will be covering the initial seven AL patterns in this book.

Using NLP and AL techniques will help you develop your skills rapidly and effectively. There are some short sets of questions in Chapter Three to help you identify your own motivational and learning patterns. Once you have completed this process, you will be better able to understand how the use of these patterns will enhance your success at networking.

The Applications of NLP and AL to Networking

I will not be constantly drawing attention to the particular techniques used, but it is important to know that NLP and AL (and particularly NLP) provide the underpinning framework for most of the ideas in the book.

NLP is particularly relevant to networking, as it concentrates on helping people to function effectively and interact with others in positive and beneficial ways, in both their personal and their business lives. It is largely the skills areas of networking that can benefit most from this application and I have included a variety of activities and exercises to help you enhance your skills.

The Specific Elements of Effective Networking

There are many ways of analysing what goes on in effective performance and, in this book, I have adopted the NLP model developed by David Gordon and Graham Dawes, which they have called "The Experiential Array". This approach to effectiveness is one which has been shown to have very practical benefits. It involves five separate elements, which are represented in the diagram below.

The Experiential Array

The elements of the Experiential Array model can be outlined as follows:

Good Objectives

To achieve a result it is important to set yourself good objectives. It is easy to think that a rough idea of what you want is sufficient but, once you use effective objective setting, you will find it helps enormously in achieving results.

A number of elements are involved in objective setting, some of which may be familiar to you and some less familiar. There is already a commonly used business model for objective setting (called the SMART model) and the procedures I present in this book use the elements of SMART, plus various additional ones. I will be covering objectives in some detail in Chapter Four.

Appropriate Behaviour

Having a good objective is important but, in order to achieve it, you need to be able to take suitable action. This means having behavioural skills which are appropriate to your goals. Much of this book is about developing skills you can use in networking.

A Positive Mental Attitude

This is very important. Over the years, much has been written about positive mental attitude (PMA) and it is often thought of as an "entity", as if you could have a pound of positive thinking. Positive thinking is not an entity, however; it is a collection of processes that can result in a positive frame of mind. These processes comprise identifiable component parts and, as they vary from person to person, it helps if you can identify your own processes and find out how to make them really work for you. In Chapter Five, I will be explaining how to create and maintain a positive approach to what you do.

Appropriate Emotional States

Emotional states, or feelings, are a basic foundation of effectiveness. Being able to choose how you feel and create supportive feelings for your actions is a real skill. For example, enthusiasm and energy are vital in many situations and in networking it really helps to maintain a good emotional state. I will be returning to this too in Chapter Five.

Supportive Beliefs and Values

This is another major factor, and one which often separates really successful people from those who simply want to be successful, but don't yet know how. Believing in yourself, believing others will be interested in what you have to offer and valuing your own efforts are vital elements underpinning success. Again, I will be considering this later in the book.

These are the elements of effective performance: having a good objective, using appropriate behaviour, having a positive mental attitude, maintaining suitable emotional states and having supportive beliefs and values. The diagram on page 5 shows the relationships between each of these elements and the thickness of the arrows indicate the most commonly found strength of movement between the elements. So, for example, our beliefs have more impact on our thoughts and emotions than our thoughts and emotions have on our beliefs and values. Of course, there can always be exceptions to this, but in general the elements to the left of the diagram are more powerful than the elements to the right.

In addition to these elements, there are various processes involved in networking and I would like to outline these here; the rest of the book will then explore these processes in more depth.

Networking Steps

There are various steps which will help you become an effective networker. I have listed 11 steps here and you may well think of others yourself, according to your particular circumstances. I will be taking you through each of these steps and suggesting ways of working with them which suit your own personal style. You may not follow this exact sequence of steps in everything you do, and you could find some steps being repeated in loops as you try things out and then go back to the drawing board. It is, however, important to consider each of the steps, so that your approach to networking is systematic and thorough.

1. Having a Purpose

This means knowing what your overall aim, mission, vision or direction is before you start. Some people have very clear "life goals", while others function more on a day-to-day basis; whatever applies to you, you are likely to be more successful if you take time to consider your overall purpose in networking.

2. Developing a Strategy

Thinking strategically will help you put your networking into a broader context. Working out strategic plans for your total range of activities, and your networking in particular, will give you the edge when it comes to success.

3. Setting Detailed Objectives and Targets

Being able to describe in detail what you want to achieve is vital. For example, do you wish to be better at initiating conversations, do you wish to improve your image, do you wish to be better at writing interesting copy for publicity material? Each of these specific objectives could form part of your overall purpose.

4. Working out Tactics

Once you have your objectives, you can begin to build a tactical framework for achieving them. This means having plans for exactly how you will translate your objectives into reality.

5. Researching

Getting information is an important link in the networking chain. For example, finding out about people you will be meeting, checking what knowledge your contacts may have about particular subjects and ascertaining details of events, times and venues. All this information is important as a foundation for your activities.

6. Planning

To be successful at networking, it is important to plan. Having a diary of what you will be doing, and when, helps focus your mind, makes it easier for other people to co-operate and is likely to ensure you take action. Not having a plan can lead to *ad hoc* activities, which may be successful, but could lack a co-ordinated drive and purpose.

7. Organising

Getting yourself organised is another important element. It is so easy to put information on scraps of paper and mislay them; it is so easy to intend to create a filing system for your information, but never set it up. Having good administrative systems and procedures will help your efficiency and make it easier to access important information when you need it.

8. Preparing

Preparation for networking is another important step. Having planned and organised, preparing for the actual activities is helpful. There are many things you can prepare, including yourself. The better your preparation, the more successful you are likely to be.

9. Doing

It is also important to actually *do* what you set out to. Some people get so involved in goal setting, planning and organising that they leave themselves no time for taking action. So make sure you set aside time for the activity of networking and then actually carry it through.

10. Monitoring

This is a real aid to success. Keeping track of your activities helps your future planning and can keep your motivation going.

11. Evaluating

This is somewhat different from monitoring and consists of assessing just how effective your activities really are.

So there are a range of processes to help you network effectively. You may not necessarily do them all in sequence, but thinking about them will assist your efforts. I will be examining each of these processes in the chapters that follow.

And finally, before getting into the detail of networking, I would like to introduce you, briefly, to the skills involved in networking; again, these skills form the basis for several of the chapters that follow.

The Skills of Networking

I have divided networking skills as follows:

- Self-management

- Impression management

- Face-to-face communications, including

    ◆ Speech and language

    ◆ Conversation

    ◆ Rapport, influence and assertiveness

    ◆ Non-verbal communications

- Distance networking.

All the skills are interrelated and contribute to effectiveness. Self-management is important because being able to control your own thoughts, feelings and actions will help you deal more effectively with others. Impression management is how you manage your image in the eyes of other people. Face-to-face communication skills are vital as, without them, networking would not be possible. And distance communications allow you to network when circumstances prevent you meeting face-to-face, or when it is more effective to do your networking without actually meeting directly.

Each of these aspects has its own chapter and, as you read on, you will find explanations of each topic, ideas on improvement, tests and practical exercises and activities to help you develop. It helps to read the chapters in sequence, but it is possible to skip forward or back if there are particular topics that interest you.

Remember, you almost certainly already possess many of the skills required to be a successful networker. Many of the skills are just day-to-day living skills and, as you go through the book, I hope you will see parallels between the current patterns of your life and those additional elements that could improve your performance even further. Skills development is a lifelong process and I believe that, by following the principles I outline, you will be able to enhance your own success as a networker and also help others in their quest for achievement.

Chapter One

What is Networking and How Can it Benefit You?

What is Networking?

Examples

Let's begin with a story of two people — Jeremy and Janice. As you read the story, perhaps you may wonder which of the two is most like you . . .

Jeremy enjoyed school, but felt happiest when he was able to concentrate on his favourite subjects, science and technology. He didn't really want to spend time on activities such as the school play, the debating society or team sports. Although he was friendly enough with other pupils, he never socialised with them outside school, preferring to spend his time on study or building working models, which fascinated him.

Jeremy was an only child and his parents spent as much time as they could with him. They often went out for day-trips as a family, but seldom invited other people over for meals, gave parties or socialised with others.

Jeremy went on to university and studied engineering. He was still a bit of a loner and spent much of his time on his course work, not really wanting to join clubs or societies, or spend much time out with other students. He did well in his finals and was successful in his application to join a large manufacturing company. The company was located in a different part of the country to his parents' home, so Jeremy moved into a small flat, on his own, to be close to his work.

Jeremy stayed with his company for ten years and still lived alone, as his work was the most important thing in his life and he had never made many friends or formed a long-term relationship with a special person. Then a recession in Jeremy's business sector made it necessary for his company to make a number of staff redundant and Jeremy's job was one which was affected. Because of the specialised nature of his work, it would not be easy for Jeremy to find another job. He responded to advertisements, with little success.

Jeremy began to feel despondent and found he had nobody close to confide in; his parents were a long way away and he had no real friends to talk to. He didn't know what else to do to find a new job and began to feel rather lonely and unsupported. He felt there must be more he could do, but didn't know where to start . . .

Janice had an older brother and sister, whose schoolfriends were always visiting them and talking about a wide range of activities and interests. Janice, like Jeremy, enjoyed school but, as well as putting in time on her studies, she made many friends and participated in various non-academic activities. She joined the netball team and took part in matches with other schools, where she met new people and saw how things were done in other places. She also helped raise money for a local charity for people with disabilities; this gave Janice the opportunity to meet people who were professionally involved in this field and also to find out about how those with disabilities lived, and what difficulties they encountered in their daily activities. Through these activities, Janice made friends outside her school environment and kept in touch with many of the people subsequently.

After leaving school, Janice did a course in business studies. The course involved trips to local organisations and projects researching how local firms ran their businesses. Janice spent a good deal of time talking to people in different fields of activity and found this both useful and stimulating. Again, she made many friends, several of whom remained in contact after her projects had finished.

When she had completed her course, Janice decided she would like to go into journalism and she began a junior job with her local newspaper. Her work with the charity for the disabled and with the local business projects helped at her interview, demonstrating her wide range of interests and experience. Janice did well at her job and was popular with her colleagues, as she was always interested in what they were doing and willing to offer help and encouragement if they needed it.

After a couple of years, two sections of Janice's paper merged and her job was no longer needed. Janice still wished to stay in journalism and as she had built up a wide circle of acquaintances, she asked around to see whether anyone she knew had contacts on other papers. One of the people with whom she had worked on the school fundraising project, and with whom she had kept in touch, knew the assistant editor on a national magazine, covering a specialist area which was one of Janice's main interests. The paper had just advertised a job which would be just right for Janice's next career step. Janice replied to the advertisement, was interviewed and, through her interest in the subject area and her past experience, including her skills at making contacts and working well with others, was successful at getting the job. One of her first jobs was to write a feature article on the charity, so helping others at the same time as she was enhancing her own career . . .

Jeremy and Janice are both intelligent, capable people, with much to offer, but their lifestyles and experience have equipped them very differently. Jeremy relies on himself and keeps apart from others, while Janice makes friends and keeps relationships going. When the need is there, Janice is likely to be better equipped to use her social contacts in a beneficial way. This is what networking is about — making contacts, developing relationships and being able to help yourself, and others, through such activity. The ideas and activities in this book are designed to enhance your own skills in this area.

How Can Networking Be Defined?

In the introduction, I offered the following definition of networking: "The creation, development and use of personal contacts for mutual benefit, or for the benefit of others." This means that networking is a process which can help you, and others, to make the most of relationships to enhance your personal or professional achievement.

This broad definition implies that networking can take place in any context: whether at work, during leisure time or in other circumstances, you can use contacts with other people to help yourself, and them, become more successful.

Some examples of networking in action are:

- Attending a meeting to discuss a work issue with people in the same line of business as yourself;

- Using e-mail to exchange information on products or services;

- Telephoning acquaintances to find out if anyone knows of a job vacancy which could be suitable for a friend of yours.

There are many more situations in which networking can be used, which I will be discussing in later chapters.

The reference in my definition to mutual benefit is important, as it demonstrates that there can be a two-way flow of advantages from networking. When you use personal contacts effectively, everyone involved can gain in some way, so I would encourage you to think of networking as an activity which can help both you and others.

If you lived alone on a desert island, networking skills would probably not be a major priority. Most of us, however, live in established communities, with family and social acquaintances, and engage in a wide range of activities including work, travel, hobbies, education and community development. This means our social frameworks are often complex and culturally diverse. Depending on where you live, you will find a variety of expectations, norms, values, attitudes and behaviours which impact on your life. Being able to function effectively within your own social framework is important, as it enables you to get on with others and work harmoniously.

So the variety of personal contacts you make acts as the foundation for networking and you could say you are networking any time you interact with others, although you may not have used that particular term yourself for everyday contacts. What makes networking different from other social or business relationships is its focus on using interaction with others for enhancing success.

How Does Change Increase the Need for Networking?

The pace of change in the world seems to increase constantly. For centuries, progress was slow. Agricultural societies had the same way of life for generations. Communities were small and self-contained. Transport limitations meant that, for most people, their movement was restricted to their immediate geographical area and their contacts were limited to their small circle of family and acquaintances. Some societies still survive in this way, although their way of life is rapidly disappearing.

As technology developed, society changed. Production methods made consumerism possible, transport made distant places more accessible, communications media telescoped distances, developments in teaching made education more widely available, increased affluence led to more leisure time and more contact between people, the world of work became more varied and the rate of job change increased. Many more examples could be given of how social and technological changes have impinged on everyone's everyday life.

Not only are interpersonal skills vital, they are becoming more and more important as geographical boundaries become flexible, trade expands and knowledge increases. People are *the* essential element in today's business world. In past times, bricks and mortar, machinery, equipment and money were the major resources; nowadays we increasingly come across terms such as knowledge management, intellectual capital and relationship management. This means that, whereas in the past we could get by with technical knowledge and process management, today we need to utilise and interact with people if our businesses are going to be competitive and thrive. Today, development depends on the effective interchange of ideas, practices and skills.

Networking in our internationally mobile society has become not just a social process, but a vital business tool. Without networking, our activities would undoubtedly be less productive and our results not so good.

Who Can Use Networking?

Networking is for everyone. It doesn't matter how old you are, what sort of education you have, what job you do, or where you are in an organisational hierarchy, you will be able to find ways in which networking can contribute to your success and to the success of others.

Nowadays, with the advent of electronic means of communication, even young children are able to communicate with people in distant places and with different backgrounds and skills. Youngsters seem to find this process quite natural, as they have been brought up in a world where it is commonplace. This kind of communication process is, however, only one way of relating to others and, in this book, I will be presenting a range of ways in which you can make personal contacts work for you.

Even if, in the past, you have not thought of yourself as very socially adventurous, you will find ideas and techniques which you can use to enhance your relationships with others and develop your professional activities.

What is a Network?

Networks exist in many forms. We speak of neural networks (networks of nerve cells in the body), transport networks (the pattern of roads, railways, water channels, airlanes and so on), computer networks (the Internet, company "intranets") and so forth. In this book, I am using the word "network" to describe people's links with each other. For example, you may have a network of friends, a school may have a network of past students, a professional institute may have a network of members, a consultant may have a network of clients and a manufacturer may have a network of dealers. It is possible to represent a network graphically, showing the links between its constituent members, a process which I will be describing in the next chapter.

Some of the networks described above just "happen"; for example, you probably did not select most of your friends deliberately, you most likely met many of them in an unplanned way. Other networks are more organised; for example, the dealership networks. So a network can be planned or unplanned, depending on circumstances.

The structure of a network can vary, depending on its purposes. For example, in a "network marketing" organisation (one which has distributors working on a self-employed basis, selling direct to the consumer) there can be different levels of people ("ground floor" sales people, team leaders, sales managers and so on) — different levels of hierarchy all forming part of the same overall structure.

The actual "shape" of a network can also vary. Some may be fairly evenly spread and others more "weighted", for example with more people at the centre and less at the periphery, or more in one section and less in another, or with some people in the network having many connections with others and other people having fewer connections. The following diagrams show some typical network "shapes".

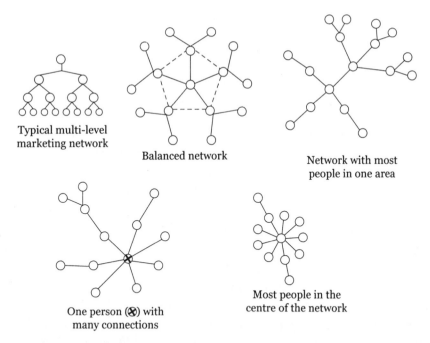

Typical multi-level
marketing network

Balanced network

Network with most
people in one area

One person (⊗) with
many connections

Most people in the
centre of the network

Finally, there can be differences between networks and organisations, or they can overlap. So, an organisation generally has specified "lines of command", where people report to others or, sometimes, work in a more flexible way, reporting to different people for different purposes or projects. An organisation also tends to have policies and procedures and people are all working to a common goal. With networks, there is generally a more fluid way of operating, so that people can interact with whatever part of the network they choose, in whichever way they choose and when they choose. There may be some "roles" if the network is more structured; for example, an administrator or a committee but, in general, networks operate more flexibly and serve the needs of their members individually, rather than serving one corporate end.

How Can You Benefit from Networking?

Networking can bring you many advantages, some of which may be obvious and others perhaps less immediately apparent. Let's look at some contexts in which you can network.

Personal and Social Applications

In your personal and social life you can use networking for many purposes. You can use it to make friends when you move to a new neighbourhood or to find good shops and leisure facilities. You can use networking for educational purposes: finding schools for your children or locating evening classes for yourself. You can use it for health purposes: tracking down a good doctor or dentist or finding a complementary medicine practitioner. You can also use it for locating professional services, such as accountancy or plumbing. You can use networking to collect information on topics which interest you, perhaps a hobby, a sport or a lifestyle issue. All these, and many other examples, are likely to be outside the world of work.

Example

Susan wanted to have a new kitchen in her house. She knew some neighbours had done the same recently, and asked which supplier they had used. They put her in touch with a local firm of kitchen suppliers, which Susan decided to use. In addition, when Susan wanted to see an item of kitchen equipment in operation before making a purchase, the kitchen suppliers gave her the phone number of another local person for whom they had installed a similar item. Susan visited this person, saw the equipment, made her decision and also found that she and this person had some mutual friends. Chatting for a while, Susan found the person was able to put her in touch with a different acquaintance, who could give her information on another product she was trying to locate. The initial enquiry to the neighbour had resulted in finding a kitchen supplier, making a new friend, and tracking down some rather hard-to-find information.

Business Applications

Within work, you can also use networking to good effect. Networking can be used to find a job, to build an effective team, to learn new business techniques, to generate finance, to source new markets and to develop internationally. You can use networking to build business contacts and to promote your business activities. You can use networking to gain greater access to information and ideas, which can help your business grow. You can use networking to find out what competitors are doing and you can use networking to identify areas for future growth. In the US in particular, women's networks are an established feature. ("Currently at least 33 per cent of Fortune 100 companies have women's networks" — Sheila Wellington, *Creating Women's Networks*.) General business networking, where people work together for mutual interests, is often called "Learning or Developmental Alliances" (see *Transformational Mentoring* by Hay).

Example

Martin was a consultant who carried out a project for a small transport organisation. The personnel officer who commissioned the work changed jobs a few months later and Martin kept in touch through sending Christmas cards and by making occasional phone calls when he had items of information which he thought would be of interest. A couple of years later, the personnel officer found that his new organisation was in need of help. He thought of Martin and called him to see if he could assist. Martin was delighted to do so and was pleased that his ongoing contact had borne fruit.

Information Handling

Networking can save you having to collect and store large amounts of information, or very specialised information, yourself; instead, you can identify others who possess this information and draw upon their expertise when it is needed.

Example

Trudy needed to write a health and safety policy for her employer. She telephoned other people she had worked with in the past to find out what they knew about the subject. One gave her contact details of a government agency which dealt with the subject; a second was able to send her examples of policies written for other companies; a third sent her a reading list on the subject. Trudy saved a good deal of time through accessing her personal network of contacts.

Social Contact and Support

Networking can also help if you are involved in an area of work which does not provide an immediately accessible social group to back you up; for example, if you are an independent contractor, work in a remote geographical area or work unsocial hours with few social contacts. In such cases, networking can save you feeling isolated and provide the kind of social interaction and support which people in more traditional communities, or in more conventional work environments, take for granted.

Example

David had moved to a small island for a three-year environmental project; he loved the work, but there was nobody in the immediate community who shared his interest in astronomy. Through the Internet, he was able to exchange ideas and information with people with similar interests and could plan to meet up with some of these people once his contract had ended. After the contract, David actually set up a small independent business with one of the people he had met in this way and ran a very successful company exporting specialist equipment to all parts of the world.

Skills Development

Networking can also help you develop a wide range of skills. For example, if you regularly attend meetings with others, you are likely to learn about handling conversations and dealing with differences of opinion. If you use the Internet to communicate, you are likely to enhance your computing skills. There are many ways in which interacting with others through networking can help you advance your social and professional skills — this process is often called generative learning, where learning becomes a continuous process of increasing development, rather than a one-off experience.

Example

Sylvia felt her public speaking skills were poor. She was persuaded to join a small society, which met monthly with the purpose of helping its members gain experience in this area. Although initially somewhat apprehensive and reluctant, Sylvia took her turn at addressing the group at informal meetings and soon found her confidence improved and her skill level soared.

Are There Any Drawbacks to Networking?

It is hard to think of negative aspects to networking, although there are a few issues of which you should be aware.

Time

Effective networking may have some time implications. For example, keeping in touch with people so they remember you can be time-consuming. If your time is costly, you may need to work out the cost/benefit implications of spending it in this way (and also the implications of *not* spending it this way, as missed opportunities can be costly too).

Availability

If you are an effective networker, it is likely that people will gravitate towards you when they want something done or need another contact themselves. Again, this has implications in terms of time and effort which you may need to consider.

Administration

It helps to keep records of contacts and plan for future activity; this will necessitate administration and possibly additional storage space.

Health

Some people combine networking with "social" activities such as eating or drinking; it helps to be in control of this so you don't find yourself putting on weight or getting other health problems due to over-indulgence.

Personal Inclinations

Your own personality and temperament is likely to influence your attitudes towards networking and the extent to which you use it. If, like Jeremy in the example at the start of this chapter, you are in-clined to prefer your own company and shy away from contact with others, you may find it challenging to network in some of the ways suggested in this book. If this is the case, you will need to decide whether you can rise to the challenge, or whether you would prefer to stay as you are, even though you might miss some wonderful oppor-tunities in the process.

What are the Implications of Not Networking?

I think it is probably impossible not to network at all, so what I am raising here are the implications of not networking proactively; in other words, not making a conscious decision to network.

Firstly, if you do not use networking in a purposeful manner, you may limit your knowledge base and, because knowledge is an increasingly valued commodity, this means you can fall behind in your general awareness and, thereby, in your value to current or potential employers. Secondly, you may fail to generate opportunities, which means you can miss out on many things such as acquiring products, finding jobs, locating services and so on. Thirdly, you may restrict your sources of connection and support, which could result in fewer friends and less back-up in times of need. Fourthly, you may be perceived as out-of-touch or lacking in social skills, which can mean you are overlooked, avoided or excluded from events and activities.

So the implications of not networking can have an impact on you and, depending on how important the above factors are to you, could result in your chances of success in your chosen fields of endeavour being limited.

Chapter Two

Identifying, Managing and Building Your Network

Identifying Your Network

So far I have explained the definitions and benefits of networking; now let's move on to how you can identify what your own personal network is and ways in which you can develop it.

Describe your Network

Firstly, let's think about what your network is. Everyone has a network of some kind. Unless you live on a desert island, alone, you interact with other people and everyone you interact with *could* be classed as part of your network.

In practice, things don't quite work out that way, because there are many people you meet who would be inappropriate to consider as members of your network. For example, if you go on a bus journey, you may talk to the conductor or ticket collector as you are travelling, but you would probably never have occasion to meet that person again and you would probably do no more than exchange a few brief words with him or her at the time.

But what about a taxi driver on a half-hour journey? In this case, you might well have a long discussion and find topics of mutual interest; you might even exchange contact details, or one of you might pass on details of the other to a third person. In this case, the taxi driver would probably become part of your personal network.

So your network consists of those people with whom you come into contact and where there is an advantage for one or both of you in maintaining the relationship. So who could be included in your network? Have a look at the following list and see how many of the entries describe relationships you have, or have had in the past:

- Family

- Friends

- Neighbours

- School, college or university colleagues

- Holiday acquaintances

- Work colleagues

- Children's friends, family and teachers

- Trade or professional services (doctors, gardeners, opticians, librarians, builders, solicitors, shop assistants, hairdressers, etc.)

- Professional acquaintances (members of trade associations or institutes)

- Club members (sports, music, travel, social, etc.).

There may well be other groups of people that you could add to your own list. Members of all these groups can be included in your personal network; once you have identified the categories, you can list all the people you know in each of them.

Sometimes these contact spheres overlap, so you may develop friendships with people you work with or who provide a service for you; or you may embark on a business venture with a member of your family or a neighbour; and so on.

Represent your Network in Pictorial Form

To work out who falls into your own network, you can either list categories and then write in the names of all the people who you know who fall into each category, or you can draw your network diagrammatically, with circles representing each category and dotted lines showing links between them and then write the names of your contact in the spaces.

Here is an example of a network diagram, partially completed. When you draw your own network diagram, you will add the names of all your contacts in each section.

Personal Network Diagram

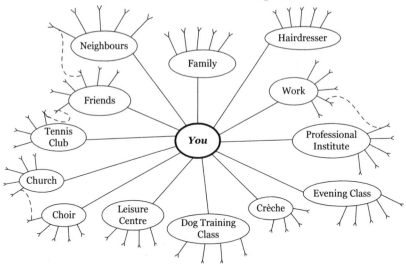

Now you have your current "immediate network". However, your network actually goes far beyond this, as everyone you know, knows others. It has been estimated that there is nobody in the world who is more than five or six steps away from you; in other words, you will know someone, who knows someone . . . who knows them.

You can also put in some dotted lines between people or groupings in your diagram. For example, your choir might be connected with the church, which would be a linkage, and some of your friends might also be neighbours, which would be an overlap. It can be useful to put these dotted lines in colour so they are easy to pick out.

Of course, you couldn't put all these indirect contacts onto your own personal network diagram, even if you knew all their names, but it is worth remembering that your network increases exponentially each time you add one name, so that effective adding to your network means considering who might be one, two or more stages beyond your own personal contacts. This means that networking can be regarded rather like a game of chess; if you think ahead a few steps you can deduce the total game plan, rather than just the next move.

Analyse your Network

As you draw your diagram, it is helpful to notice the balance in your network. For example, are your contacts mainly work or business ones, or are they mainly family and social? Are they mainly long-standing relationships or short-term interactions? Are they mainly women or men? Are they mainly people who live close to you or people who live far away? Are they mainly people you interact with frequently or people you deal with on very few occasions? Or are they a combination of all these things?

Remember that, although you may have many names on your network diagram, the people included are only *potential* network members until you interact with them in some way. So, you may know many people at your evening class, but may never actually do more than chat to them briefly. There can, alternatively, be others with whom you have developed mutually beneficial relationships. Because of this, you might consider assigning each person in your network diagram a "rating", regarding their potential usefulness in different contexts. For example, you might use a letter, number, symbol or colour to indicate:

- Their potential for producing further contacts;

- Their willingness to help you in the past;

- Their relevance to your career development;

- Their potential for generating business for you;

- Their skills or knowledge in a particular field; and so on.

Target your Network

Once you have analysed your network into categories such as those I have just described, you will be able to understand your network better and come up with ideas about the extent to which it could be developed in particular directions. You may feel you need more contacts in a particular area, such as a business sector, a geographical area, or a work function. In this case, you can work towards targeting your network so it is more likely to help you achieve the goals you set yourself.

Managing Your Network

You may feel it is sufficient to take part in networking activities but, without proper procedures for managing what you do, you may fail to optimise the efforts you put in. So what goes into network management? I will be considering three elements here; they are:

- Keeping your information up-to-date;

- Keeping in touch with your network;

- Responding to contacts from others.

Keep your Information Up-to-date

It is very easy to collect lots of information about people you meet. You will probably receive business cards, e-mails, publicity flyers and so on. All this is simple to collect but, unless you do something with it, its value is negligible.

You can assess the value of information by using two different terms to categorise it, as follows:

- *Data*: This is "raw facts", such as a list of members of an organisation.

- *Information*: This is data you have processed in such a way that it becomes usable; for example, sorting the list of members to select those with particular skills which you would like to find out about.

You could also add to these categories the words *Knowledge*, the state that exists when you have assimilated, and understand, the information you have collected; and *Wisdom*, the state that exists when you are able to apply what you have acquired in a judicious manner.

So it is only when you do something useful with the information you have available that it becomes truly valuable. What can you do to make the information you gather work for you? There are a number of steps you can take, and I will be using the term "information" to cover both data and information in what follows.

Annotate Information as you Receive it

As soon as you receive useful information, it helps to have a system for annotating it, so you know what it is and where it came from. For example, if you are given a business card, write on the back where and when you met the person, and something to remind you about the person and the conversation you had. If you do not do this, you may find you have a pocketful of cards and don't know why you have them. This is particularly important when you are at an event where you meet several people; you could easily collect five, ten or twenty cards and then be confused later about which person was the friendly outgoing one and which the remote and uncommunicative one; which was the person with an interest in flying foxes and which with the interest in old microscopes; which was the person who promised to call you and which was the person you were going to contact.

So, putting some reference against information helps keep it in your memory and makes it easier for you to take the next step of sorting what you gather into useful categories.

Sort your Information into Categories

This means deciding which classification would be most useful to you and then adopting it. For example, you might choose to group business cards under the geographical location of the people concerned, the specialist areas of the people, the events at which you collected them, and so forth. By doing this, you will have a coherent system for information storage and be better able to retrieve items quickly and easily. You might also group "active" and "inactive" contacts together; active ones being those with whom you deal on an ongoing basis and inactive ones those who are simply potential contacts, or with whom you have had no contact for a while.

Choose Appropriate Systems on which to Store your Information

The choice of whether to use a manual or electronic system for storing, handling and retrieving your information is up to you; there can be benefits both ways. A manual system is generally easy to use, easily accessible and can be inexpensive (not always, however). An electronic system is easy to update, can work through commercially available software packages which avoid you needing to create your own formats for information handling, and can be accessed at a distance if you have appropriate equipment, which is a benefit if you travel a good deal and need regular access to your information.

Manual systems can include diaries, calendars, index card systems, files, filofaxes, wall charts and so forth. You can also obtain magnetic boards or sheets which enable you to display, and manipulate, information simply and clearly. Electronic systems include computers, electronic diaries and notebooks and a range of portable items which can link up with computers to provide integrated data-handling systems.

If you use a computerised system, there are packages, such as Microsoft Outlook, available as part of the software with most PCs (personal computers). These packages provide facilities such as spreadsheets, diaries, reminder systems, databases, e-mail and so forth, allowing you to keep and update all your network contacts easily and effectively.

Review and Update your Information

It is important to review the information you hold so that it is still current. For example, are people's contact details still valid? If you don't do this, you may find your information rapidly becoming unusable and you can waste time and money trying to contact people who are inaccessible or no longer working in a relevant field. Discard any information which has been unused for very long periods of time and use your time and space to gather contact details which are likely to be more productive.

It may be tempting to think that all information on possible contacts is of value, but if it does not fit with your requirements, or your time availability, it will just be useless data. An example of this is collecting exhibition catalogues, or conference proceedings with lists of delegates. It gives you dozens of contact details but, unless you can do something with them, they are just a waste of space.

Keeping in Touch with your Network

Once you have your information in a usable form, you will be able to make it work for you. Having names and contact details on file is only a potential resource; to activate it, you need to do something with it. Although you could keep details of people on file in case you find them useful in the future, it is more constructive to keep in touch with your network, so you don't only approach people when you need something from them.

Contact People in your "Active Network"

This means keeping in touch with those people who seem the most useful to you. Chapter 11 provides some specific ideas on ways of contacting people, so you can select the most suitable approaches. For example:

- Mailing a newsletter. Remember that graphics brighten up a newsletter and if you can include photographs as well, you are likely to make even more of an impact.

- Telephoning periodically.

- Sending items you think may be of interest to them: newspaper cuttings, details of events you have heard about or are organising, articles you have written, etc. It is generally acceptable to attach a post-it note to such brief communications simply saying: "Thought you might be interested in this" and signing your name; there is no need to write a lengthy letter.

- E-mailing regularly with news, information, tips, offers, etc. Remember to be concise and relevant so your communications are not seen as "junk-mail".

- Sending Christmas or other holiday cards, with a handwritten note, an annual newsletter or a small gift if appropriate.

- Some people and organisations make a point of sending their clients or associates cards on their birthday. This may be appreciated, although it could also be seen by some people as intrusive, frivolous or unbusinesslike.

Example 1

A multi-level marketing organisation in the fashion industry has forms for its distributors to give to their customers when they sign up. The form asks for birth date. On each birthday, the distributor sends the customer a card to keep in touch.

Example 2

Many consultants send their clients a card at Christmas/New Year or other suitable holiday times. Again, it is a way of keeping in touch and reminding the clients of the relationship.

Example 3

A mail order service sends its regular customers a periodic letter offering them discounts on items they order most frequently. Again, keeping in touch helps remind people of their existence, even if they do not place an order there and then.

Keeping in touch will keep your name and activities in people's minds and you may also find that your contact comes at a time when they actually have a need for some of the things you offer. Even if they have no immediate need for your products or services, they are likely to welcome your contact as long as you do it in an appropriate way and offer them something of value. It has been estimated that there is a point at which contacts begin to produce responses and it seems that it needs several contacts a year to do this — possibly around five. In any case, you should aim to contact people on your active list at least two or three times a year if they are to remember you.

Keep Records of when you Contacted People

It is useful to keep a note of when you have contacted people. It is easy to forget when you last spoke to someone; it could be only a short while ago or it could be months or years. Having details of when you spoke, what you discussed and any action taken will help you keep track of contacts and find out which people need contacting again. If you keep your information on computer, you can devise a system to let you know which people should be contacted in any given period; if you have a manual system, you can add a note to the record. By the way, do remember that fax paper may fade and so manual records should be photocopied if they are on flimsy fax paper; otherwise your files will become unusable over time.

It is also useful to include some personal touches when contacting people. If you know someone has been on an interesting trip, has recently married or had a baby, has bought a new pet or moved house, you might refer to this. You might also mention something you discussed last time you spoke, so it is obvious that you remember the occasion and it stayed in your mind (although do not assume that the other person will remember everything and embarrass them by expecting they do). Small touches like these can make all the difference between an impersonal contact and one which makes the relationship seem more direct and supportive.

Check Whether People in your "Inactive" Network Still Wish to Remain on your Files

When sorting your records, you could simply discard details of anyone with whom you have not been in touch for, say, a year or so, or you could send out a simple mailshot asking whether they wish to remain on your list of contacts.

If you say you will remove their name unless you hear from them by a particular date (do allow sufficient time for replies in case people are away or unwell, and remember, letters could get lost in the post), you may find it easier than wondering if they are going to reply and waiting indefinitely.

If you attach an offer of some kind to your communication, people will be more likely to reply. The offer might be a discount on an event, a copy of a report, a newsletter, a voucher or information on something that you think they will find attractive.

Responding to Contacts from Others

This is an important part of network management. I have discussed how you can be proactive in organising and contacting your network, but it is also important to react appropriately when members of your network, or others, contact you.

React Promptly

A good principle is to reply to all contacts within 24 hours, even if it is only by getting someone else to say you are not currently available, but have their message and will respond by a particular time. In this way, people will know that you have received their message and have not forgotten about them.

Keep Records of Contacts from Other People

It is important to keep records of such contacts, as it can be easy to mislay notes taken from telephone messages, particularly if you pick up your calls at a distance, or to forget messages given to you orally by colleagues. So do have a system for recording these messages; possibly a particular notebook or file. If you have a portable electronic system, you may well have the information easily to hand, but you will still need to put it into an appropriate file if it is to be dealt with suitably.

Keep Records of Action Taken

It is also important to keep records of action you have taken following requests from others. If you send someone an item of information, pass their details to others or speak to someone on their behalf, do keep a record of what you have done. In this way, if there is any doubt later on you can check to be certain you have actually taken the intended action.

Building Your Network

So far I have dealt with understanding and administering your personal network. Now let's think about how you can build your network.

Plan for Success

I will be covering objective setting and strategic planning in Chapter 4, so I will just make the point here that, in order to build your network, you need to know what your purposes are and have ways of achieving them. Remember that you can easily build up a large number of contacts but, if they are not targeted well, they will not give the results you want.

Utilise Every Suitable Opportunity

This means taking steps to think about networking in every area of your life. It doesn't mean you have to be networking actively at all times, because sometimes this will not be appropriate; it does mean that you should think about possible contacts as a matter of course, rather than as an add-on activity. To this end, it is worth considering *where* you can network.

Almost any situation can be a networking opportunity, but there may be a few situations you have not thought about in this context. You will find, from personal experience, that there are some situations in which you feel very comfortable about networking, while others may not come so naturally to you yet. It is worth persevering, however, as it is often the unexpected situations which present the most interesting chances.

The situations I will be covering here are:

- Meetings of professional bodies
- Business meetings
- Travelling

- Social gatherings
- Clubs and associations
- Conferences
- Exhibitions
- Training events
- Leisure activities
- Education
- Utilising waiting time.

Do remember, in any of these situations, to be prepared by having relevant items, such as business cards, available to give people. Also remember to have a particular place to store cards or information given to you by other people. There is nothing worse than knowing you have been given some really useful information but not remembering what you have done with it — and I speak from personal experience here!

Let's take the various contexts in turn and see how they can be used for networking; I will give some examples from my own experience of networking in these contexts.

Meetings of Professional Bodies

For many people, this is a major focus of their networking activities. If you are a member of one or more professional organisations, going to local and national meetings is a good source of contact with others in a similar field.

In order to make the most of these events, it helps to arrive reasonably early, talk to as many people as possible and stay on after any presentation to chat informally to attendees and speakers. Remember to take your business cards or other relevant material and have a target for each meeting of how many contacts you hope to make and what results you would like. You may not achieve all your goals, but there is a good chance that you will get close if you plan and organise things carefully.

You may well find that, in time, you get invited to serve on committees or sub-groups of such bodies. This can also be helpful to your networking plans, as it brings you into closer contact with others working in the field and, through your work for the organisation, you are likely to become known to others, both in your own field and possibly in others.

Example

At a meeting of a professional body, I chatted to someone new during a break between sessions. He was looking for an external course on a particular topic, so that a number of employees could attend. I happened to have such a course running in the near future and several people signed up for it following our discussion.

Business Meetings

Meetings within an organisation, between organisations, or between an organisation and its clients and suppliers can all be used for networking.

If you do use such meetings for this purpose, remember not to behave inappropriately by using official time and resources for your own personal aims. There is a difference between discussing mutually interesting subjects with others and using your employer's, client's or associate's official business time to conduct your own activities. It is also unacceptable to network with clients of an employer or third party if your contractual arrangements with them preclude such activity.

So when you are acting as an agent for another organisation, be certain of the boundaries within which you can operate; with this in mind, however, business-based networking can be one of the most productive forms of all.

Example

Many years ago I attended a group set up for personnel directors of organisations in a particular sector to exchange ideas and information. One of those attending a meeting of the group had been working for a past client of mine and, on renewing the acquaintance, we found an opportunity to work together on a project.

Travelling

People use travel time in many different ways. Some people use the time to think, others to relax; some to work, others to socialise.

Whatever your preference, it is worth being open to the possibility of making useful networking contacts while on the move.

Whether you travel by public transport or by other means, there will always be times when you can come into contact with others.

Train travel is good, because you are likely to be seated close to other people, all of whom are potential networking contacts. You might wonder how to start a conversation with someone you don't know, but there will be many appropriate opportunities. For example, you could comment on an interesting view from the window. Or the food trolley could come round and you could compare notes about the refreshments. Or you could make an observation about an article in the newspaper if you are both reading one.

Alternatively, you might notice someone working on documents relating to an area with which you are familiar and you could use this as an opportunity to speak. Whatever you do, remember to respect the right to privacy and do not impose your conversation on people. If in doubt, use the observation and rapport skills I will be presenting in Chapter 9 and elsewhere, which will give you a good indication of whether the person is likely to be receptive to conversation.

If you really want to maximise networking opportunities, you can look around the train carriages before you sit down and select someone to sit near who looks as if they could be interesting — as long as you don't do this when the rest of the carriage is completely empty, in which case it could seem rather strange!

There are other chances to network while travelling. Waiting rooms or restaurants are useful, as people there are likely to have time on their hands and may welcome a friendly chat. Delays on public transport also offer opportunities for people to talk — even if the circumstances are not, initially, ones you might relish. Car travel also provides chances to network, generally at stops at service stations, shops and so forth. The important thing is to consider your networking objectives at all times, so you make the most of any opportunities that present themselves. And flying has many chances to offer the networker, especially as there can be lengthy delays when the only "entertainment" on offer is talking to your fellow travellers.

Example

On one train journey, I met another independent trainer, working in a slightly different field from my own. We exchanged cards and have since passed on various leads to each other over a period of some years.

Social Gatherings

Social gatherings present ideal opportunities to network, as people are there with the purpose of talking to others. Be careful, though, that you don't come across as concerned solely with what you can gain on a personal or business basis. Networking is a two-way process and there are also times when it isn't appropriate to network actively — so remember, you can still go to events simply to enjoy them.

You can maximise your chances of success at social gatherings by circulating and talking to as many people as possible, rather than staying with just one or two people. The more people you speak to, the more likely it is that you will come away with new information, ideas and opportunities.

If you are moving between groups, remember to find a way of leaving the person you are speaking to without appearing rude or uninterested, and don't overstay your welcome if the other person wants to talk to others. Also remember that it is as important to listen as to talk (remember the adage that you have two eyes, two ears and one mouth — so use them in that proportion!); keep your ears open and make the most of the occasion.

Example

At a dinner party, the person next to me, who owned a small shop, began to talk about appearance. After a while, we found we both had an interest in how one's business dress could influence others. She mentioned a person who worked for her who could do with some help with personal appearance and I agreed to have a couple of sessions with this person to give her some advice.

Clubs and Associations

There are many kinds of organisation that could fall within this category. Business clubs, charitable bodies, associations such as the

Scouts or the Women's Institute and so on are all places where contact with others has an important function.

Your networking activities can be very well served by such organisations but, again, do be careful that you aren't just serving your own ends; helping others as well as yourself will probably be more productive overall.

Example

While helping a body of which I am a member carry out a recruitment drive, I telephoned a number of people to find out their views about joining. During one of the conversations, the person to whom I was speaking asked me about my own activities. This resulted in a long-standing association whereby I became actively involved in this person's new business. I should add that I did not volunteer information about myself when contacting people on behalf of another body and I would not encourage you to do so either unless asked directly, as I was, about your activities.

Conferences

Conferences offer many possibilities for networking. Breaks, mealtimes and social events during the conference provide opportunities to exchange ideas and information, and you may also find that your neighbours at sessions are interested in chatting about matters of mutual interest, so select where you sit with networking in mind.

You may also find that some of the speakers at conferences are potentially good contacts, so make a point of approaching them after their session to see if some kind of follow-up is possible.

Example

I currently chair the Association for Neuro-Linguistic Programming and edit its magazine, Rapport. *At our conferences, I make a point of talking to both delegates and presenters to see if they will write items for the magazine, whether views on the conference, articles on their specialist topic, interviews and so forth. This kind of direct request often achieves better results than simply issuing a general invitation to people to contribute.*

Exhibitions

Exhibitions can be an excellent place to network. If you have a stand at an exhibition, you will be able to meet visitors and target your communications to them directly; this is more of a marketing exercise, however, than a networking one.

But as a visitor to an exhibition, you can walk round and look at other people's stands, choose those which seem potentially rewarding, and then talk to the people there. You can ask for information on their products and services and, at the same time, offer information on yours if you feel it is relevant. People on stands often become very tired and bored doing the same thing all day long; having a different kind of conversation can break up their time and lead to a useful exchange of ideas on both your part and theirs.

Example

At a recent exhibition I met some people who had a trade stand. They had previously attended one of my training courses and it was good to renew the acquaintance. There was no specific outcome to this contact, but it did serve the purpose of re-establishing a link that had been created earlier. In future our memories of each other's activities will be refreshed by the continued interaction.

Training Events

Training courses, workshops, talks and other similar activities can also be helpful in extending your personal network. You may go to these events to learn, to be entertained and also to network.

Be careful, if you do use these events for networking, that you don't do so at inappropriate times; save your networking activities for breaks or times when you and others do not need to be attending to the agreed business of the day. Also remember, it is not very courteous to promote your own activities at a training event if the training provider could be seen as a direct competitor to you — enticing other people's customers away from them will not put you in a good light as a networker.

Example

I first met one of my oldest friends at a training course. We subsequently found ourselves continually sitting next to each other at various training events and this developed into a long-standing association, both personally and professionally.

Leisure Activities

Perhaps you don't think of this as an immediately obvious source of networking contacts, but it can actually be very productive. If you are involved in a sport, music, gardening, photography, showing animals, dancing, keeping fit, walking, collecting antiques, visiting country houses or any other kind of activity, there will be others around who could form a focal point for contact.

Even though you might think that people interested in a particular topic might not have other interests that coincide with your own, you could be mistaken. Often an excellent networking opportunity can arise from unlikely settings and there is always the possibility that speaking to someone in one context could lead you to a useful contact in another. So keep an open mind about what benefits there can be from activities in any sphere in your life.

Example

I have attended a local leisure centre for some years. At one stage I gave some talks on NLP in sports performance at the centre. Subsequently some of the people who attended the talks asked if I could run some longer sessions and that was how one of my open courses began life. Later, the people on the initial courses introduced me to others who came on later ones. So, from the visits to the centre being for purely personal reasons, they developed into both social and professional ones later.

Education

If you are a parent, or if you attend further education classes yourself, there is a good chance that you will be able to network with others at educational establishments. Parent/teacher meetings, evening classes, crèches and open days can all be contexts for meeting people. Using these opportunities well can be an excellent addition to your networking armoury.

Example

Another of my activities, some years ago, involved Indian Dancing. Although it is some time since I took part in this, I subsequently came across another fellow student in a totally different context, where we were both members of another association. It was nice to renew the acquaintance and interesting how contacts can overlap in different spheres.

Waiting Times

I have already mentioned this under travel, but it is worth remembering that there are many other situations where waiting time could be used for networking. Some situations where this could apply are:

- Doctor or dentist's waiting rooms

- Checkout queues in shops and supermarkets

- With fellow job interviewees

- With fellow radio or television show guests.

There are many more, so you can be certain that waiting time will not be wasted.

Example

While waiting to do a radio interview, I chatted to some other people who had come to do an item for the same programme. It turned out we had a mutual contact in common and worked in fields which overlapped in several ways. We exchanged cards and there is every possibility we will be able to use this contact in future.

Final Comments

Managing your network effectively will have many beneficial results. You will be able to access the information you collect easily and swiftly. You will remain at the front of people's minds. You will make the most of opportunities to benefit from your networking activities.

Conversely, if you don't manage your network well, you are likely to have stacks of out-of-date information, be forgotten by people who could be useful allies and lose out on chances to benefit from a wide range of relationships.

The choice is yours.

One of the most important elements of managing your network is relating to people well. The chapters that follow deal with this element in depth.

Chapter Three

Identifying Your Current Networking Skills, Styles and Preferences

Everyone possesses networking skills to some extent, because these skills are prerequisites for everyday life. How you network, though, will depend on your own personal characteristics, experience and attitudes and this chapter addresses these.

In the next few pages, you will find various sets of questions. By completing them, you will gain useful information about yourself and about how you can use your own particular strengths to advantage. Everyone is different, and by understanding your own ways of operating, you will be better equipped both to enhance your own skills and to understand how other people function.

The questions differ in format; some dealing with things which are likely to be familiar to you and others focusing on issues which may be unfamiliar and, possibly, unusual. You may find it useful to have a pen and paper to hand as you go through the questions.

Your Experience of Networking

Take a little time to think about the networking you may have done in the past. Have you ever:

- Looked through your address book to find old acquaintances to contact about a new venture?

- Attended a social event with the main purpose of promoting your business?

- Passed on a colleague's details to someone else to whom they could be of help?

All of these involve aspects of networking.

Now think about whether there have been other occasions when you have deliberately taken steps to interact with others to further your, or their, efforts. List these occasions on a sheet of paper.

Now consider whether there are patterns in what you have written. For example, have you:

- Mainly listed activities which benefited *you*?

- Mainly listed activities which benefited *other people*?

- Mainly listed *face-to-face* activities?

- Mainly listed processes which you have carried out *without* other people being present?

- Mainly listed *one-to-one* activities?

- Mainly listed activities involving *groups* of people?

At the time, you may not have thought of these activities as networking, but doing this exercise will give you a good idea of the extent to which you have used networking processes in the past.

If you find this exercise a little hard to do, you could ask people you know whether they can think of occasions when you networked with others; you may find that things which you don't consider as networking are in fact thought of in that way by other people.

Now think about organisations you are, or have been, involved with. It is possible to network in all kinds of organisations and, even if you don't feel you have done much networking in this way, you may have observed other people engaged in networking in these organisations. So do you have experience of any of the following?

- A social club

- A parent/teacher association

- A professional institute or business organisation

- An activity club or association (sports, arts, travel, etc.)

- A women's or men's club, association or institute

- A school, college or university club or association

- A local community action group

- A union or staff association.

Are there any other kinds of organisation of which you have personal experience that you can add to the list?

As you work through this exercise, notice whether you recognise each of these organisations as contexts in which networking can take place. You may find that you naturally think of such contexts as ones where you can network, or you may be surprised that some of them appear on the list.

Now, although it is only a subjective measure, give yourself a score from 1 to 10 (with 1 being low and 10 being high) on how much experience of networking you believe you have. You might like to compare your own experiences with those of friends, family or colleagues, before giving yourself a score. You could also ask these other people to score themselves too, to see how you all compare.

If your score is towards the lower end of the scale, it may be that you have little direct experience of networking, or it may simply be that you do not yet recognise all the features of networking and so do not realise that some of the things you have done in the past are actually networking processes. Once you have finished reading the book, you might like to come back to this question and score yourself again; you may find the results interesting.

Your Attitudes towards Networking

Now consider your attitudes towards networking. Ask yourself the following questions:

- Do I think networking can help improve personal and business success?

- Do I think people who network a lot are doing something admirable or something pushy, devious or otherwise reprehensible?

- Do I think networking can be learned?

- Do I want to become good at networking?

- Do I think networking is likely to take up a good deal of time?

- Do I feel envious of people who are good at networking?

- Do I think networking can help me personally?

These questions are simply meant to help you explore your own thoughts, feelings, attitudes and beliefs about the subject; there are not necessarily "correct" answers for all the questions.

Having a positive attitude towards networking is a step towards success. When you believe that networking is a useful and effective process, you are likely to use it and to broaden your range of contacts and opportunities.

You might also like to consider whether your own attitudes towards networking are influenced by others. For example, has anyone ever tried to persuade you that networking is useful (or that it is pointless)? Has anyone ever said you are a good networker (or that they think you could use networking to better advantage)? Have your opinions on networking been affected by seeing others network well (or badly)?

Once you have thought about your opinions on networking, you might want to spend a little time on the following activities:

- Ask a few other people (say five or six to get a reasonable spread) their views on networking and see how they compare with your own. This will also give you ideas on different ways of approaching the topic.

- At the next social or business event you attend, observe how other people interact — notice particularly how much they circulate between groups and how much time they spend with any particular individual; listen to the topics of conversation and notice how many of them involve exchanges of information or arrangements for future meetings; notice how people respond to the approaches of others. Doing this will help you "role model" networking and evaluate for yourself some of the different ways of doing it.

Doing these exercises will help you clarify your own attitudes and feelings in relation to networking; having positive attitudes and feelings is an important factor in success.

Your Networking Skills

Now you can begin to think about your own networking skills. I will be covering networking skills in some depth in later chapters so, for the time being, don't be too concerned about whether you know what all the skills are; just think about your answers to the following questions:

- Am I generally good at initiating contact with others?

- Do I make a point of attending events in the hope that I will meet someone who can be useful to me?

- Do I have a wide circle of acquaintances?

- Do I get many calls from people asking for my advice or opinions?

- Do I have many people I can contact if I have a problem or want information?

- Do I take every opportunity to promote my own activities?

- Have I become better at interacting with others over recent years?

- Do people copy the way in which I relate to others?

- Do I take opportunities to promote other people's activities or to pass on useful information to them?

These questions will begin to give you an idea of some of the things that contribute to successful networking. You may know very well what your current skill levels are and be reading this book to enhance them in specific ways; alternatively, you may be unsure of how good you are at networking and want to find out what useful skills you can adopt to improve your performance. Either way, I hope you will find this process of analysis enlightening and helpful.

Another thing you can do to check your skills is to ask other people what they think of what you do. The next exercise is designed to give you some external feedback on your networking skills.

For this, you need to find a few people — three or four would be good — and ask them some questions about yourself. The following questions are examples, but you might well add others of your own to build up your information base even further:

- How well do you think I handle meeting new people?

- How do you think I come across in social situations?

- How well do you think I promote my own activities when talking to others?

- How helpful do you think I seem to others?

- What do you think of my professional image?

- What do you think I do particularly well when meeting other people?

Listening to the answers to these questions and adding the information you receive to your self-assessments will give you valuable assistance in your networking programme. You might like to ask the people you speak to whether they would like to do it as a one-way, or a two-way process; they may well benefit as much from your input on them as you do from their input on you. See also Chapter 14 for information on getting feedback from others.

Remember, when doing this exercise, to choose people with differing attitudes, experience and lifestyles if you can. This will give you a broader range of opinion to consider; if you only select people who have similar approaches to your own, you may limit the range of views you receive.

How You Learn New Things

Understanding how you learn will be useful in developing your networking skills. There are many ways in which people learn and I will describe two approaches here so you can find out about your own style. The two approaches I will be covering are:

- Honey and Mumford/Kolb's "learning styles"; and

- Accelerated Learning's "types of intelligence".

Let's take them in turn.

Honey and Mumford/Kolb

The principle behind the theory developed by Honey and Mumford, based on earlier thinking by Kolb, is that people can learn in any of four different ways (or combinations of these ways). The four learning styles are Activists, Reflectors, Theorists and Pragmatists.

These styles also influence how people solve problems and make decisions, so understanding your own style(s) will help your networking success by enabling you to select appropriate ways of developing your skills and choosing networking methods that will fit with your own preferences and abilities. Let's take each of these styles in turn.

- *Activists* like to **do things**. They like getting involved in hands-on activity and enjoy new experiences and immediate action. They often want quick results and can get impatient, with both themselves and others, if things don't happen rapidly. Activists may get bored quickly if the pace of things is slow and if they are swamped with detail, explanations, justifications and example; they may also get bored with long-term planning and with implementation of their plans — they just want results. Activists tend to be self-motivated and enjoy initiating activities, which can make them good networkers.

- *Reflectors* need **time to consider** their opinions of things. They value information and explanation. They can be slow to act unless they have all the information they need to hand. Reflectors rarely make snap decisions and can get frustrated and immobilised if others don't provide them with the information they need. Reflectors may hold back and let others speak or take action, so face-to-face networking activities may not always come naturally to them. Reflectors often like to take other people's opinions into account as well as their own.

- *Theorists* like to **understand the principles** underlying things and to be able to put them into a context or framework. Having access to evidence and to precedent will help theorists come to a conclusion. Theorists tend to be logical thinkers and use analysis and rational thinking to get results. Theorists can be very detached and objective and may feel that being subjective is not an appropriate way of acting. Theorists will like to understand the principles behind networking before embarking upon it.

- *Pragmatists* like to be able to **apply things**. They need to know the practical value of something before they will take it on. Pragmatists like to try things out to see if they will work; they prefer to get on with applying what they have found out, rather than necessarily spending time discussing things and exploring options. They can be very down-to-earth people who get frustrated with academic discussion and impractical thoughts. The practical uses of networking can really appeal to pragmatists.

Now you have had a brief overview of each of these styles, you might like to take some time to think about which style or styles is most like you. Ask yourself:

- Do I like getting on and doing things?

- Am I able to act even though I have little background information?

- Do I need plenty of time to consider new ideas?

- Do I have to have a good deal of information on any new venture?

- Do I need to understand the principles behind different issues?

- Do I like to know how ideas have originated?

- Do I need to be able to use ideas as practical tools?

- Do I want to find out how I can benefit from new things?

Although this is a very simplistic approach to the topic, if you answered "yes" to the first two questions you may be closest to the activist style; if you answered "yes" to the second two you may be closest to the reflector style; if you answered "yes" to the third two you could be closest to the theorist style; and if you answered "yes" to the last two you may be closest to the pragmatist style. However, do remember that you may have a mix of styles, especially if you answered "yes" to several of the above questions.

Answering these questions will give you useful information about your preferences and needs and, as you go through the rest of the book, you might like to consider how the suggestions made fit with the styles you think are closest to you. If you feel that activities I suggest are right for you, that's great; if not, you could think how they could be adapted so they fit better with your own personal style and preference.

For example, if I suggest you listen to different people talking, analyse the various tones of voice they use and notice what difference their tone of voice seems to make in the reactions they get from others (an approach which could suit reflectors and theorists), you could change this to trying out different tones of voice yourself to see what difference it makes to your personal results (an approach which could suit activists and pragmatists).

So knowing your own style and being flexible on occasions will help you network better and understand better how to get through to people with whom you are interacting.

Accelerated Learning

Accelerated Learning, as I mentioned in the Introduction, defines a number of different ways in which people learn; the first three of these relate to NLP concepts as well. I will outline these below and you can consider each of the following categories to see which are closest to the ways in which you prefer to learn; we will then go on to see how you can use this information in networking. Remember that you can have more than one learning style, depending on the subject matter or the situation in which you are learning.

Visual

Visual people need to see things in order to learn well. They find it helpful to observe demonstrations, see pictures in books or posters, watch videos and look at exhibitions. Visual people need the stimulation of seeing things in order to register them in their minds.

As an example, if a visual person is told how to get somewhere, they may find it hard to take in the directions by simply listening, but may find it easier to understand if they are drawn a map.

If you are strongly visual, you may find networking easier when you can see people face-to-face and observe their appearance and expression. In fact, you may be exceptionally good at "reading" people from their expressions and postures (see also the section on Action Profiling on page 180 in Chapter 10). You may find your own visual image important and want to dress in a visually appealing manner; you may also want to create business stationery which illustrates clearly your approach to your activities. You may also find it easier to learn from this book by making mental images of the situations I am describing and picture yourself doing some of the things suggested.

In addition, visual people tend to use a good deal of visual language, with words such as "clear", "picture", "see", "look" and "bright". This kind of language is good for communicating with other visual people but, for those who do not rely on their visual sense to a great extent, this kind of language may be inappropriate. In Chapter 7, on speech and language, I will be exploring this concept further.

Auditory

Auditory people need to hear things in order to learn. They like discussion, reading, listening to audiotapes, playing music and so on. Talking things through is often helpful to them. An auditory person will be quite content to be given directions orally rather than being drawn a map.

If you are auditory, you may be happy with telephone networking, as you can hear people's tone of voice and assess how they are responding. You will also want any material you produce to have the right words to convey your message. You will probably be good at detecting people's feelings and attitudes through their intonation and phrasing and may find it easy to work out other people's styles through their language.

Auditory people often use words such as: "hear", "sounds", "listen", "wavelength" and "resonate". While such language will work well with other auditory people, for those who do not use their sense of hearing to the same extent, such words may be less meaningful.

Kinaesthetic

Kinaesthetic people need hands-on experience. They often express their feelings openly and can be affected strongly by such things as comfort and emotional balance. Kinaesthetic people also tend to enjoy physical contact and may put their arms around people's shoulders or shake hands enthusiastically when they meet.

Kinaesthetic people may use words like "feel", "grasp", "weighty", "struggle" and "move". Again, these words will work well with other kinaesthetic people but may seem inappropriate to some others.

In networking, kinaesthetic people will probably surround themselves with things that feel good; nice textured clothes and stationery and brochures which have a good weight and surface feel. They are likely to feel most comfortable with people who express their own feelings openly and can acknowledge other people's feelings in turn.

Mathematical/Logical

Mathematical/logical people need to understand the reasons behind things and how they work. They like facts and figures and want to see the connections and relationships between things. They may find it hard if they can't do things in an ordered way.

The language such people use could include words such as "reason", "analyse", "facts", "system" and "order". They will want their communications to be rational and systematic and will learn best when they understand the principles behind issues. The danger for these people is that their language may sound cold and detached to others.

In networking, mathematical/logical people will tend to plan their activities well and enjoy organised events and conversations which are structured and progress in a systematic way.

Musical/Rhythmic

Musical/rhythmic people like to use music and patterning in what they do. Learning multiplication tables by chanting the figures is an example of this process, or remembering other information by saying it to yourself in a rhythmic form (for example, to the rhythm of "Hiawatha"). These people may find it hard if they aren't able to follow rhythms in what they do and may prefer to have patterns to their day, taking into account their natural body clocks.

Words used by these people could include "chord", "pattern", "cycle", "timing" and "flow". When with other people, they can be put off by voices which sound harsh or guttural and may be attracted by speech which has naturally interesting patterns and tones.

In networking, these people may be able to help others appreciate the nature of flow and pattern in interactions.

Interpersonal

Interpersonal people like being, and working, with others. They are at their best when they are involved in joint activities and may find it hard if they have to do things on their own.

Words used by interpersonal people could include "we", "our", "team", "collective" and "joint". This language works well with similarly inclined people, but may give the impression of a lack of individuality or independent thinking to those who are of a different nature.

Interpersonal people will like to include reference to others in their speech and written material and, in networking, interpersonal people are likely to find contact with others rewarding and easy to engage in. They may prefer face-to-face activities, as this brings them into closer contact with others, and they are likely to join organisations or associations for the social contact this brings.

Intrapersonal

Intrapersonal people like being on their own and doing things themselves. They may find it hard to be with others, as they can feel their presence intrusive or overpowering.

Words used by intrapersonal people could include: "I", "me", "myself", "my" and "one" and this may come across as pushy or self opinionated to others.

In networking, intrapersonal people may find it hard to feel at ease in social situations or, alternatively, may try to take over events and activities with which they are involved. In their written material, intrapersonal people may give examples of their own activities and suggest their own approach to things.

In addition to the seven modes outlined above, Howard Gardner, who originated the idea of different kinds of "intelligence", has posited a further one ("Naturalist") and a possible second one ("Existential"). I will not be dealing with these in this book but, if you are interested in this topic, you might like to read some recent books on Accelerated Learning, including *7 Kinds of Smart* (see the Bibliography).

Let's think now about which of these styles is closest to your own. Consider the following scenarios and decide which one, or ones, seem most like you.

Anne

Anne thinks ahead to the events she attends and, in her mind, conjures up images of how they might be: how the place will look, how people might be dressed and how she will appear to others. Once she has arrived at the event, she likes to take a good look around and notices the surroundings, the furnishings, the décor and the lighting. She also notices how people are dressed, the expressions on their faces and any small movements they make with their eyes, their mouths and their hands which indicate to her how they are reacting to things around them. When she talks to people she paints pictures in the air with her hands, so they can see the scenarios she is describing. Her language is full of words which describe how things appear to her.

Mark

Mark thinks ahead to events, recalling conversations about similar events and imagining the kind of conversation which will take place at the forthcoming occasion. When he arrives, Mark notices the noise level in the room and listens out for voices which sound pleasant and on the same wavelength as himself. He notices people's language and pays attention to what they are saying. He is also very aware of subtle changes in voice tonality, volume and pace, noticing how people speed up or slow down according to their interest levels. He is also aware of the sound of his own voice, noticing when he is speaking quietly or loudly and how much of the conversation he is leading. He sometimes chats to himself (silently, in his head) about what is going on. Mark's language effectively communicates what he intends.

Stephanie

Stephanie thinks ahead to events and runs through her feelings about attending. She considers her energy level, her enthusiasm for the occasion and her chances of finding the event pleasant and rewarding. When she arrives, Stephanie notices the temperature of the room and how soft the carpets feel underfoot. She is aware of the atmosphere overall and the effect it has on her feelings about the occasion. Stephanie likes to pick up "vibes" from others and guess their feelings about the event. When talking to others, she tends to stand fairly close to them and will often touch them lightly on the arm if they tell her about something which they have found difficult or upsetting. If she meets a friend, she will probably give them a hug and tell them how pleased she is that they are there. Her language is very descriptive of the feelings she is experiencing and the activities she is engaged in.

Steve

Steve thinks ahead to events and considers how long it will take to get there, what he will wear, what preparation is needed, what items he should take with him and exactly what he wants to achieve from the visit. He works out what other people are likely to be interested in and decides on how best to present himself and his ideas. When he arrives, Steve calculates which people are likely to be most useful to talk to and heads straight for them. He responds to questions and opinions in a straightforward way, giving reasons for his views and countering any ideas with which he disagrees in a systematic way. Steve's language is concise and unambiguous and he keeps very much to the point.

Jenny

Jenny thinks ahead to events and wonders how they will fit with the rhythm of her week. As she thinks about the event, she hums softly to herself, enjoying the combination of the sound in her head and the anticipation of the event. When she arrives she is very conscious of any background music and also of people's movements and voices — whether they move in a graceful and elegant manner and whether their voices are melodic and pleasant to listen to. Her own language is full of words which make patterns with sounds and with the pauses between.

Chris

Chris thinks ahead to events and wonders how many new people he is going to meet. He enjoys being with others and likes the opportunity to join in discussions. Chris remembers other occasions when he has been part of a group venture and knows he is able to contribute well to the achievement of results for the group as a whole. At the event, Chris makes for the liveliest group and quickly joins in the conversation. He enjoys listening to other people's views and ideas and is always able to help others with their activities. Chris's language is full of references to collaboration and mutual support.

Lesley

Lesley thinks ahead to events and tells herself what she will do and say. She likes to organise her arrival and departure to fit in with her personal schedule and to be in control of her own timetable. Lesley prefers events where she can "do her own thing"; perhaps listening to an interesting speaker or studying the ways in which people are interacting. She is likely to stand on her own until she is approached by someone else and even then is likely to remain fairly wrapped up in her own thoughts and ideas. Lesley's language refers to her own views and opinions a good deal and she is good at motivating herself to do things and at assessing her own performance.

Which of the above do you think is most like you: Anne (visual), Mark (auditory), Stephanie (kinaesthetic), Steve (mathematical/logical), Jenny (musical/rhythmic), Chris (interpersonal) or Lesley (intrapersonal)? Working out which of these styles are ones you use personally (and remember you may use more than one style overall, or in particular situations) will give you useful insights into your own behaviour. When you come to work on skills in later chapters, you will be able to adapt the suggestions given to fit in with your own personal approach.

For example, if you like working on your own, you may well do best by following the information and doing the activities by yourself. If you prefer working with others, you may find it helpful to share the activities with different people. If you are kinaesthetic, you will probably need to physically try out a lot of things before assessing them and if you are visual you may need to picture how things could work for you. And so on . . .

When you are networking, it is helpful to think of both your own preferences and those of the people with whom you are in contact. For example, if you are very auditory, you may talk a good deal and ask questions a lot, but if the person you are with is visual, they may want to be shown examples of what you do, rather than simply hearing about it. Similarly, if you are kinaesthetic, you may think nothing of putting your arms round someone's shoulder, but someone who isn't kinaesthetic may find this intrusive. So thinking about your own personal style(s) is useful and can help you in practice when it comes to relating to others.

What Motivates You

There are many ways in which people become motivated. In this section, I outline a few so you can assess which motivational patterns you use most yourself. Once you understand your own motivational patterns, you will be better equipped to decide which networking activities will suit you and how to keep up your energy levels while engaged in networking processes. Knowing about the motivational patterns is also one of the keys to relating well with, and influencing, others — an aspect which I will develop further in the skills chapters.

It is important to remember that motivation can change over time, and from one situation to another so, although I use general labels in the sections that follow, these may change and so should only be thought of as shorthand for the range of individual responses which are possible. It is also important to remember that none of the patterns are good or bad in themselves, but they may be more or less suitable for particular purposes.

The "categories" which follow are used in NLP and have been explored in depth by various people, including Rodger Bailey, in his development of the LAB (Language And Behaviour profile), and Shelle Rose Charvet (in her book *Words that Change Minds*). See the Bibliography for more details.

Carrot and Stick

This is a commonly used term for the pattern which, in NLP, is given the name of "Towards and Away From". "Towards" people tend to be motivated by goals, targets and striving for things they desire (carrot). "Away From" people tend to be motivated by avoiding problems, resolving difficulties and preventing discomfort (stick).

To find out which is most like you, have a go at the following questions:

1. Would you prefer to:

    a) Be praised for things you have done well?

    b) Have your mistakes pointed out to you?

2. Would you be more likely to change jobs:

    a) For a greater challenge, to earn more money or to further your career?

    b) Because you didn't feel sufficiently stretched, you felt under-valued or you thought your present job wasn't leading any-where?

3. Do you prefer to:

    a) Set yourself goals or targets?

    b) Overcome obstacles or difficulties?

4. Do you more often:

    a) Find the positive side of things?

    b) Complain about things going wrong?

5. If a colleague asked your opinion on a piece of work they had done, would you be more likely to:

   a) Tell them which parts you thought were good?

   b) Tell them which parts needed improvement?

If more of your answers to the above questions were "a" rather than "b", you are likely to be a "towards" person; more "b" answers than "a" means you are more likely to be "away from".

Knowing these patterns is a great help in self-awareness and in choosing networking activities which are appropriate both for you and for those you deal with.

Example

In organising a social event at which people could get together, chat about topics of mutual interest and exchange ideas on business development, you could do the following "towards" things:

- *Circulate a leaflet showing the benefits of attending;*

- *Ask people what their preferred format for the event would be;*

- *Have a checklist so you can work through each item you need to plan.*

And you could do the following "away from" things:

- *Check that nobody had transport problems and needed to be collected;*

- *Have alternative foods so that non-meat-eaters aren't left out;*

- *Anticipate any problems that might arise.*

Me or You

In NLP, this category is referred to as "Internal and External". Internal people are self-reliant, make decisions without referring to others and have strong opinions, which they defend vigorously. External people like to have support and feedback from others and can put off decision-making until they know that what they have in mind has other people's approval.

Although this may sound similar to the previously mentioned "Interpersonal/Intrapersonal" AL categories, there is a difference. Internal and external relate very much to decision-making strategies and the extent to which a person is reliant on others for guidance and support. Intrapersonal and interpersonal is more about the extent to which a person enjoys being with others or lives in their own self-contained world.

To find which of these two you most resemble, have a go at the following questions:

1. Do you generally:

    a) Find it easy to decide such matters as which car to buy or where to go for an evening out?

    b) Prefer to ask around to find out what others recommend?

2. Do you:

    a) Feel happiest when making your own choices?

    b) Need someone else to tell you what to do?

3. Do you:

    a) Know when you have done something well?

    b) Need another person to give you feedback?

4. When you see an advertisement for a product or service do you:

    a) Make up your own mind about its benefits?

    b) Believe that it must be good if other people endorse it?

5. When you are with friends, are you more likely to:

    a) Take the lead in making decisions on things such as where to go for a meal?

    b) Be influenced by other people's opinions or wishes?

If you have more "a" answers than "b", you are more likely to be internal and if you have more "b" answers than "a" you are more likely to be external.

In networking, as an internal person you are likely to be good at giving people ideas, initiating contacts and evaluating the effectiveness of your own networking activities. As an external person you are likely to be good at getting others to consider their own thoughts and activities, listening to other people's problems and suggestions and getting feedback from others on your own performance.

Again, both categories have their place. By knowing which you favour, you can gain insights into how you behave and into what could be appropriate ways of dealing with others.

Example

If you were driving to a meeting and someone stepped out in front of your car, it would be useful to be internal and just take action instantly to avoid them; if you behaved externally instead and asked your passengers whether they thought you should put your foot on the brake, you might be involved in a serious accident.

What about the Rule Book?

Some people like to follow established customs and practices; they prefer to know what is the "right" thing to do and then to do it. Others like flexibility and choice; they prefer to explore options and variety. In NLP, this category is called "Options and Procedures".

To find out which is your common way of approaching things, consider the following questions:

1. In your office or home:

    a) Do your possessions and equipment have set places that you do not like having disturbed?

    b) Are you comfortable with other people moving things you have on display?

2. Do you prefer:

    a) Predictable situations?

    b) Spontaneity?

3. When attending a new event do you prefer:

    a) A structured timetable, so you know exactly what will happen and when?

    b) A fluid format so there is opportunity to make choices and respond at the time?

4. Do you like to:

  a) Organise and plan so you always know what you will be doing?

  b) Leave room for flexibility and unexpected occurrences?

5. If someone tells you "This is the right way to do this . . ." are you more likely to:

  a) Accept what they say?

  b) Look for alternative ways of doing it?

If you have more "a" answers than "b", you are more likely to be a procedures person; if you have more "b" answers than "a", you are more likely to be an options person.

In networking, you can use procedures effectively to plan and organise your activities, to keep records of contacts and to talk regularly to people in your network. You can use options to explore new ways of doing things and different places to network; you can also use options to give you a range of ways of responding to questions or proposals.

Example

If you were organising an event, on behalf of a networking group, to which a number of people had been invited, it would be good to have some procedural elements, such as a list of those attending, so you can check who came and add the names to a database. Another procedural element which could be useful would be giving people an idea, at the start, of who to speak to if they need information on the group organising the event. It would, however, be counterproductive to make the entire event so structured that people couldn't choose who to speak to or how long to spend on particular discussions. So thinking about both procedures and options is helpful in networking contexts.

Depth of Information

People vary in their need for detail. Some people need detailed information on most things if they are to be able to function effectively while others prefer to have a broad overview of things. The NLP terms for these are "Detail and General".

To find out which is your preferred way of functioning, answer these questions:

1. Do you:

    a) Read instruction manuals word-for-word?

    b) Skim to get a rough idea of what to do?

2. When giving someone else instructions, are you more likely to:

    a) Give them precise information on every aspect of what they have to do?

    b) Leave many of the finer points to them to work out?

3. When selecting what to wear for an event, do you:

    a) Check that everything is correct and in good order?

    b) Not worry if there is an odd button missing or your belt isn't exactly the right colour?

4. When telling someone about an event you attended, would you probably:

    a) Tell them all about it, including everything that happened?

    b) Give them an overview of what happened?

5. When working on a project, do you:

    a) Like to make sure it is all done correctly?

    b) Prefer to leave it to someone else to check that each specific element is completed?

If you have more "a" answers than "b", you probably have a high degree of need for detailed information, and if you have more "b" answers than "a" you probably have a high tolerance, or liking, for the broad picture.

In networking, detail is important for some purposes — for example, making sure you have people's contact information accurately and remembering how and when you met them. A broader approach can be useful when you want to give people a general idea of your background and experience.

Example

When meeting someone new at an event, you could collect the following detailed information about the person: their name, their contact details (preferably on a business card) and their particular field of activity. You could then ask them some general questions, such as: "What kind of events do you find it useful to attend?" or "What are your views on the economy at present?" Using such general questions is likely to get the person to talk broadly and give you a good feel for their approach and interests, whereas very precise, detailed questions are more likely to restrict conversation.

What do you Notice?

Some people go through life noticing things that stand out, while others tend to look for things they recognise. NLP calls these "Difference and Similarity". To find out which you are, which you tend to favour, you can answer the following questions:

1. When visiting someone's home, do you:

    a) Notice if a picture on the wall is at an angle, and want to straighten it?

    b) Not notice such things?

2. When shopping for clothes, do you:

    a) Like to try out new styles and colours?

    b) Tend to stick to the same ones you have always worn?

3. When you meet new people, do you:

    a) Look for people who are different from you?

    b) Try to find people with whom you have things in common?

4. In a group, do you:

    a) Notice how you differ from the others?

    b) Notice the similarities between you and the others?

5. When you think about how you network now, do you:

    a) Think how what you do has changed over the years?

    b) Become aware of how similarly you still do things?

If you have more "a" answers than "b" answers, you are probably aware of and may seek differences, and if you have more "b" answers than "a" answers, you are probably more aware of and prefer situations where things are broadly similar to those you have experienced in the past.

In relation to networking, this information can help you decide how to approach situations. For example, if you prefer difference, you may well wish to try out new approaches and meet people with different opinions and experience. If you prefer similarity, you could well be more comfortable with contexts that are like others you have experienced.

Example

If you are thinking of having your business cards redesigned, you could look at those of a number of other people. You could then check how they are similar to yours and how they differ from yours. Noticing both similarities and differences should give you some ideas about your own redesign. Some of the things you can look out for are the size of the card, the colour, the print style, the logo, the information included and so on.

With all these categories, you can use the information you have obtained in a couple of different ways. You can use it to help you do things that will fit with your own patterns. Alternatively, you can use it to extend your capabilities by trying out different things that will extend your range of skills and stretch you somewhat. The choice is yours, but the more you use different approaches, the more likely it is that you will enhance your development further.

What do You Think of Yourself?

Finally, a rather deeper issue than some I have outlined. Your self-concept, self-esteem, confidence levels and belief in yourself are aspects which are important in success generally and networking in particular.

The higher your self-regard, and the more trust you have in your own abilities and self-worth, the easier it is to achieve success. This is because a low opinion of yourself often means that you limit what you do because you don't think you are capable, or because you think others will criticise, blame or make fun of you.

Of course, you may have more confidence in some situations than in others, but this issue is more about your underlying sense of self-worth.

The following questions will help you assess just how confident you are in yourself.

1. If someone criticises something you have done, can you put their criticism into context or do you tend to take it as an overall criticism of you as a person?

2. If you were asked to take on something which you were potentially able to do, although you had no previous experience of it, would you be willing to give it a go, or would you feel unable to take the risk?

3. Do you feel you have achieved as much in your life so far as most of the people you know personally?

4. If someone compliments you, do you find it embarrassing or are you pleased by the attention?

5. Do you often find yourself being critical of yourself, perhaps saying negative things to yourself in your head, or thinking you can't do things very well?

Take a little time to review your answers to these questions. You may already have a good sense of how much you value yourself, but your answers might give you some additional food for thought.

In networking, if you have a good self-image, you are more likely to feel good about yourself and also to help others feel confident in you. You may also find that your own confidence inspires confidence in others, through you acting as an example, or role model, for them.

If you feel that you have a lower opinion of yourself than you would like, some of the exercises in the skills chapters that follow will help you develop confidence. Continued practice can assist you in developing a higher regard for yourself generally.

Chapter Four

Preliminaries to Networking

In the Introduction, I described 11 networking steps, and I will be exploring them in more detail here and in the chapters that follow. I will be spending more time on some than on others, as their practical uses to you are likely to be greater. Just to remind you, the 11 steps are as follows:

- Having a purpose

- Developing a strategy

- Setting detailed objectives and targets

- Working out tactics

- Researching

- Planning

- Organising

- Preparing

- Doing

- Monitoring

- Evaluation.

I will be exploring the first eight of these steps in this chapter.

Having a Purpose

This is the initial stage, and a vital one. In order to achieve a result, you need to know why you are aiming for it. Sometimes different words are used in place of "purpose". You may find people talk of "Vision", "Mission", "Goal", "Ambition", "Direction" and so on. I am using the word *purpose* here to encompass all these things; to mean whatever it is that is motivating you to strive for success.

Your purpose can be set at different levels (as can your objectives, to which I will turn soon). So you could think in terms of a "Life Goal" or of a "Specific Purpose". I would encourage you in this part of the book to think about what it is that networking would bring to your life and work which would be welcome and add benefits to your overall endeavours.

Example

Peter was a middle manager in a large consultancy organisation, where part of his role involved selling. He had been with the company for five years and, at his last appraisal interview, one of the areas identified for his personal development was using networking in a more effective manner. Some of the specific issues he needed to address were:

- *Broadening his circle of contacts in order to open further opportunities for business within a defined geographical area;*

- *Enhancing his communication skills, especially in relation to developing good rapport with people, quickly;*

- *Using his contacts within the organisation in a more effective manner, so he could get support from other functions when needed.*

Peter began by considering whether the appraisal was something he wished to "take on board". He decided it was and started to think what his purpose might be in doing so. He decided that he wished to continue his career within the consultancy function and that, to do so, he needed to enhance his personal and business skills in any way that would further his career aims.

Peter's purpose was connected with his career and his personal development; he was quite explicit about why he wanted to follow up the action suggested in the appraisal.

Developing a Strategy

Strategic thinking about networking is vital in today's climate. Thinking strategically means taking a long-term view of what you want to achieve and relating different aspects of your activities to one another. Some strategies for networking could include:

- Using networking as one element in your campaign to advance your career;

- Developing your networking skills so you can coach others in it;

- Taking every opportunity to incorporate networking into your life as a means of enhancing your personal development.

The differences between *strategic* thinking and *tactical* thinking can be quite small at times but, if you approach strategic thinking as the process of setting your activities into a broader context and a longer timeframe, as opposed to the detailed process of identifying very particular, and sometimes short-term, courses of action, you will find it makes sense.

So how can you develop your own strategy for networking? There are a number of factors you can consider in doing this:

- Your personal situation and lifestyle

- Your commitments and responsibilities

- Your preferences, abilities and experience

- Your resources

- Your needs and desires.

Let's take each of these in turn and see how they can affect your strategic thinking.

Your Personal Situation and Lifestyle

It is important to take some time to think about your life overall, so you can put your networking into a broader context. You might find the following questions helpful in reviewing your life situation:

- Am I studying, in employment, self-employed, unemployed or retired?

- How active is my social life?

- What is my general state of health and fitness?

- How mobile am I?

By assessing your present situation in this way, you will be able to take stock of your resources, your constraints, your assets and your activities. Once you are clear about where you are at present, you will be better able to consider how networking could fit into your overall lifestyle. For example, it may be that you have spare time at weekends, which could usefully be devoted to extending your networking activities.

Your Commitments and Responsibilities

Thinking about commitments and responsibilities will also help you work out how networking can fit into your life. You might ask yourself the following questions:

- Do I have a job which takes up a substantial amount of time?

- Do I have family responsibilities or act as a carer?

- Do I have financial commitments which make a major impact on my life?

- Am I undertaking study which takes up a good deal of my time?

By doing this assessment you will be better able to know what time and effort you can put into networking and also which networking processes are likely to work best for you. For example, it may be that your commitments make it difficult for you to do much face-to-face networking, but that telephone or e-mail contact would be workable.

Your Preferences, Abilities and Experience

Understanding what you like and what you do well will also be an invaluable aid in thinking broadly about networking. If you completed the questions in Chapter 3, you will already have many insights into these issues, and you might also like to answer the following questions here:

- Do I enjoy meeting others, socialising and exchanging ideas and views?

- Am I good at getting others to talk and to exchange opinions?

- What past experience do I have which could be useful to other people?

These questions will help you understand whether you like the process of networking and what it is that you could offer in a networking relationship. For example, if you have experience of working with young people, you may be able to offer advice to others on how to relate to youngsters or, possibly, how to get a job in the youth services.

Your Resources

Knowing what resources you have available will also help you think about your strategy. You might like to ask yourself the following questions:

- How much time could I make available?

- What support do I have from others?

- What finances are available to me?

Again, knowing what resource base you are starting from will both tell you where you are at present and indicate what resources you might need to acquire in the future. If you have limited finances, you might choose to engage in activities with a minimum cost implication (perhaps attending free meetings of a local interest group); or you could make fundraising a priority so you can afford to put more into your networking (perhaps joining a professional body or hosting an event).

Your Needs and Desires

And finally, it is helpful to think about your own needs and desires; what you actually need to have and what you would like to have. You could ask yourself the following questions in this context:

- What are my major needs at the present time?

- What particular needs can I predict for the future?

- What are my specific short-term needs?

- What kind of life do I wish to have?

- What particular things would I like to attain?

Working out what it is that you want or need is important, because otherwise you might be side-tracked into striving for things which are not really of major importance to you.

I hope these sections will have given you some ideas on how to assess your current situation before embarking on strategic planning. We can now move on to strategy development itself.

Creating your Strategy

When you work out your networking strategy, you should consider the factors I have discussed above, because they act as frameworks for what you do. For example, it would be difficult to form strategic plans to use face-to-face networking as a business tool if you live in a very isolated area where you have little opportunity to meet other people. In this instance, your strategic plans might be based more on using electronic media, such as e-mail discussion groups, to conduct your activities.

Some questions to ask yourself in developing a strategy include:

- What is my main purpose in using networking?

- Will networking be a major element of my activities?

- Do I need to develop my skills in networking even further?

- What might be the focus for my networking activities?

These and other similar questions will help you create a strategy to use networking in whichever areas of your life you feel it would be most useful.

To physically produce your strategy, you can use either manual or electronic systems. Whatever the means employed, you will need to take an overview of your future direction and work out how networking might fit into your overall aims.

Example

Let's return to Peter. In discussion with his manager, Peter agreed to develop and implement a strategy for addressing the three issues.

He spent some time doing what is called a SWOT analysis (taking stock of his own current Strengths, Weaknesses, Opportunities and Threats — a commonly used business technique for thinking about individual and organisational change and development). Having assessed what he was good at, what he could do better, what he could take advantage of and what could pose a problem, he went on to create a strategic plan.

Peter listed the following points as important ones on which to base his strategy:

- *The need to incorporate this development into his normal working life as much as possible, as he already had an extremely full working week and could not extend it too far without his health and energy being drained.*

- *His preference for face-to-face learning, in a practical, experiential way.*

- *His support from a colleague within the same company, who often acted as a mentor to Peter, especially being a sounding board for Peter's ideas and suggestions.*

Taking these three points into account, Peter produced the following strategy:

- *To explore what "good networkers" in his own organisation currently did to achieve their results.*

- *To learn from these people's ways of working and incorporate some of them into his own daily activities.*

- *To use his colleague as a point of contact in turning his strategy into operational plans and activities.*

Having considered the process of strategic thinking, we can now turn to the next step — setting objectives.

Setting Objectives and Targets

Having created a strategy, your next step will be to formulate detailed objectives for achieving your strategic plans. In the Introduction, I set out the five elements of effective networking:

- Having good objectives

- Having appropriate behavioural skills

- Having a positive mental attitude

- Having positive emotional states

- Having supportive beliefs and attitudes.

This section will cover how to set good objectives and later chapters will go into more detail on the other elements.

Having objectives for networking will help you considerably. You can set both long- and short-term objectives for what you do. Long-term objectives could include becoming a member of a particular professional body, once you have completed a qualification. Short-term objectives could include how to handle a particular telephone call or how to persuade a particular person to meet you for a discussion.

Having objectives even for small activities helps focus your mind and makes it easier to go on to plan and organise what you need to do to achieve a successful outcome. It may sound strange to think of objectives for telephone calls, for instance, but it is really useful to think out in advance such things as when you will call, how you will open the conversation, what tone of voice you will use, which questions you will ask and what results you would like to achieve.

Getting used to setting objectives in this way will help your overall success in networking and will make it easier for you to check how far you have come towards reaching your goals.

I referred in the last chapter to the NLP approach to objective setting. This goes beyond the "SMART" way of setting objectives (the commonly used business objective-setting framework) and its elements are as follows.

Making your Objective Positive

People often set objectives in a negative way, such as "I don't want to be under so much pressure" or "I would rather not take on additional responsibility". Such an approach makes it difficult to achieve results, as it does not define what you actually *do* want. Changed into positive language, these two objectives could be expressed as: "I want to have more time for each of my tasks" and "I prefer to limit my responsibilities to what they are at present". In each of these cases, it becomes easier to move on to working out how to achieve the result, rather than simply being dissatisfied with the present situation.

Example

Peter might state his overall objective as "I want to identify and learn from excellent networkers in my organisation."

Defining the Context for your Objective

This means specifying where and when your objective will apply. For example, you might say to yourself "I want to be able to socialise better." However, this doesn't define the context for socialisation. A better objective might be "I want to be able to talk to people at our office lunches."

Example

Peter might define the context for his objectives as follows: "I want to learn from people in my workplace, finding time within my working day to meet them, talk things through and observe them in action in work-based meetings and events."

Being Specific about your Objectives

Being imprecise about your objectives also makes it hard to achieve them. Instead of saying "I want to be better at speaking to people on the telephone" you might say "I want to sound friendly and approachable, state clearly and simply why I am calling and use words which are clear and understandable." The second statement is more precise and thereby easier to achieve.

Example

Peter might make his objective specific by saying: "I want to identify five people within the organisation whom I can approach, spend one to two hours with each in discussion, observe each of them in action at one meeting and one other event, write down my observations and talk them through with my mentor at the end of the exercise. I then want to use some of the behaviour I have observed in ten situations, to enhance my own skills at doing similar things."

Weighing up the Pros and Cons

There are generally positive and negative points associated with the achievement of any objective. This is because achieving something means bringing about change, and change in itself can have a range of accompanying factors. For example, you might wish to attend more events of a local branch of your professional institute. This would benefit you by allowing you to meet other people and find out about new developments. It could also mean that you were out for two evenings a month and did not see your family as much as previously. Assessing the pros and cons of making the change allows you to check whether you really want that particular objective. You could also weigh up the pros and cons of *not* making the change; e.g. "If I don't go to the meetings I could take up a new hobby or interest, but if I do go I could find I am bored and wish I had stayed at home." Doing both will give you a good overview of the situation you are aiming for.

It is also worth considering that sometimes there are "hidden" advantages in keeping things as they are. A term used in therapy is "secondary gain", which means that people sometimes maintain "unproductive" behaviour because of accompanying benefits it brings. For example, a person could claim that they couldn't learn to use a typewriter, or computer, and thereby have someone else type their letters for them. If they admitted they could learn, they might lose the benefit of the help they were getting. These things can sometimes occur unconsciously, so I am suggesting that you really delve into why it is that you do, or don't do, particular things; being as honest as you can with yourself in the process.

Example

Peter could consider the pros and cons of his objectives as follows:

Pros

- *This process will help me become more effective as a networker;*

- *This process will give me useful information about how other people function;*

- *This process will enhance my skills so I have added value in my present job and more to offer any future employer.*

Cons

- *This process will take up time (at least twenty hours over the next two months);*

- *This process will mean I have to fit my other work activities into a shorter time, creating more pressure on me in the short term;*

- *This process will mean admitting to others that there are skills I still need to develop.*

Pros

- *When I become better at networking I will perform more effectively;*

- *When I become better at networking I am more likely to get promoted.*

Cons

- *When I become better at networking I may find more time is needed for involvement in social and business events;*

- *When I become better at networking I may be asked to spend time in coaching others in these skills.*

Pros

- *If I don't pursue this course of action I will have more time for my present business activities.*

Cons

- *If I don't pursue this course of action my boss will be disappointed in me and I may not be as highly regarded within the company.*

So there are many factors to consider when thinking about pros and cons: what will and won't happen if you make the change and what will and won't happen if you don't make the change. Working out the pros and cons can be one of the most important elements in objective setting.

Ensuring What You Want is Achievable, Realistic and Within Your Own Control

However much you want to achieve your objective, it may actually be something which you cannot attain. This could be because it is actually impossible (being promoted in an organisation which is too small to have another tier of management), because it is not realistic (doing ten hours' work in five), or not within your control (making someone else behave differently towards you). Checking that your objective does meet all these criteria is an aid to success.

Example

Peter's objective is quite achievable, realistic and to a large extent within his own control. The elements that may not be within his control are getting agreement from all his "subjects" to assist him in his development project. There may also be occasions when other work becomes more urgent and his plans have to be temporarily put aside to devote time to other priorities. Overall, however, he is well able to conduct this project in a realistic and achievable manner.

Considering the Ethics of your Objective

You may have the best objective for you, but have you taken into account other people's feelings and attitudes? Have you considered the "politics" of the situation? There may be some things that are simply not appropriate in particular circumstances. Thinking these out is important. For example, you might want to impress a potential business contact with your sense of style, but if this involved "outdressing" everyone else at a low-key event, this could be quite inappropriate.

Example

Peter's overall project is well within the bounds of corporate ethics; there is no problem here. He might, however, consider whether all the people involved are willing to disclose their practices to him, have him sit in on their meetings and events, and collaborate in a venture where their behaviour might be compared or contrasted with others within the same organisation. Peter will need to take these issues into account in doing his planning.

Working out whether you have the Resources to Achieve your Objective

Often forgotten, but an important element. You may wish to impress potential clients with your style, but if it involves entertaining them at expensive restaurants or taking them to the opera, it could prove extremely costly. Thinking about resources such as money, time, support from others and so forth is also an important factor.

Example

Peter's main resource is time, and he will need to think carefully about how he allocates it. His other resources include the people who are co-operating with him and his mentor who is acting as a source of support and advice. He will also need to consider his energy levels and enthusiasm as renewable resources to be drawn upon as the project continues.

Knowing whether your Objective is actually the Final Goal or simply a Step on the Way

People often strive for things that are substitutes for what they really want; for example, losing weight when what they want is to be liked, or getting a higher salary when what they want is recognition. People also sometimes set objectives at too high, or too low, a level; for example, wanting to get fast promotion to a job several steps above your present one (too high) or wanting to produce a report on a subject when what is really needed is a face-to-face meeting to talk things through (too low). Being really clear about your ultimate goal will help you get to where you want to be.

Example

Peter will need to keep focused on his real objective, of enhancing his own skill levels, and not be satisfied with doing a research project providing useful information which he does not then apply. He will also need to make sure that he does not take up too much (or too little) of his subjects' time for the purpose in hand. When he is clear about what he wants, and the standards he needs to set in order to achieve it, he will be well on the way to success.

Knowing Yourself

Finally, and very important, is the issue of self-concept. Your goal may be an admirable one, but not right for you. For example, you may aspire to be the life and soul of the party but if you were naturally shy and retiring, this would not really be "you". You could learn the skills involved, but would you still be *you* if you did so? Only you will know whether your goal would fit well, or whether this course of action would lead to a feeling of discomfort or a sense that you were "playacting". Assess yourself honestly and then decide on goals that really fit with who you are.

Example

Peter has agreed to the development process after considering whether it would be appropriate for him. Both he and his manager agree that he is capable of doing what has been discussed and that it will fit well with his overall activities. He should be more than capable of doing the project, and using his findings in a beneficial way in both his work and his social ventures.

Exercise

So, now you know how to set good objectives. You might like to have a go at some of the following activities to improve your skills in this area. Do as many as you feel are useful:

- Set a networking objective for the next talk you attend, e.g. "I will identify at least one person in a key position in businesses who is prepared to give me advice on how to further my job search campaign."

- Set a networking objective for each of your telephone calls for one day this week, e.g. "I will use a positive tone of voice with each of my telephone calls today, so people will find me enthusiastic and helpful."

- Set a networking objective for your next outing with friends, e.g. "I will ask three people this week if I can offer them any assistance with useful contacts in their particular line of work."

Working out Tactics

The next step in the process is to think about tactics. I have already given you ways of setting detailed objectives and some of the elements of objective setting are tactical. When you decide that you will best achieve success by joining a particular organisation, this is a tactical move. However, there is more to tactics than objective setting and I would just like you to consider, for a moment, that there are possible options in achieving any objective.

Suppose you decide that your conversational skills need enhancing (I will be covering this topic in Chapter 8). This is your objective. You could work towards this objective in a variety of ways. You could do it by attending a class on conversation skills; you could do it by practice in real life situations; you could do it by reading more about such skills and listening to audiotapes. Or you could do a combination of all these things. Your tactics for achieving your objective can vary.

Example

Peter could decide that, tactically, he could encourage people within his organisation to help him by letting them know that acting as a support to him would also look good on their own appraisals, later on. So part of the way he will achieve his objectives is through helping others benefit from the process as well.

So when you consider your own networking activities, do make sure that, as well as setting objectives, you think through your possible tactics for achieving them.

Researching

Now you can move to the next step — researching. Doing research is useful in networking for many reasons; for example:

- You can find out more about people with whom you will be dealing;

- You can check what kind of event you will be attending;

- You can work out what kind of image will work best for the occasion;

- You can explore the kind of organisations which may be useful to you;

- You can check whether other people have already carried out activities you are considering.

Research can help you assess whether your intended activities are likely to be useful and check the best course of action to follow.

There are many ways of doing research; here are a few that many people find helpful.

Contacting Information Departments of Local or Specialist Libraries

There is a wealth of information available in libraries, which you can tap into once you know where to begin. Remember that, as well as public libraries, there are also libraries in public companies, hospitals, colleges, professional bodies and so forth.

If you are not sure how to access these resources, your local reference library will have a list of libraries and information bodies and there are many directories listing information sources available to the public. Information science is a growing discipline and you will find many resources available once you ask.

Checking Details in Company Registers

If the information you need is on a public company, you will find this available through open registers. You may have to pay for access to this service, and you can access it either in person or at a distance. Information held on companies includes details of directors and staff, financial records and information on operations.

Asking Telephonists in Companies for Contact Details of Their Staff

If you need details of individuals in order to contact them, phoning the switchboard of the organisation in which they work can be helpful. Asking the telephonist for the person's full name and job title will usually produce a positive response, although some organisations are reluctant to give out such information without knowing the purpose to which it will be put. In fact, company information can be so closely guarded that, in one instance I heard of, a consultant working for a major national organisation had to use indirect means even to gain access to the contact details of senior staff within the organisation.

Once you have details, it becomes much easier to contact the person in question and a letter generally looks better when it is addressed to the person in question, rather than just saying "Dear Sir or Madam".

Contacting Professional Associations

Professional bodies can be an excellent source of information on specialist areas. Many such bodies have a library or information department, as well as a range of publications relevant to their field of activity. Although some bodies will only make their information services available to members, you will generally be able to get answers to basic questions and may well be able to access information in more depth if you use your influencing skills well.

Speaking to People Who Have Already Done Things you are Considering Doing

When researching, it can be helpful to speak to others who may already have taken time to find out the information you need. You may have colleagues working in a similar field who you think could have relevant experiences or you might need to look at listings of people who could be useful (for example, membership directories of professional bodies, if these are publicly available). Once you know who to contact, it becomes easier to ask the relevant questions and gain useful information.

Looking at Registers of People and Organisations with Particular Interests

I have already referred to this briefly above, but it deserves a section of its own. There are many listings which you might find helpful, such as lists of personnel and training officers; lists of local councillors; lists of people who are self-employed; and so on. Some of these lists are only available for purchase through commercial organisations supplying mailing lists, and this can be an expensive process. However, some lists are also available through public sources, such as libraries, and this is well worth following up.

Reading Publications, Listening to or Viewing Tapes and Accessing Websites on Particular Topics

Finally, you can carry out research through published material. Material can be published through documents, such as books, magazines, reports and leaflets; it can also be found on audio or videotapes or can be published on the Internet. If you are using the Internet, you will find listings of sites containing information on most areas of interest. These sites are found by using appropriate "search engines". A search engine is an initial site on the Internet (and nowadays there are literally hundreds of these) which is used as the starting point for research. If you do not yet use the Internet, do find a colleague who can help you.

Finding out what is available will be a good starting point and will give you useful information. Do remember that information can become out of date, so check the publication dates of what you read or view, if available. Also remember copyright restrictions and be careful about reproducing information without permission or crediting sources.

Example
Peter could research which people in his organisation to contact by asking his manager or by going to the personnel manager to find out more about who might be receptive to his needs. Researching your networking activities is important and I hope the methods outlined here will prove useful to you.

Planning

Having done your research, the next step is to plan your activities. There are many ways of planning and many processes and products available to help you do so. Some useful approaches are covered here.

Planning Processes

There are two planning techniques you may find useful: the first is a highly structured technique and the second a less structured one.

The first technique is to list the things you want to do. You can keep your lists on a manual or an electronic system, depending on factors such as personal preference, available space and existing information retrieval systems you possess.

Your list can be very simple, just an itemised sequence of activities, or it can be classified or subdivided in various ways. One useful way to subdivide activities is to put them into three columns with the first for those activities which are essential, the second for activities which are desirable and the third for activities which are possible if time and resources permit. A sample list might look like this:

Planning List

SUBJECT: PLANNING TO JOIN A PROFESSIONAL BODY		
Essential Activities	**Desirable Activities**	**Possible Activities**
1. Research which bodies might be suitable 2. Contact each body for an information pack 3. Check you have the required qualifications or experience to join 4. Complete relevant application forms 5. Check agreement from anyone needed as a personal or professional referee	1. Speak to a membership officer in each organisation to get additional information 2. Speak to existing members of each organisation to get their opinions on the benefits of membership 3. Attend a meeting of the organisation to see how you feel about how they function	1. Read back copies of the organisation's publications

Once you have this list, you can check whether you have put down too many essential items, given the time available and whether you need to revise your priorities to fit everything in. You can also check you have the relevant resources and skills to actually do the things you intend. Seeing your plans listed in this way is a real aid to effectiveness.

The second technique is to use mind mapping, a technique popularised by Tony Buzan, who has written several books on the subject. Mind mapping allows you to consider the various elements associated with your activities in a more fluid way. You can think of a mind map as an aerial view of a tree, with a trunk, branches and twigs. When making a mind map, you put your main topic in the centre of a page, draw lines radiating from it to represent each idea you have for one aspect of the topic you wish to consider, then continue drawing branches off each line as you think of more aspects of each of the topic elements. You can continue this process until you have exhausted your ideas (although you could ask a friend or colleague to help, in which case the mind map is likely to expand even more as their own ideas are added to yours).

Once your mind map is completed, you can review it, work out which structure seems to emerge from it and then transfer the elements of it to a different sheet of paper, where it can be turned into a more linear sequence. Alternatively, you could leave the mind map as it is, if you prefer that kind of visual diagram showing connections as well as separate items.

Example of a Mind Map Diagram
SUBJECT: PLANNING TO JOIN A PROFESSIONAL BODY

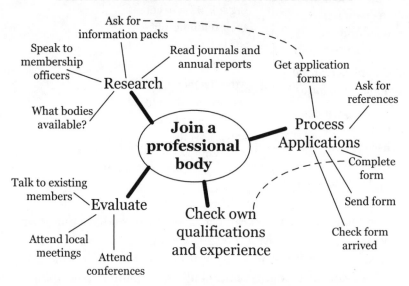

Mind mapping is a good alternative to simple listing and can show you clearly the interrelationships between the different parts of your plan. It is also a good way to think about a topic without having to force it into a structure right from the start.

Whichever approach you use (and you can combine them if you wish), your planning process will be improved by using some kind of analytical and recording device to support your thinking process.

Making Time

Planning takes time. It is easy to underestimate the amount of time you may need, so it is important to allow yourself sufficient time for what you need to do. It is also useful to have a place where you can concentrate without being interrupted.

And while we are talking about time, if you find time management hard, it can help to imagine all the tasks you need to do and, if possible, represent them graphically, say on a sheet of paper. Once you can see all the things you need to do, it is often easier to assess how much time each element will take. A simple method for doing this is called a flow chart, where each element leads to the next.

Flow Chart Diagram

SUBJECT: PLANNING TO JOIN A PROFESSIONAL BODY

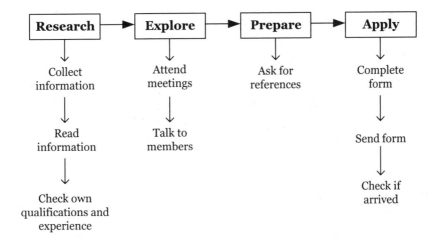

There are many other techniques which are useful in time management, including rapid reading, and there are many good books on the subject. I have listed some of them in the Bibliography.

Planning Methods

People plan in different ways and it helps to know your own favoured approaches. For example, do you like working on your own, or do you plan better when you can discuss your ideas with others?

Some people find that planning is easier when it is done visually; if this is the case, you may want to use wall charts, your computer screen or other processes which will give you a visual display.

Example

Peter could plan his "campaign" by listing the steps he wished to take; deciding which people to contact, and in which order; deciding the format for each session; and deciding to get himself in a good frame of mind for the discussion and to encourage the people he was visiting to look forward to the conversations as well.

Organising

Being organised will help you network successfully. Some of the things you can organise are:

- Yourself

- Your physical environment

- Your information

- Your activities

- Other people who support you.

Let's take each in turn to see how organisation can help you succeed.

Yourself

This can be easy if you are naturally self-disciplined, or harder if you like to be spontaneous and respond as circumstances change.

Useful aids to self-organisation include a diary, a personal organiser system in a binder or on your computer, a wall planner and post-it notes in places where you can see them as reminders. It can help to have a duplicate diary, partly in case you lose the first one and partly so that you can leave one with a colleague to enable them to check your availability if people need access to you, and make provisional appointments, to be confirmed on your return. Having these simple aids can help enormously and keep you on track with your activities.

Your Physical Environment

It is easier for most people to work in an organised environment. Having specific places for things helps you access them quickly and saves time. It is also useful to have a dedicated place to carry out your administration, where you can place your office furniture, your storage systems and your equipment in the most appropriate places.

Keeping your desk tidy will help you feel in control and give a good impression to any visitors. Keeping things clean, having a nice atmosphere — perhaps with some plants or interesting objects around or pictures on the wall — will all add to the sense of order and balance.

Your Information

Having a well-organised filing system will help you access records easily. You might want to have files for subject areas, named people or organisations, active contacts, current projects and so forth. A coloured system, with different coloured files, or labels, for particular topics, can aid retrieval.

Having a system for incoming papers and calls also helps. In-trays or folders for the day's activities, or for things held over from the day before or things to do over the next few days, will help you get a sense of order into your paperwork.

Organising your computer files is also important, making sure their names accurately reflect their contents, so you can remember what they contain. It can also be useful to add a "tag" to the names of files which are similar, so you can see at a glance which ones contain information of a particular class.

Your Activities

Arranging your activities so you do similar things during certain parts of the day can help you manage your time and organise things well. For example, making telephone calls during one period, rather than interspersing them throughout a whole day, or dealing with correspondence at one time rather than letting it drag out for a long period can give you a sense of achievement and make the most of time available.

Organising activities well in advance is also useful. Thinking ahead in this way will ensure that you have time to prepare and give you a sense of what lies ahead. It is also helpful to other people if you can plan activities which may involve them well in advance, rather than springing requirements on them at short notice.

Other People Who Support You

Sometimes it is necessary to organise other people as well as yourself. If you have family, friends or paid staff or associates who assist you with your activities, or look after your other commitments while you spend time on networking, it can help to make sure they are well organised too.

So give them the resources they need (time, encouragement, money or whatever), check their availability, make sure they know what is expected of them and dovetail their activities if more than one person assists you. Doing all these things will provide a real support framework which will help you become more effective overall.

Remember to show your appreciation if you do get the support you need — your supporters are part of your network too, so treat them in a way which will ensure your relationship with them thrives and is mutually beneficial.

Example

Peter could organise his time so as to allow sufficient gaps in his diary for the planned meetings. He could also organise his recording system before he embarked on the visits, so he had a consistent format for recording the information he collected, such as by setting up a system on his computer to handle it.

Preparing

Finally, preparation is important in networking, as it allows you to maximise the impact you create and alerts you to potential opportunities. There are many things you can prepare, such as:

- Yourself

- Your clothes and accessories

- What you will say

- Your timing

- Material you will have available to give out

- Requests you would like to make.

I will be covering many of these elements in later chapters, so I will just illustrate them here by looking one last time at our friend Peter:

Example

Peter could prepare himself before each meeting by taking time to collect his thoughts, get all his questions in note form and take some time to relax and motivate himself for the discussions. He could also prepare the ground by telephoning each person prior to the meeting, just to make sure they were expecting him and still had time available as agreed.

This chapter has covered various elements which are important as first stages in networking. By taking time to consider all these things, you will be better able to conduct yourself well and make the most of any events you attend and any interactions you engage in.

Chapter Five

Self-management Skills

In this chapter, you will find a range of techniques which will help you get into a good state for networking success. One of the most important things in networking is to convince yourself, and others with whom you come into contact, that you are confident, capable, interesting, knowledgeable and effective. Self-management helps you develop a persona which is engaging and attractive; it enables you to manage your feelings and your behaviour to good effect.

So what does self-management consist of? There are a number of factors which I will cover here:

- Self-awareness

- Confidence and self-esteem

- Motivation and energy

- Memory training.

You have almost certainly already developed skills in these areas and the information which follows will enable you to further develop the attributes you have. In this chapter you will find some questions to help you identify your current skill levels in each of these areas and then some ways of further enhancing these skills. The higher your skill levels in self-management, the more successful you are likely to be in interacting with others.

Self-awareness

Let's take self-awareness first. Sometimes people talk of feeling "self-conscious". When they use this term, they often mean that they feel uncomfortable or embarrassed as they think about themselves in relation to others. When I use the term "self-awareness", I am not considering this kind of negative reaction to oneself, but rather a skill in monitoring your thoughts, feelings and behaviour so as to be able to do things which help you to achieve your objectives (and stop doing things which hinder this process).

So self-awareness is an aid to effectiveness by helping you be more in control of what you do. How exactly can you develop self-awareness? The first point I would like to make is that it *can* be developed, because it is a skill. Some people are highly self-aware, while others have not yet developed the ability to monitor themselves. The term for using self-awareness is "dissociation". Being dissociated means that you are detached from yourself in some way — able to monitor your own behaviour by "watching" yourself and listening to yourself, as if you were an observer.

In contrast, the term "associated" is used for a person who is so wrapped up in their own experience that they are not distancing themselves from it at all; until it is pointed out to them, they can be oblivious to exactly how they are behaving.

Now both of these states, associated and dissociated, have their uses. Being associated is appropriate when you really want to immerse yourself in an experience; for example, listening to music or bathing in the warmth of the sun. At such times, you probably don't want to be detached, but simply to enjoy experiencing the event.

Being dissociated is appropriate when you need to check your performance and progress. For example, in a negotiation or presentation, it would probably be very useful to check how you are getting on, how you are coming across and how you might look or sound to the other people with whom you are interacting.

So both association and dissociation have their places and both are well worth developing. Before I discuss how to develop each of these, you might like to take a few moments to answer the following questions:

• Are you often aware of the sound of your own voice?

• Do you often imagine how you appear to other people?

• Do you often have a discussion in your head about people, issues or events?

- Do you often notice your feelings about things at the time you experience those feelings?

If you answered "yes" to most of these questions, you probably spend quite a bit of your time in a dissociated state and if you answered "no" to most of them you probably spend more time in an associated state.
Now take a few moments to answer the next set of questions:

- Do you often wish you had noticed yourself doing things at the time, rather than simply in retrospect?

- Do you often realise you have reacted to something instinctively, without really thinking it through?

- Do you often allow your emotions to control you?

If you answered "yes" to most of these questions, you probably spend more time in a state of association, and if you answered "no" to most of them you probably spend much of your time in a state of dissociation.

Example

Jane *is the manager of a small retail organisation. She is quite an excitable person and has to work hard at controlling how she feels when someone behaves in a way she finds annoying. At times, she allows her temper to get the better of her, feels angry and shouts at people. Her staff find it hard to relate to Jane and find her emotional outbursts difficult to handle. Jane spends much of her time in an associated state; as feelings well up in her, she doesn't "step back" from them to manage what she is doing, but simply reacts, often with negative consequences.*

John *is the administrator of a small professional body. He is a quiet, reserved person, who seldom shows his feelings or tells people what is going on in his mind. When a potentially difficult situation arises, John deals with it calmly, thinking about all the aspects involved and taking care to manage his behaviour so he presents a competent image. John's staff like him, but sometimes find it hard to relate to him in a personal way, as he can appear a little distant. John spends much of his time in a dissociated state, being distanced from what he is doing rather than fully engaged in it.*

Both Jane and John could benefit from enhancing their skills in managing their "states". Jane would benefit from learning how to dissociate more, so she is aware of her emotional state before it gets the better of her and impacts on other people. John would benefit from learning how to be more associated, so he experiences different emotions and comes across to others as engaged and lively.

If your answers to the above questions indicated dissociation, you might like to work more at the skills of being associated, whereas if your answers indicated association you might like to work more at the skill of being dissociated. The exercises that follow explain how you can do this and you will find that working on these skills can enable you to be more successful in personal interactions.

Exercises

Association

Let's take association first. Being associated means really being "in" an experience; to practise association, take yourself back to a past experience that left a lasting impact on you. A good way to do this is to find a comfortable place to sit, or lie down, free from obtrusive noises and interruptions, put on some calming music, if this helps you to relax, and then go through the instructions that follow.

Once you are comfortable, think about an event you remember well. Select a pleasant event, rather than one with unpleasant associations. Examples of events you might choose are being at a concert, taking part in a sporting activity, going to a celebration, walking in beautiful countryside and so on. Just select whatever event comes to mind and make sure it is a *specific* event, not a generalisation from a mixture of events.

Now think back to the actual occasion and remember what you could *see* at the time; for example, the scenery, room furnishings, people's clothes, objects and so forth. Put in as much detail as you can of shapes, colours and juxtapositions.

Now think about what you could *hear*. Notice whether people were talking, music was playing, birds were singing, water was flowing and so on. Recall the volume and intensity of the sounds, the direction from which they were coming, pitch and tone and so forth.

And now think about any *physical sensations* you had at the time; for example, were you warm or cool, keeping still or moving, holding or touching anything, and so on. Notice how you were breathing — how quickly or slowly, deeply or rhythmically.

Now bring back your actual *feelings* at the time; for example, were you relaxed, energetic, excited, amused, etc. Truly re-live these feelings.

You may wish to ask a friend to read these instructions out to you — in a pleasant tone of voice and at a fairly slow pace — as you relax. Once you are immersed in this process, you should find the experience comes flooding back to you. When this happens, you are likely to be in an associated state, i.e. experiencing the feelings fully, rather than being distanced from them.

Doing this exercise regularly, using different situations to give you a range of experiences, will help you get in touch with your feelings about things and is also likely to help you become more relaxed and stress-free as a by-product.

Dissociation

Now let's think about the state of dissociation. To dissociate yourself, you need to become aware of what you are doing as you do it. One parallel to this is an advanced driving test where you may be asked to talk the examiner through your thoughts and actions as they occur — for example, commenting on the speed at which you are driving, road conditions, the actions of pedestrians and other drivers and so on.

A good way to practise dissociation is to do a running commentary on some of your everyday behaviour. For example, as you use the bathroom in the morning, you might say to yourself (in your head if anyone else is around!): "I am picking up my toothbrush"; "I am turning on the tap"; "I feel quite warm"; "I can see my reflection in the mirror"; "The water feels cool"; "I am thinking of which route to take to work".

By using such "internal dialogue", you are telling yourself exactly what you are thinking, feeling and doing as it happens and this will enhance your skills in self-observation.

Having learned the skills of association and dissociation, you will be better equipped to manage yourself when dealing with others. Being associated will allow you to participate fully in activities and come across as engaged and involved. Being dissociated will allow you to monitor your actions and select different behaviour if you think it is more appropriate in the circumstances.

Both association and dissociation have their place in networking. Being associated will allow you to fully experience the situation you are in, and help you come across as participating fully. Being dissociated will allow you to monitor your own behaviour and decide whether you need to alter it in any way. The more you practise these skills, the more your interactions with others are likely to benefit.

Confidence and Self-esteem

Let's move on to ways of becoming more confident and feeling more positive about yourself. Some people just seem to exude confidence; they appear convinced that what they do is right and they seem comfortable in any social situation. How do they become like this?

It is sometimes said that people are naturally either confident or not, but I believe that confidence is another attribute which it is possible to develop. I know from personal experience that it is possible to gain confidence as you go through life and I am convinced that it is possible to shortcut this process by applying a range of simple and easily learned techniques, some of which I will be introducing you to shortly.

It is important to remember that your thoughts, feelings and beliefs about yourself are contributory factors in confidence. We sometimes call these things collectively "self-esteem", and this also needs to be boosted if you are truly able to be a confident person.

In Chapter 3, there were some questions about confidence and self-esteem; I hope you answered these, as they will have given you some useful information. If you did not do the questions, I suggest you go back and look at them now.

Exercises

Before starting the exercises, I would like to introduce you to the concept of "self-talk" or internal dialogue. Some people are more aware than others of having discussions with themselves in their heads. If you do this, you will know instantly what I mean; if you don't, you may wonder what I am talking about. Self-talk is a kind of internal debate, a conversation about things. Some people find that if they have difficulty in sleeping at night, it is self-talk which keeps them awake.

The first two exercises involve the idea of self-talk. Monitor yourself over a period of two or three days. If you find it a little time-consuming, you can simply select particular periods in which to do the exercises, but it would be really helpful if you could keep alert to the processes throughout a two- to three-day period. Make sure that when you do these two exercises you are in a "typical" state of mind; do not pick a time when you are in an exaggerated emotional state, such as being excited about a forthcoming event, upset about a past occurrence, annoyed with yourself or others, or lacking in energy through tiredness or overwork. Just pick a few days when life is fairly average for you.

1. Becoming aware of your thoughts about yourself

To do this, you will need to notice any thoughts you are having about yourself. For instance, you may be thinking ahead to a future event and be either positive or negative about how you are likely to handle it; you may be picturing something which has happened and be either criticising or praising yourself for what you did; you may be engaged in an activity and thinking that you are doing it well or badly.

Each time you think about yourself, make a note and be sure to notice, and record, whether your thoughts about yourself are positive or negative.

2. Becoming aware of your thoughts about yourself in relation to other people

Now, notice anything that goes through your mind in relation to yourself and other people. You might be comparing your health, dress sense, academic ability, skill at relationships, financial situation and so on. Each time this happens, notice the thought and then notice whether you are comparing yourself favourably or unfavourably with others. Notice if what you are comparing is your behaviour (what you *do*) or your persona (what kind of a person you *are*).

These two exercises will help you become aware of your thoughts and give you an idea of how positive or negative they are.

Now you can move on to the rest of the exercises, which should help you boost your confidence and self-esteem. I would suggest you practise these daily for a month; they will only take a few minutes to do and will pay real dividends in how you feel about yourself and how you come across to others.

3. Generating positive self-talk

First, think of one or two things you believe you can't do, or don't do very well, and which you would like to be able to do. For example, you might think that you can't speak to strangers very easily, or that you aren't very good at organising your paperwork.

Now, in your head, say these things to yourself; e.g. "I'm not a good organiser" or "I find it hard to speak to people I don't know".

Now for the nice bit. Have a go at substituting some different kinds of self-talk for the ones you have just experienced. There are a few options here, for example:

- Say the same words to yourself ("I'm not a good organiser"; "I find it hard to speak to people I don't know"), but say them in a funny voice — for example, that of a favourite cartoon character. Notice how difficult it is to take these words seriously when they are being said in this way.

- Add the words "yet" or "at the moment" to your sentences; for example, "I'm not a good organiser, *yet*" or "I find it hard to speak to people I don't know, *at the moment*". These sentences will allow you to consider that it is possible to change your present behaviour to become more successful in the future.

- Reverse the words, so for example you say: "I *am* a good organiser"; "I find it *easy* to speak to people I don't know". Again, this makes it seem much more possible and can give you confidence that you are able to do these things.

- Say: "I wonder *how quickly* I will be able to be a good organiser" and "I wonder *how soon* I will be able to talk easily and comfortably to people I don't know". These words give your mind the idea that it is possible to act differently, and that it can happen quickly. It is then much more likely that these things will come about.

Whether or not you are aware of your own self-talk, this exercise will help you become more confident about yourself. The reason for this is that your actions and feelings are often governed by what goes on in your mind. If you have negative thoughts in your mind, your behaviour is likely to be influenced by them. By substituting more positive thinking, you can move on and become more effective.

4. Generating positive physical states

This exercise concerns the relationship between your physical and your mental states. If we say someone is depressed, they are not simply mentally depressed. Their body reflects their state also, so they tend to round their shoulders, drop their head, speak slowly and quietly, move slowly and so on. Conversely, when someone is enthusiastic, they tend to be active, move and speak quickly, hold their head high and so on.

Once you understand the relationship between physical and mental states, it is possible to improve your mental state by altering your physical one. This exercise will help in this way.

Find a quiet place and sit down. As in the earlier exercise on association (on page 96), remember a past time — for this exercise it should be a time when you felt *very confident* about something specific. Think yourself back to that time by remembering what you could *see*, what you could *hear* and how you *felt*. Turn back to page 96 if you need to remind yourself of the process in more detail.

Once you have remembered the occasion fully, your body will take on the physiology it had at that time, for example the posture, the breathing, the movement and so forth. Once this has happened, describe to yourself, in as much detail as you can, what your posture is, your breathing pattern, the expression on your face and so on. Now stand up, keeping the feeling of confidence, and notice your posture, breathing and movement as you stand. Now move around, still keeping the feeling of confidence, and again notice your posture, breathing and movement.

What you have done is recreated what your body does *when you are confident*. By consciously describing it to yourself you will make it easier to remember. In future, when you want to feel confident, you will find that by getting your posture, movement and breathing aligned with how it was when you *were* confident in the past, you will be able to re-access the actual feelings of confidence you are capable of generating.

5. *Extending your boundaries*

The last exercise in this section is about working within boundaries which you set yourself. One reason for lacking confidence could be a concern about venturing beyond your own comfort zone. When you are in a familiar situation, you can be confident. However, once you move into unknown territory, there is a new scenario. To be good at networking means making contact with people, often ones with whom you are unfamiliar, and maintaining the contact effectively. If there is any element of the situation which is new to you, it may be that you feel less than confident about it.

You *can* enhance your confidence in networking through gradually extending your boundaries. To do the exercise, take one context that is relevant to networking, such as speaking to people on the telephone. Now consider what you are already comfortable with when telephoning; perhaps you feel confident about making very specific requests, or about calling to check information you have been given.

Now, extend your telephone conversations to include other aspects which you may not have considered, or may have thought were more complicated. For example, the following list gives you some ideas of what you could include in your conversations:

- *Make a statement* about how useful you have found the call;

- *Make a request* that the person calls you back if any further information arises;

- *Offer to find out* something for the other person;

- *Ask for* the names of any other people whom you may approach for additional assistance;

- *Invite* the person to an event of mutual interest.

Now, each time you make a phone call, where appropriate, add some of these elements to your conversations. What you will be doing is gaining confidence in extending the boundaries of your interactions. Begin with one statement or request that stretches you a little, and build up until you feel comfortable with asking for, and offering, suggestions, advice, assistance and support.

If you find the particular aspects I have suggested irrelevant to the kind of calls you make, you can simply substitute different ones of your own.

Motivation and Energy

Now let's think about motivation. Being able to motivate yourself is a key skill in networking. Many people want to network, intend to network, know exactly what they would get out of networking, but never actually do it. One reason for this is lack of motivation; it simply isn't important enough for them to carry it out; something else always seems to take precedence. This part of the chapter will give you some ideas on self-motivation.

Motivation is what drives us towards achievement. Without motivation from ourselves or others, we would probably cease to function. Motivation is needed to get out of bed, look after ourselves, go to work, interact with others, achieve goals and grow and develop. So what makes motivation possible?

There are many theories of motivation and if you work in management you have probably heard of some of them. Popular theories have included those of Abraham Maslow (hierarchy of needs), Frederick Herzberg (hygiene and motivation factors), David McClelland (achievement orientation), Victor Vroom (expectancy theory) and many others.

The theories seek to explain motivation through different factors including the need for survival, social contact, recognition and so on. All the theories have their place in academic thinking and in practical application, but they all presuppose that people can be categorised in different ways. While this is a workable principle in broad terms, in practice people differ and are unique. Because of this, if you wish to increase your motivation, it helps firstly to know something of yourself as an individual and secondly to know something about techniques which anyone can use to raise their motivation levels.

The tests in Chapter 3 presented some motivational patterns; here are some additional questions on motivational *level*:

- Do you feel your motivation levels are generally high for most things?

- Do you usually find it easy to motivate yourself?

- Do you have periods when you find it harder to motivate yourself?

- Would you like to have more ways of increasing your motivation?

In the section which follows, I will give you a few ideas for working on your motivational levels.

The exercises mainly rely on the principle that once a concept is *real* for you, you are more likely to work towards it. What I mean by "real" is that you have formed such a strong mental representation of the concept that you are almost compelled to work towards it. This idea will become clearer as you work through the following activities.

Exercises

These simple exercises will give you more flexibility in how you use your mind and are a good foundation for positive motivational thinking. You will probably find it easiest to do the exercises sitting comfortably in a quiet place, where you will not be interrupted. In any event, do not do them while driving or using equipment or machinery.

1. Strengthening your mental skills

- In your mind, picture a table and chair. Now, in your imagination, make the table larger and the chair smaller. Now make the chair much larger and the table smaller, so it would fit under the chair. Now return them to their original sizes. Now make the table green and the chair yellow. Now make the table red and the chair purple. Now see a tablecloth on the table and a cushion on the chair. Now see stripes on the tablecloth and spots on the cushion. Now picture someone pulling the chair up to the table and sitting on the chair.

- In your mind, as you see the person sitting on the chair, imagine him or her speaking. Notice the sound of the voice and the words being spoken. Now make the voice louder and louder, then softer and softer. Make the voice speak slowly, then fast. Make the words sound serious, then funny, then angry, then friendly. Now hear the person get up from the chair and walk across the floor; listen to their shoes as they take each step. Hear the person turn on a radio and hear music come from it.

- In your mind, imagine the smell of fresh bread, the smell of oranges and the smell of perfume. Now imagine the taste of cheese, of tomatoes and of peppermint.

- Now remember feeling warm and then feeling cool. Remember how it feels to walk in sand and how it feels to walk on a hard floor.

- Now remember what it is like to feel energetic, happy, curious, relaxed, excited and contented.

2. Visualising Success

Think of a networking objective; for example, being comfortable with asking someone for a contact name or enjoying giving a talk at a local society. Now, in your imagination, create as clear an image as you can of what you have selected — for example, asking someone for a name or giving a talk. You may be able to create very clear images in your mind but, if you find it hard at first, simply get a rough idea of what your goal would look like.

Now make your goal as enticing as possible. To do this, I am going to give you a few sets of alternative things to do with your mental image. For each pair of alternatives, see which makes the image more appealing to you and select that particular option. Work through them all and then look at your image again, with all the best options in place. Firstly make your mental image a) clearer, and b) hazier. Now make the image a) very large, then b) very small. Now make the image a) very close then b) very distant. Now make the image a) a moving picture (like a video), then b) a still one (like a photograph). Now make the picture a) black and white, and then b) in colour. Now a) see yourself in the image, and then b) see the image as if you were there seeing it with your own eyes.

This technique will be useful when you want to motivate yourself to achieve something; just make the image of achieving it (or having achieved it) really enticing and it will draw you towards it.

3. Listening to things going well

Now take another networking goal — perhaps handling telephone calls well, or organising a social event. Now, in your mind, tell yourself you are going to do it really well. Now imagine the voice of someone whose opinions you respect also telling you that you can do it well and that you will be really good at it.

Now imagine actually doing the thing you wish for and, in your mind, hear other people complimenting you on doing it, or having done it, well. Make all the voices sound very positive, very enthusiastic and very friendly.

This exercise should enhance your motivation by making it seem that the activity really is achievable.

4. Imagining achievement

This mental rehearsal exercise was created by Judith DeLozier. Again, select a networking goal, maybe being more assertive or perhaps encouraging someone else to take a course of action. Now, make a mental image of yourself, in the future, doing the activity really well. (If you find it hard at first to imagine yourself doing it, recall observing someone else doing something similar and notice how they do it; how they sit, stand or move; how they approach and speak to people, etc. Once you have remembered what they do, just picture yourself behaving in a similar way.)

As you picture yourself, make the picture as large, clear, bright and colourful as you can. See as much detail in it as you can. Now, imagine "stepping into" this picture so that you imagine how it would actually *feel* to be doing those things. As you do this, become aware of any sounds in the environment, any things people might be saying, how people around you would look and how you feel physically as you behave in this way.

This mental rehearsal achieves a number of things. Firstly, it makes it seem more possible, because your mind takes such images and sensations as if they were real, so it believes you have already done the activity really well. Secondly, it gives you an opportunity to try it out in your mind before having to do it in real life, and in this way you can anticipate different possibilities and go for the course of action which will produce the best results. Thirdly, research indicates that such mental rehearsal of skills produces as good (and possibly even better) results as real life practice; many sportspeople, arts performers and others use these techniques to practise their skills and are delighted with the results.

What seems to happen during mental rehearsal is that, unlike real life where we occasionally get results which are less than perfect, when we practise in our minds we can go over "perfect" behaviour time and time again, establishing networks of nerve connections in our brains, which then allow the real-life experience to take place easily and smoothly. There is much more written on this topic; for more information see the Bibliography.

Example

It now seems, according to recently reported research, that not only does mental rehearsal improve skill levels in sports, it may even — amazingly — cause enhanced physiological responses, such as increased muscle development. In addition, imagining coming first in a race, winning a tournament or beating a record is likely to make it more real to your mind and therefore more achievable.

A final point on motivation. One writer, Csikszentmihalyi, has explored the relationship between challenge and skill. When the difficulty of a task just stretches your skill level comfortably, you are likely to perform at your best and achieve what is called "flow", where activity seems effortless and your focus is complete. See the Bibliography for more on this.

Before we leave this section, a brief word about energy. We all have times of the day when we are at our best. By keeping an "energy diary", you can work out your daily rhythms and then use your peak times for demanding, or creative, activities. Having regular breaks to replenish your physical energy is also important, and responding quickly to signs of tiredness (lack of concentration, hunger, restlessness, etc.) is important. See the Bibliography for relevant books.

Memory Training

A good memory is important to networking. There are many things you can do to improve your memory skills and this section will give you some ideas on how to do that.

Just take a few moments to answer the following questions about your memory:

- Do you think your memory is generally good?

- Do you think your memory has become a little worse over the years?

- Do you find there are some things you can remember easily and others you are more likely to forget?

- Do you already use specific techniques for remembering things?

- Would you like to enhance your memory even further?

There are many different ways of remembering things, and probably the most important thing is to *intend* to remember. Simply putting that idea in your mind will make it more possible. Until you are confident that you will remember facts you need, it is probably best to make notes. Jotting down brief detail of things, as soon as you can, will help you re-access information. So, after meeting someone new, you might write their name in your diary; when hearing a useful piece of information on TV, you can write it down on a sheet of paper or notepad which you keep close for that purpose.

It is not always possible or appropriate to take notes; for example, at a formal dinner, you may not want to produce a notebook to record details of your fellow diners. So here are some other ways of remembering.

Association

By associating one piece of information with another, you can make it easier to recall. I once had a neighbour, whose name I always remembered, but I tended to forget the names of her husband and daughter. The daughter's name was Vicki, and she had a turned-up nose. I recalled that, as a child, there was a product called Vick, an ointment that was put on your chest if you had a blocked-up nose, so you could breathe more easily. I thought that if you had Vick spread on your chest, your nose would probably turn up if it could. In future, I remembered the girl's name by seeing her nose and remembering the association with Vick ointment. The husband's name was Andrew, so I thought, when I saw his wife: "It's her and who . . . Oh, Andrew" and I always remembered his name too! I have now forgotten my neighbour's name, but still recall the name of her husband and daughter because I made a point of making these associations at the time. Once you have made associations in this way, the links tend to persist over lengthy periods; it is ten years since I last had any contact with this family, yet I still recall this information.

To use this technique, especially for remembering names, simply find a physical feature of the person which has strong characteristics and associate it with something else which will help you link the two. Make sure you only use a characteristic which persists through time; nose, mouth or ear shapes are good; hair colour is not because it can be altered.

Humour

By making a situation seem funny, it can be easier to remember. Suppose you are on your way to a meeting and don't have time to make a note, but want to remember to tell your colleagues there about a new kind of filing system you think would be useful to them. You can imagine the filing system and, inside each file, a miniature version of your colleagues, peeping out from the top and waving to you. As soon as you see the people, you should remember this amusing scene and remember to mention the new system. Be as creative as you like with this; it really helps you recall things effectively.

Exaggeration

Exaggeration is another aid to memory. Suppose you want to remember which platform your train departs from on a business trip. Just imagine the platform number as if it were a firework display; see the number lit up with colourful flares, hear the sound of the fireworks as they fizz and pop. Really make the scene as bright, dazzling and exciting as you can. You should remember the platform number and may well take some of the excitement of the firework display onto the train with you.

Telling Stories

This technique is really useful for remembering lists, or sequences, of items. Suppose you have to buy some stationery — a few lined pads, some pens, a bottle of eraser fluid, some overhead projector transparencies and some staples. You can make up a story which incorporates all these items and, by utilising the elements of humour and exaggeration, as well as association, it will be even more effective. An example follows; I have indicated the items to remember in bold:

*A bus driver started a new job and was told to take the first in a line of buses which were standing in the depot. As he climbed into the cab, he found the driver on the previous shift had left a pile of **lined pads** on the seat. There were so many of them he couldn't get in at all; they filled the space and had overflowed so that a few of them had fallen onto the floor. He picked them up, one by one, and put them on the ground by the side of the bus. As he did that, he noticed some **pens** on the ground; he noticed the pens because they were making an unusual bleeping sound, which he had never heard a pen do before. He bent to pick them up but, before he could do so, a spray of **white fluid** came from above and completely obliterated the pens; he just couldn't see them any more as they had blended into the background as if they had been **erased**. Leaving the pens behind, he climbed into the cab. The windscreen was rather dirty, so he cleaned it; he did such a good job of it that it appeared to him quite **transparent**, like a sheet of **clear plastic**. He was really pleased with himself. He set off in the bus, putting his new route on the ledge beside him, with each sheet **stapled** neatly so they were in the right order. A new day had begun . . .*

Once you get into the habit of making up little stories like this, you will find that lists are easier to remember; the technique works really well.

Mnemonics

In this case, you use the first letters of the items you want to remember to create a word, then use the word to help you remember the original list. Let's take the items in the example above — lined pads, pens, eraser fluid, transparencies and staples. The first letters of these are L, P, E, T and S. You don't have to keep the letters in the same order, or even make up a "correct" word with them. If you rearranged these letters you would form the sequence SPELT. By remembering this one word, you will be able to work back and remember the separate items on your list.

There are many other memory-training techniques and, for further reading, see the Bibliography.

Chapter Six

Communication Skills —
Impression Management

Having considered self-management, I now turn to how you manage the impression you convey to others around you. Firstly, though, a few words about the different elements of face-to-face communications to introduce you to this chapter and the four that follow.

The Elements of Face-to-Face Communication

There are generally considered to be three main elements to face-to-face communications: a) your appearance — how you *look*; b) your voice and speech — how you *sound*; and c) your message — the *content* of what you communicate. The first two of these are what are called "process" elements — in other words, they are about *how* you communicate — and the third is what is termed a "content" element — *what* you communicate. Both process and content are vital to effective communications and some research indicates that the process elements far outweigh the content ones on many occasions, especially initial contacts. This means that how you look and sound can attract or repel other people. If the impression you create through your appearance is inviting, then it is more likely that people will listen to what you are saying and pay attention to you. However, if you put people off through your appearance, it will be far harder for you to persuade them to listen to what you have to say. Both initial and continuing impressions are important and getting your appearance "right" can be vital.

Whether you like it or not, people form opinions of you, and these opinions are often based on how you look. In western society at least, how you *look* is often of primary concern. Apart from telephone conversations, we generally see people before we hear them speak; for example, at an interview, the interviewee generally enters the room before talking, so visual impressions are especially important. Because of this, being able to manage your physical appearance and vary it appropriately for different circumstances is an important skill.

How You Look

Visual impressions include a) your appearance (clothes, accessories, hair, cosmetics, etc.); b) your non-verbal messages (posture, movement and gesture); and c) the accoutrements of your social and business life (car, phone, business stationery, etc.). This chapter concentrates on visual elements.

How You Sound

How you sound is also important. Years ago, having a particular "accent" was considered important in the UK. Now, regional variations in speech are more valued and you can find radio and television presenters speaking in a much wider range of voice patterns than previously. However, it is still important that your voice is clear and understandable and that the sound you make is pleasing rather than discordant. I will be returning to voice in Chapter 7.

What You Say

Finally, what you say counts. The content of your message is, after all, what you want to convey, so being good at communicating messages will create a positive impression. The actual content of what you say can only be decided by you and is an important part of communication, along with appearance and voice. I will be returning to this topic in Chapter 8.

Image

You can create an impression well before anyone actually meets you. Take the following scenarios:

• You drive into a company car park for a meeting with some senior managers. You didn't allow time to organise yourself properly before starting out, and so the things you need for the meeting are scattered on the seat or in carrier bags. You are also wearing old shoes to drive in and have not brushed your hair. You intend to tidy yourself, and your papers, in the car before going into the building. One of the people you will be meeting looks out of the window and sees you, looking untidy and harassed, and shuffling papers about. What impression might this person have of you at that stage?

- You answer a job advertisement, but your letter contains some spelling mistakes and you inadvertently stood a cup of coffee on it before sending it and it has a brown ring at the side. What impression is the personnel officer receiving your letter likely to gain as a result of this communication?

Exaggerated examples? Perhaps, but I know of many such cases that have led to people missing out on opportunities or being perceived in a negative way. Better to think about image well in advance, and at all stages of your activities, if you really wish to be effective.

If you believe that this approach is superficial and that people should not be concerned with surface appearance, or if you feel it is not what you wish to spend your time on, fair enough. However, do remember that some people find it important and by ignoring such conventions you could limit your chances of success. A delegate at a recent conference said he was treated very differently when he wore a suit; it generated much more positive responses from people.

Exercise

Here are some questions about image:

Your Own Image

1. Given that you may create different impressions in different situations, how many of the following do you think describe the image you give to other people?

   ◆ Casual
   ◆ Smart
   ◆ Stylish
   ◆ Trendy
   ◆ Sporty
   ◆ Professional

♦   Classic.

Maybe there are other categories that you could add to this list if they describe your own image better.

2.   Is there a difference between the image you think you create and the one you would like to create; if so, what is the difference?

3.   Would you like to have more flexibility in how you come across to others?

Other People's Images

1.   How aware are you of the way other people look?

2.   What do you think a professional image consists of and how do you recognise it in others?

3.   What do you admire in the way other people look?

We can now move on to considering how image is actually created.
There are a few simple keys to effective impression management:

- Being consistent
- Dressing appropriately
- Meeting expectations
- Creating harmony
- Creating focal points and optical illusions
- Organising and planning your wardrobe
- Grooming
- Optimising expenditure
- Being up-to-date
- Being yourself.

Let's take these in turn and see how you can capitalise on them.

Being Consistent

This is about not sending "mixed messages". Suppose someone asked you how you felt a meeting went and you said "Very well" while shaking your head from side to side. You would be giving a mixed message; your words would be positive but your gestures would be negative. The person you were speaking to could well be confused and, if so, would probably go by the non-verbal element of your message rather than the verbal one.

So being consistent means delivering the same message through your appearance, your body language, your speech and language and the content of your message and it includes having the various items of what you wear co-ordinated, so you present a "together" image.

Example

Many years ago I had some involvement with a leisure organisation. The men wore grey suits with a pink shirt and the women wore grey skirts and jackets with a pink blouse. One woman I met wore her outfit with gold evening shoes — during the day. I thought this was a good example of a mixed message — one which confused the observer. Also, while noticing the woman's oddly matched shoes, it was hard to concentrate on what she was saying. Given that the major part of a communication is the process (how it is communicated) rather than the content (what is communicated), this kind of mixed message makes it likely that the listener will be so wrapped up in trying to untangle the visual cues that the main thrust of the message will be missed entirely.

So, being consistent in your appearance is important. This means that, if you are dressing formally, make it all formal; don't wear some casual items. If you are dressed for summer, avoid items that look wintry such as boots or heavy scarves.

Formal winter wear for men generally means wearing a suit, a plain shirt, a tie, dark shoes and socks and a dark belt. Summer wear is similar, but the suit colour can be lighter and the shoes, socks and belt matched accordingly, although very pale colours for shoes and belts, and also white socks, are usually considered inappropriate for business wear and formal occasions.

Formal wear for women generally means a co-ordinated outfit (skirt and jacket or trousers and jacket), again with matching shoes and belts. In some situations, trousers are not conventional, so it is worth checking in advance if you are unsure. Again, dark colours will be more appropriate in the winter and lighter ones in the summer.

For both men and women, dark colours tend to convey more of a sense of authority, as do plain, rather than highly patterned, fabrics.

Informal wear for men and women can vary considerably; the main thing to consider is that it should be clean, tidy and in good condition.

Thinking about these details will ensure that you look "right" and people can concentrate on your message rather than your appearance. Consistency can also matter over time. If you look very smart and elegant one day and somewhat scruffy the next, people may wonder whether you will select the appropriate dress for particular occasions or whether your underlying approach is disorganised. This doesn't mean you have to be formal all the time, but simply that thinking about how you come across and assessing how to appear on particular occasions can matter.

Dressing Appropriately

If you were going to a wedding or to a funeral you would be expected to dress appropriately and the same goes for business occasions too. If you are not sure what is expected, find out what others will be wearing. Check if the event is formal or informal; whether the location is likely to be warm or cool; whether it is likely to extend into the evening when alternative clothes will be needed and so on.

It is perfectly possible to turn up to a formal event dressed casually and still be accepted, but it is more likely that this will happen if you have already been "socially" accepted in a broader context. There are some notable public figures who consistently wear casual clothes to business occasions and are still accepted, but this is probably because they already have a reputation for effectiveness and professionalism which outweighs their physical appearance. For most of us, image is important and, especially when making new contacts, it is our image on which the other person is likely to form an initial opinion. If you look very different from others at the same event, you may well stand out from the crowd, but there is the possibility that you will simply come across as inappropriately dressed and lacking in social skills.

Example

Richard Branson is an immensely successful entrepreneur who deals with people at all levels, on the national and international scene. For years he was noted for attending important meetings wearing very casual clothes and, in particular, knitted sweaters which were completely out of line with conventional business dress.

Although he does not always dress in this manner, Branson has been able to defy convention — partly because his business acumen has made him acceptable even when he is unconventionally attired, and partly because his friendly personality has helped create a feeling of acceptance where a less socially skilled person could have had difficulty in establishing a good rapport.

Meeting Expectations

It is worth checking what people's particular expectations of you are likely to be, so you can decide to what extent you will conform. For example, if you are a consultant, you might wish to dress in a similar manner to your clients in order to make them feel you are like them. Alternatively, you might wish to dress as you think they may expect you to look — which could be different — so that you meet their expectations of you. Knowing if there are particular expectations of you, and then meeting those expectations, will help you create a good impression.

Example

A designer I know once said he felt that, if he didn't have a beard, wear corduroy trousers and drive an old car, his clients would not think he was any good at his job. This may or may not have been true, but illustrates well the importance of other people's perceptions on your own success.

Creating Harmony

In general, people look good when their clothes complement their personal appearance. This goes for colour, style and scale. If you have a dark colouring, you will probably look best in deep colours; if you are an elegant person, you will look best in sophisticated styles and shapes; if you are petite, you will look best in small-scale designs. Let's consider these elements in more depth.

In general, if people compliment you on your appearance, rather than on your clothes — by saying "You look well" rather than "I like your blouse" — the clothes are doing their job. Suitable colours can make you look healthy and energetic; the "wrong" ones can make your skin look sallow or too highly coloured; they can overpower you or they can seem drab and uninteresting.

Example

I saw a woman on a train who had put together an outfit where virtually nothing worked to complement other elements. Her jacket was too tight and pulled at the seams; her clothes were navy (a "cool" colour) and her shoes were brown (a "warm" colour); she had an expensive handbag but very cheap-looking jewellery, and there were many other unharmonious elements. With a little attention, she could have looked much better, and more professional too.

Colour

There are three principles related to harmony in colour:

- Intensity

- Warmth

- Brightness.

Intensity refers to how light or dark a colour is. Warmth refers to whether a colour is "warm" (yellow-based) or "cool" (blue-based). Brightness refers to whether a colour is bright (vivid) or soft (muted or pastel). Each person has an individual combination of these elements in their colouring, which can be seen in their skin, hair and eye colours. When I say skin colour, I don't mean racial characteristics, but the overall impression that skin pigmentation creates.

So, if you have dark hair, you will tend to look good in dark colours; if you have light hair, you will tend to look better in light colours. If you have a clear complexion, you may look better in bright colours and if you have a more muted skin colour you may look better in softer colours. If you have a lot of blue pigmentation in your skin, you will probably look better in blue-based colours and if you have a lot of yellow pigmentation in your skin, you will probably look better in yellow-based colours.

As an example, a person with ginger hair and freckled skin is likely to look good in golden, soft shades, while a person with jet black hair and a pale skin is likely to look good in deep, cool shades.

Example

A newsreader on television had a warm tone to his skin and hair. He often wore cool coloured (navy or grey) suits which made him look washed-out. When he wore warmer-toned (sand-coloured) suits, he looked much better and healthier.

Style and Shape

Two elements of style and shape are:

- Line (rounded or angular) and

- Personality (sophisticated, romantic, casual and so forth).

If you are angular in appearance, with long limbs and straight lines to your body and face, you will tend to look better in sharp-lined clothes, while if you are more rounded in appearance, with broader hips and shoulders, a round face and shorter limbs, you may look better in softer shapes with some draping or softness in the cut.

If your personality is sophisticated, you will come across well in clothes which are stylish and elegant; if you are romantic, you will come across well in garments with softer outlines; if you are casual you will come across well in informal, relaxed clothing and so on.

Example

Before she became UK Prime Minister, Mrs Thatcher wore some-what unsophisticated clothes, with large bows at the neck and an unstructured hairstyle (and her voice was also fairly high pitched). After image training, her clothes and hair became more sophisti-cated (and her voice was trained to be lower in tone). Many other politicians have been through similar processes to alter their image.

Scale

The elements of scale are:

- Height

- Size of bone

- Weight.

If you are tall, heavy or large-boned, you will be able to wear clothes and accessories with bold designs and chunky cuts. If you are short, petite and small-boned, you will probably look best in neat clothes, with detailing and accessories kept small and unobtrusive. You can go against your natural body scale, but it could look either over-dramatised or insignificant, depending on what exactly you wear.

Example

If you consider mass-produced clothing, you will often find that, as the size alters, the elements of the clothes do not always vary to the same extent. So, you may find oversized buttons that look good on a size 18 person, but terrible on a size 10 person. So when shopping, do look out for the details as well as the overall fit.

So, matching your clothes to your skin tones, your body-line and structure and your personality will help you dress more successfully.

Examples

These examples illustrate some "extremes". Many people come somewhere between the different elements of colouring and body shape mentioned here.

Aziz has extremely dark hair and eyebrows; his eyes are also very dark and his skin is quite pale, with a slightly bluish look to it. He is tall and large-boned, with long arms and legs and an angular face. Aziz looks good in black, dark grey, dark navy, dark green and burgundy. He can wear bright red, icy blue or white for contrast. His accessories, such as belt buckles and cufflinks, look best in silver rather than gold. He comes across best when wearing clean, sharp lines to his suits with bold designs on his ties or sweaters.

Jonathan has curly ginger hair, a slightly sallow complexion and is short, with plump arms and legs. He looks good in warm colours, such as olive green, brown and cream. He comes across well when he wears gold accessories, such as cufflinks and belt buckles, and brown shoes rather than black. His suits look best when they have soft, unstructured tailoring and his ties look good when they have rounded designs rather than stripes or jagged lines.

Bhanu has brown hair, and a soft, dusky complexion. She is slim and long-limbed, with narrow shoulders and hips and small hands and feet. She looks good in pastel colours, such as pale pink, blue or green, off-white and light grey or navy. Her clothes look best when they are tailored and classic, with tiny detailing and small items of jewellery in silver or muted colours. Her make-up is best when it includes pale pinks, soft blues and mushroom shades.

Sandra has golden blonde hair and light blue eyes, with a warm glow to her skin. She has large hips, short arms and legs and an oval face. Sandra looks good in ivory, coral and bright blue. She comes across well when she wears soft-shaped clothes, with shawl collars, pleats and slightly padded shoulders. Her make-up is best when it has shades of peach, coral and green; gold jewellery suits her best.

Creating Focal Points and Optical Illusions

This is about gaining maximum interest and minimising any physical "problems". Focal points can be used to good advantage for a number of purposes. For example, if you are doing a presentation, or being interviewed, it helps to have something close to your face which adds interest, such as a bright tie or scarf, a brooch or earrings. This helps people focus on your face and gives them something interesting to look at. Focal points can also draw attention away from areas you wish to "hide". So, if you believe you have heavy hips, chubby arms or thin legs, you can draw attention away from these by putting a bright colour, pattern, or interesting accessory somewhere else. The observer's attention will then focus on that area rather than your "problem" one.

Optical illusions work in a similar way to focal points, by appearing to change your body proportions. The following are some ways in which you can create optical illusions.

- *To look taller.* Use colour and pattern high up on your body (for example in shirts or blouses), avoid turn-ups on trousers, wear the same, or similar colours in your whole outfit.

- *To look shorter.* Use colour and pattern low down (for example in skirts and socks), have turn-ups on trousers, wear different colours above and below the waist.

- *To look lighter.* Causing people's eyes to go up and down, rather than from side to side, can make you look lighter, so using vertical seams and pleats and vertical stripes in designs can be slimming.

- *To look heavier.* Conversely, horizontal lines, which attract people's eyes from side to side, can give the impression of bulk to people with a very slight frame, as can gathers, especially at the waist or hips.

- *To look longer-waisted (more length above the waist).* You can make your top half look longer by extending your shirt or blouse colour through adding a belt of a similar shade. This decreases the apparent length of your skirt or trousers.

- *To look shorter-waisted (less length above the waist).* Conversely, if you match your belts to your trousers or skirts, you will apparently decrease the length above your waist, creating an impression of a shorter top half.

- *To make your arms or legs look thinner.* When you have a garment ending at a narrow point of your arms or legs, it gives the illusion of the whole limb being thinner than it is; this applies to blouses, shirts, skirts and shorts.

- *To make your arms or legs look fuller.* When you have a garment ending at a wide point of your arms or legs, it gives the impression of the whole limb being wider than it is; again, this applies to blouses, shirts, skirts and shorts.

- *To make your neck and face look longer.* What you have around your face alters its apparent dimensions; to lengthen these, you can wear your hair longer and closer to your head and wear long, pointed collars and deep or V-shaped necklines.

- *To make your neck look wider and your face rounder.* Conversely, you can have a fuller hairstyle, with more width near your cheeks, and you can wear cut-away shirt or blouse collars, or polo necks.

- *To widen your shoulders and level out sloping shoulders.* For this you can wear shoulder pads and wide necklines. If one shoulder is lower than the other it can be "corrected" with different depth shoulder pads and wide pads can extend narrow shoulders.

- *To narrow your shoulders.* In this case you should avoid shoulder pads which extend beyond your natural shoulder line. You can also wear deep or V necklines, rather than boat-shaped ones.

- *To make your jaw-line look less square.* Again, what is near your face affects the appearance of your jaw; to make it less square, you can avoid square necklines on blouses, T-shirts or sweaters.

These are just some examples of what you can do with optical illusions and I hope they have inspired you to take a critical look at your own wardrobe.

Example 1

A personal one this time. When I gave talks on image, I would very often find that people thought I was much taller than I actually was (5'3"). This is because I tended to wear long tailored skirts, with a belt and boots of the same colour, a matching jacket and a blouse under the jacket so that a vertical line of blouse colour showed through. I also wore bright earrings and necklaces which drew the eye upwards. Although I did not intentionally dress in this way to add height, the result was that I did appear taller.

Example 2

Another television presenter almost always looked good in the outfits selected. She had one, however, which did not work at all well for her. This one had a square neckline, which made her squarish jaw look heavy; in all her other clothes, the jawline was not noticeable and the necklines were much more flattering.

Organising and Planning Your Wardrobe

Thinking about your clothes in a systematic way can help you enhance your appearance and make the most of your resources.

Sorting

Sorting clothes into outfits and aiming to purchase missing items to complete an outfit will be more effective than collecting random items of clothing simply because they seem attractive. Set aside some time to sort your clothes into those that go together to form a whole outfit.

Once you can see all the items together, you will know whether you have total outfits, or simply a collection of random garments. Put any aside which need cleaning or mending and discard any which are out-of-date or too worn to be wearable. What you have left will form the basis for the next step in your activities.

Planning

Now you can make a shopping list of items to complete your outfits, which will make the most of your expenditure. Remember that items which are interchangeable between outfits, or which can be layered, will give you many more possible combinations of clothes than if you buy items which only work well with one or two other garments.

Organising

Keeping clothes of the same kind together in your wardrobe will make it easier to find things quickly. It is a good idea to keep all your shirts together, all your trousers or skirts, all your sweaters, and so on. You may also wish to keep summer and winter clothes in separate areas, or you can take unseasonal items out of your wardrobe and store them until needed again, which will give you more space for the current season's clothes.

And a final point on organisation. If you have to attend an important event the next day, and an early start is needed, it is helpful to get your clothes ready the evening before and have them waiting on a chair or hangers ready to put on. This can save you time and frustration when you may be in a hurry.

Example

I worked with a client once who had two basic outfits, neither of which was very co-ordinated. She had no belts or scarves and wore no make-up. The impression given was that she was rather underdressed for the job she did. After a couple of sessions, when we went through her wardrobe and considered what she needed for her social and professional lifestyle, she bought a few additional items which allowed her to put together some very elegant outfits. She also had a new haircut and wore a small amount of make-up and some good pieces of jewellery; doing this enabled her to create a professional and elegant image which enhanced both her looks and her business success.

Exercise

Female readers might like to think about the "accessory balance". Wearing no accessories tends to make you look underdressed and wearing too many can make you look fussy and unprofessional. Count up the number of accessories you wear with business clothes (one point each for necklace, bracelet, ring, earring, belt buckle, hair band, decorative button, watch, brooch and so on). The more you have, up to ten, the more "finished" you look (as long as the accessories do work well together and are not too fussy). See how you score.

Male readers might like to think about making their clothes look more expensive than they really are. To do this, simply change suit buttons for more elegant ones, have jacket sleeves altered so their length is exactly right and collars altered to make sure your jacket doesn't ride up round your neck when you sit down. Small touches can make all the difference between a cheap and a quality garment.

Grooming and Maintenance

Taking time to look after personal hygiene and finishing touches is also important. Simple things like making sure your clothes are regularly cleaned, mended and altered helps you look immaculate. Taking time to look after hair, nails, teeth and skin also helps. Bathing regularly and avoiding eating strong-smelling foods before meeting others will keep you fresh and pleasant to be near.

It is useful to take out of your wardrobe anything that needs attention so it can be dealt with; there is nothing worse than deciding to wear a particular garment and then finding it needs cleaning or mending when you have no time to do it. It also helps to carry spare items, such as tights or a clean tie, in case of accidents.

Example

I am sometimes asked to give advice to people who look very professional, but do not complete the picture by paying attention to those personal details. One person sent to me had hair which was always out of place and, because of anxiety about visiting the dentist, needed attention to his teeth. After a couple of trips to the hairdresser and dentist, his appearance was much improved and he had greater credibility with his employers and business associates.

Optimising Expenditure

This is about the cost-effectiveness of your purchases. Take the purchase cost of items (plus any dry-cleaning or alteration costs) and divide the final sum by the number of occasions on which you expect to wear the item. Cost-per-wearing is a good way of assessing how economical your purchases are and may help you avoid buying items which will have an astronomically high cost-to-wear ratio. If you really need expensive items for just one or two occasions, it can be cheaper to hire them.

Example

Fiona needed to have an extensive wardrobe, as she was constantly involved with PR activities where she was seen on several occasions by the same people. She had a couple of favourite "nearly new" shops, which sold designer clothes at very reduced prices. When she had worn her clothes a few times, she took them to the shop to sell and usually came back with one or two new acquisitions. She was able to buy expensive clothes at a fraction of their original price and the cost-per-wearing was affordable and realistic.

Being Up-to-date

This is not about being trendy, but about avoiding looking outdated. People often keep favourite items of clothing for years, maintain the same hairstyle they have had for decades, or wear the same type of make-up they have had since adolescence. Keeping up with developments can help you look "of the moment" and, if you do this, people are more likely to think your ideas are up-to-date also.

To find out what is up-to-date, read fashion magazines (make sure the ones you buy reflect your own lifestyle) and you can also keep an eye on what people are wearing generally and on what is in shop windows. Sometimes fashions can change in major ways and at other times very small details (such as tie and lapel widths, shoulder-pad sizes and the presence or absence of turn-ups) are all that make the difference between a modern image and an old-fashioned one. So taking a little time to consider this can be useful.

Example

A member of staff in a client organisation looked very smart and well turned out, but his suits were ten or fifteen years old. Although well presented, he always looked somewhat out-of-date. He had little money to spend on new suits. A visit to a men's nearly new shop resulted in him acquiring two new, and current, suits at a quarter of their original price. He looked better and was pleased with his savings.

Being Yourself

Finally, remember that you cannot be anyone other than yourself, so it is best to be aware of your individual strengths and attributes and work with, rather than against, them. Check your own likes and dislikes, work out how you want to come across, rather than how others want you to or how you think you should be, and then keep to that where possible. You will find it easier and your own persona will shine through as a result.

Example

Sheila's husband admired earthy colours on her — browns and golds, rusts and purples. He also liked her to wear loose, flowing garments, which looked peasanty and natural. Sheila, however, was tall and elegant and her colouring was better matched to pale, cool colours and lean, straight lines. Once she discovered her best styles and colours, she both looked and felt better. (Her husband had to make do with cushion covers in the house in the shades he liked!)

Etiquette

Many people have genuine concerns about what is the "correct" thing to do in different situations. In past times, etiquette was generally much stricter than it is now and there were very specific expectations about social interactions. Nowadays, etiquette is more a question of custom and, as such, can vary from one area to another, one culture to another, one age group to another and so on.

I will simply give you a few general pointers in this section. If you are interested in the subject, there are other books written on it specifically.

Use of First Names

Part of people's expectations could relate to the use of first or second names. If you are in a relaxed, informal environment, people may well prefer to be addressed by their first names. In a more formal situation, or sometimes when speaking to people much older than yourself, second names (surnames) could be preferred. Checking this if you are not sure will avoid embarrassment and help you create an appropriate impression.

Handshakes

It tends to look more assertive if you offer your hand first, rather than waiting for the other person to offer theirs. So, if you wish to come across as more powerful, this is one thing you can do. Make your handshake reasonably firm, without crushing the other person's fingers and avoid a limp "dead fish" handshake. I used to just hold out my hand and let the other person grip it until I found other people who did the same and realised that taking hold of a totally unresponsive hand was not a pleasant experience. It is also not generally considered appropriate — in business circles at least — to grip the other person's hand with both of yours, or to turn your hand so it is on top of the other person's. Matching the pressure you exert in a handshake to the pressure exerted by the other person is generally the best option if you are unsure as to what is appropriate.

Perfume

If you are going to business meetings, it is probably best to avoid strong perfumes or aftershave lotions. Some people are allergic to scents and it may give off the wrong messages.

Distance at which to stand

I will be covering this in Chapter 9, but it is useful to know that conversational distances vary from culture to culture and from person to person. Check you don't get too close to people and make them feel uncomfortable or that you don't stand so far away that they cannot hear you speak.

Courtesy

Being prompt with replies, thank you's and other expected contacts will help you come across in a professional and reliable manner.

So, impression management can raise your profile professionally; it can also give you a stronger sense of self-confidence. The better your image, the greater your personal impact will be, and the more people admire and respect you, the better you can feel about yourself. Well worth investing in.

Chapter Seven

Communication Skills —
Speech and Language

In this chapter, and the next three on face-to-face communications, I will be introducing you to the following topics:

- Speech and language

- Conversation

- Non-verbal communications

- Rapport, influence and assertiveness.

Speech and Language

I have separated speech from language in this chapter. I propose that speech is what you do with your voice (process) and that language is the words with which you communicate (both process and content). So it is important to consider both *what* you say and *how* you say it.

Under speech, I will be covering many aspects of vocalisation and taking elements such as tone of voice under this section, rather than under non-verbals. Although these elements do not relate to words as such, they do relate to the use of the voice, so I will be covering them in this chapter.

Under language, I will be covering a variety of speech patterns and discussing how you can modify your language to have more impact on others.

Let's consider speech first.

Speech

Speech can include the following elements of voice:

- Speed
- Volume
- Pitch
- Tone
- Resonance
- Rhythm
- Use of pauses
- Clarity.

I will also be covering the following, which are important influences on how you speak:

- Good posture
- Effective breathing and
- Allowing your voice to warm up.

Let's take each of these aspects in turn.

Speed

How quickly or slowly you speak can make an impact on people. Fast speech can indicate enthusiasm or excitement and, if this is the case, the person to whom you are talking may well be enthused by your own motivation and interest. Speaking rapidly could also indicate a sense of urgency and the need for quick action. However, speaking quickly could irritate or confuse a listener, making it difficult for your words to be understood and absorbed; it could be seen as being inconsiderate and it could also be taken as a sign of nervousness.

Speaking slowly could indicate thoughtfulness and a concern to emphasise the importance of particular issues. However, it could also be thought that slow speech is an indication of slow thinking and it can be irritating to people whose speech is naturally faster.

How the speed of your speech is received depends on the person to whom your remarks are addressed. It is not necessarily your own intention that matters most in the communication, but the interpretation and response of the recipient. If the person has preconceptions about speed of speaking, or if your speech draws a strong response at the time, you may have prejudiced your chances of communicating positively with that person at that time and possibly in the future.

So, thinking about the other person's responses matters; there is no right or wrong speed of speaking; how you speak needs to be related to the circumstances and the person to whom you are speaking.

Volume

As with speed, volume creates differing impacts on recipients. If you speak loudly, you will ensure that your voice carries; this can be useful when speaking to a large gathering or when talking to someone with hearing difficulties. Loud speech can, however, be somewhat overpowering and sometimes others will overhear what may be sensitive or confidential information. Have you ever been in a railway carriage where one person's voice carried throughout the entire space (perhaps using a mobile phone, which could increase the annoyance)?

A very quiet voice can seem calming and sympathetic, but could also make you come across as unassertive and lacking in confidence. And have you ever been in a theatre or cinema where someone was trying to talk without being too audible and simply succeeded in making everyone aware of their whispered conversation?

So, choosing how loudly to speak is important and can convey a multitude of messages about you to your listener.

Tonality

The tone of your voice is a significant aspect for many people. Some people have a pleasant tone and others have a tone which seems less attractive. People will often say, "I didn't like his/her tone of voice" or "Don't speak to me in that tone of voice". If you listen to different people speaking, you will notice which tones of voice are appealing to you and which you find off-putting; you can then work to vary your voice accordingly.

"Intonation" is a related term. By varying the intonation when you speak, or when you read, you can emphasise different parts of what you say. For example, you can put emphasis on particular words, such as: "**very** important"; "**now**"; "**don't**"; "really **helpful**".

Pitch

Men's voices generally have a lower pitch than women's. On the whole, a high pitch in both men and women come across as less authoritative — another example of how process can overtake content when judgements are formed.

So, being aware of your own vocal pitch, and being able to vary it to some extent, can influence the impact you create.

Another interesting point is that, in the UK at least, a question is indicated by the voice going up at the end of a sentence, while a statement is indicated by the voice staying the same or going down. So, if you want to sound positive, keeping the pitch/intonation of your voice down at the end of sentences is helpful, while the opposite is true when you want to sound enquiring.

Resonance

Resonance is the quality brought about by the reverberation, or frequencies of vibration, of the sounds you make. The major places where reverberation can take place are the throat, the mouth and the nose. Depending on how these areas are used, your voice can take on a different quality — for example, a nasal quality, a husky quality and so forth. Each of these can create differing impressions on listeners; nasal sometimes sounds whiny, while husky sometimes sounds muffled. Selecting and managing the resonance of your voice will add variety and interest to your conversation and make your presentations more compelling to an audience.

Rhythm

Some people's speech is more rhythmic than others. In general, consistency of rhythm leads to rather dull, monotonous speech, while variation in rhythm adds interest and variety.

There are marked regional and geographical variations to rhythmic speech, with some languages and dialects being more rhythmic than others. If your speech lacks variety, it is well worth practising to make it more interesting.

Pauses

Pauses serve a variety of purposes in speech. They act as natural punctuation to phrases or sentences, indicating when one element has ended and another is beginning. They can also be used to create effect or emphasis. Pauses can also give the impression that the speaker is very confident and at ease with taking time to speak; on the other hand, they may sound rather longwinded or somewhat uncertain, as though they have to hunt around for what to say next. So, pausing may seem authoritative, tedious or pedantic, according to the interpretation of the listener.

Pausing before you speak can be a good way of collecting your thoughts and allows you time to take a breath so you can continue speaking confidently and with enough oxygen in your lungs to fuel the speech. Voice projection absolutely requires adequate oxygen to make sounds and transmit them at distances.

Clarity

Your voice should be clear if you are to communicate well. To speak clearly, you should ensure you say each word completely and don't tail off or run one word into another. Each sound should be formed distinctly and, if you have a particular accent or dialect, you should check that it is understood by the person to whom you are speaking. Looking at the other person as you speak also helps, as it is then possible to see your lip movements, which can aid understanding.

Posture and Breathing

How you use your body has an impact on how you sound. In order to use your voice effectively, you need to take in sufficient oxygen to allow your body to function well and your voice to be projected; breathing is the foundation of effective speech.

In order to breathe effectively, you need to use your body in an effective manner. If you slump your shoulders and tip your head down, you make it difficult for your lungs to work properly and for air to circulate well in your mouth and throat. This in turn makes speaking harder and can make your voice sound dull and lifeless.

Warming Up

Warming up your voice will assist you to speak in an effective and pleasing manner. Warming up is also one of the keys to good platform skills.

Exercises

The exercises that follow relate to the elements discussed so far. Taking time to work on them will help you become a more appealing speaker, both in conversation and in presentations.

With the exercises, you can first practise on your own, then speak into a recorder, then enlist the help of a friend to listen to you and give feedback, then try things out in real conversations.

1. Speed of speech

Practise speaking slightly faster and slightly slower than usual. When actually speaking to others, don't vary your speed too much, but simply change it a little at appropriate times during the conversation.

2. Volume of speech

You can do exactly the same here as with the previous exercise; simply substitute changes in volume for changes in speed. When doing this in conversation, make sure the volume changes are appropriate, otherwise you will create a rather strange impression!

3. Tonality

To practise tonality, say the same sentence in differing ways, as if conveying different meanings. For example, take the words "It's all in your mind". You could say this in a dismissive way, as if suggesting that something doesn't really exist. You could say it in a neutral way, as if it were simply a matter of fact. You could say it in an encouraging way, as if to imply that something could be achieved simply by thinking positively about it. The tone of voice you use to convey these different meanings is likely to create totally different impressions upon the listener.

4. Pitch

When varying pitch in speaking to others, you are more likely to find that dropping the pitch works better than raising it, as a raised pitch can sound somewhat childlike at times. You can also practise pitch by speaking first of all in a monotone, with each word sounding much like the others, then gradually raise or lower the pitch of your voice into more of a "sing-song" quality. If you ask someone to listen to you, you can get feedback on which sounds create particular kinds of impact and which ones make your voice most attractive. Do remember, however, that what is attractive to one person may be unattractive to another, so ask a few people for opinions on your voice, rather than just one.

5. Resonance

Exercises on resonance are somewhat technical to describe, without going into much more depth on the acoustics involved in speech generally. If you would like to work on resonance, it would be useful to enlist the help of a voice or singing coach, who could guide you.

6. Rhythm

To work on rhythm, begin by spacing each word equally. Then vary the rhythm in different ways. For example, you can say words in groups of three, with the emphasis on the first of each three, then the second of each three, then the third of each three (for example: **One** fat cat, **my** brown shoes; one **fat** cat, my **brown** shoes; one fat **cat**, my brown **shoes**).

7. Pauses

To work on pauses, you can say sentences, pausing for one second between each word, then two seconds, then three seconds. You can pause for five seconds between sentences. I suggest you time this on your watch as, if you count the numbers in your head, you may well overestimate how much time has passed and not pause for long enough.

If you naturally pause a good deal when speaking, you may wish to do this exercise in reverse, so you shorten the pauses rather than lengthening them.

8. Clarity

To work on clarity, it is useful to read aloud extracts from books or newspapers, preferably to a friend. Make sure you pronounce every part of each word, and also put in pauses for punctuation and emphasis for words which need to stand out. Look ahead to a whole phrase before starting to speak, which will make it easier to convey the meaning intended.

You might like to work on combining some of these elements as well as practising them separately. For example, speaking faster and softer, or speaking at a lower pitch with fewer pauses than usual. It is easy to get into the habit of combining particular elements of speech and, the more variety you can get into your vocal patterns, the more interesting your voice is likely to be. And practise on your own any exercises that require very exaggerated speech patterns!

9. Posture and breathing

To work on these, you can do exercises both to relax and balance yourself, as follows:

- Take a few paperback books and place them on the floor so you can lie down with your head on them. The quantity of books you use will vary, depending on your usual spine and head alignment (you could need anywhere between 2.5 and 15 centimetres (1"–6") depth altogether — put as many books as feels comfortable to you). Lie on your back with your head on the books, so that your head is relaxed and your neck is free from tension. Bend your legs so that both knees are pointing to the ceiling and your feet are flat on the floor. Rest your hands on your stomach or alongside you, with the palms facing down. You should feel that your whole spine is relaxing and lengthening. Stay in this position for ten to twenty minutes at a time, breathing evenly and keeping your mind as clear as you can. Doing this daily will help you relax and bring your spine into better alignment.

- When standing or moving, make sure your shoulders are relaxed rather than pulled up. Don't deliberately force your shoulders downwards or backwards; simply allow them to drop naturally, freeing them from tension. Allow your head, neck and spine to be comfortably aligned.

- Relax your body, so your head, neck, shoulders, arms, legs and torso are all gently poised rather than tense. Doing these things will not only allow you to speak more freely and in a more lively manner, they will add to your general wellbeing through removing unnecessary tension and freeing you to sit, stand and move more easily.

These exercises are based on the Alexander Technique. For more information on the Alexander Technique (and also the Feldenkrais Method) you can do some further reading or, better still, have a series of lessons with a qualified practitioner, which will benefit you in many ways and help you avoid aches, pains and strains. See the resources list for more information.

- Hold your hands on the lower part of your ribcage and notice what happens to them when you breathe normally; do your hands stay still, do they move up and down, do they move in and out, do they move together and further apart? Now, keeping your hands in place, take a deep breath and let it out, expelling as much air as you can from your lungs and, as you do so, feel your hands moving inwards, towards your spine. Now breathe in deeply, pushing your hands as far forward as you can and taking as much air as you can into your lungs. Repeat two or three times and then return to your normal breathing. Notice how your hands move as you do the exercise and compare this with your "normal" breathing. Aim for your hands to move away from you as you breathe in, indicating that you are filling your lungs with air.

10. Warming up

It helps to warm up your voice, and your facial muscles, which help control sound, before any important interaction, especially presentations. The following exercises are useful:

- Talk to someone on the phone; this will get your vocal chords moving and make it easier to speak to others face-to-face later on.

- Talk to yourself. If you are alone, this can be good; if you are with others, it could attract strange comments, so be careful about where you practise this.

- Use "tongue twisters". Saying sentences such as "She sells seashells on the sea shore", will help to get your mouth moving and warm up your vocal chords; it will also give you greater fluency, making it easier to speak in a fluid and interesting manner.

- Again, on your own, move the muscles of your face so you are "making faces". This will exercise the muscles around your mouth and throat, again making it easier to speak and to continue a conversation.

Example

A personal one. Some years ago, I produced a series of audiotapes on personal effectiveness. I didn't know about vocal technique, so I had to speak in what I thought was the best way at the time. The recording studio was only available in the evenings, so I went there after travelling some distance from where I had been working during the day. After a day's work, and a journey in the car, my voice was both tired from the day's activities and not warmed up sufficiently for recording. Although most of the sessions went well, I found from time to time that I was losing my voice or sounding croaky. If I had known then what I know now, I would have taken time to relax, then warmed up my voice before starting. I think the results would have been better if I had done so.

So far, we have been working on voice and speech; I would now like to move to considering the role of language and how you can use language to good effect in networking contexts.

Language

The aspects of language I will be covering here are as follows:

- Precision
- Indirectness
- Metaphor
- Sensory language
- Motivational language
- Familiarity.

As motivational language will be included in more depth in Chapter 9, I will only deal with it briefly here.

Precision

There are many times when precision in language is important, especially in giving or receiving information. The NLP approach to precision in language, called the "Meta Model", was developed by Richard Bandler and John Grinder and outlined in *Structure of Magic, Volumes 1 and 2*. Utilising some earlier linguistic concepts, the Meta Model deals with three main things people do when using language:

- Generalisation

- Deletion

- Distortion.

The result of these things is that communication is only partial. Generalising can mean that certain instances are overlooked, deletion can mean that whole categories of information are omitted and distortion can lead to misinformation. A precision approach to language aims to overcome all three of these limits to clear communication.

Example

I watched a training video on time management some years ago. In the video a person had been asked by his manager to produce a report; he had not done so. The manager was cross and asked why the report had not been completed. The reply was: "Well, you said I should do it as soon as possible . . . and it hasn't been possible." More precision in the request could have produced a better result.

The Meta Model also considers that communication is a "surface structure", which describes real experience ("deep structure"). The words we use are therefore symbolic of our real experience, but are only a way of representing what we really think, feel, believe and do. By using precision, we can unearth more of the deep structure to understand other people, and ourselves, better.

Example

If someone refers to their "family", you might make an assumption about what that means but, because the word "family" only represents their personal experience, it could mean any of the following — or something different entirely:

- *Their spouse or partner and children*

- *Their lesbian or gay partner*

- *Fellow members of a commune*

- *Their pets*

- *Their parents and siblings*

- *Their entire network of relatives.*

So you can see how words can be interpreted very differently from how their speaker intended and anything you can do to make your own communications more understandable, and to question others so you can understand them better, is helpful.

Linguists often talk in terms of "transforms". Two "transforms" in particular are relevant. The first is that when we experience external "reality", it is transformed into our perception through our senses. So, if we are colour blind, there may be certain colours which exist, but we can only see them in more muted shades, as our sense of sight has "transformed" them. The second is that when we have an experience, we "transform" it through language. So, we might feel extremely excited about an event, but say we are "quite interested" in it, or we might see sunlight and describe it as "bright", while it actually has many more qualities for which we do not have the words. So the language has transformed our perceptions.

In these ways, our experience is "filtered" through our senses and our communications are "filtered" through our language. Quite a wonder, then, that communicating with others works at all.

The point of precision in language is to attempt to minimise the effects of distortions, so that what gets communicated is as "pure" as it can be. The Meta Model suggests ways of enhancing communications by posing questions of ourselves or of others in order to be more precise. Let me give you a few examples:

Questioning Other People

- If someone says: "I can do that quickly", you could ask "So when *exactly* do you think you can do it?" This makes the word "quickly" more precise.

- If someone says: "I always find it hard to talk to new people", you could ask "Are there *any* people you could talk to easily when you had only just met them?" This makes it more likely that they will find an example to counteract their generalisation.

- If someone says: "It's a good thing to keep your opinions to yourself", you could ask: "*What would happen* if you didn't?" or "*Who said that* was true?" The first response gives the person a chance to think about alternatives and the second can lead them to question the absolute truth of what they have suggested.

Giving Other People Information

- If you want to tell someone how to get to a destination, you could say: "It's *exactly one mile* to the roundabout" rather than "It's not far". The precise measurement is likely to make it easier for the person to find.

- If you want to say how you feel about someone's behaviour, you could say: "That made me *feel very disappointed*" rather than "I didn't like what you did". The first explains your actual feelings, whereas the second does not give the person a true indication of your response to them.

Precision language can really help understanding, but it needs to be used appropriately. If you constantly question people very precisely, they might feel they are being interrogated and if you go into too much detail yourself, you might be thought of as pedantic, so use precision as and when it is really needed and it will be useful.

Indirectness

Indirect language is almost the opposite of precision. There are times when it is very useful to be indirect; for example, when you don't want to be too inquisitive, when you want to leave the other person free to consider your points in a range of ways and when you want to encourage someone to be innovative or creative.

Just as the Meta Model helps with precision, another NLP model, the Milton Model, helps with indirect language. The Milton Model is based on the language skills of Milton Erickson, a famous hypnotherapist working in the 1930s and beyond. Again, Erickson's patterns were explored in some depth by Bandler and Grinder. Erickson was very fluent, very creative and adept at speaking to people in just the right way for their needs. Using similar processes to Erickson can help your interactions become highly productive.

The first way you can use indirect language is to deliberately speak in a somewhat vague way. For example, if you say to someone "I wonder what *thoughts* you have about running meetings?", you are leaving it open to them to consider what thoughts they might have. This is very different from saying "Do you think meetings should be run in a structured way?" or "Do you think there should always be a formal agenda for a meeting?" Each of these two questions leads the person down the route of responding to your particular question and limits their thinking and their response to that particular aspect. By asking what thoughts they have in general, you are inviting them to consider a wide range of aspects and select those that seem relevant to them.

You can also use indirect language through suggestion. You might ask, "How long do you think it will be before you *have a break from work*?", emphasising the last five words through your tone of voice. This implies that they *will* have a break and, even if this had not already been in their mind, your question might well put it there.

A further way of using indirect language is to use the future tense to indicate possibility. For example, saying "*When* you understand the new computer system" implies that they will understand it, whereas saying "if you understand it" implies they may not. Another example: saying, "*After* you have taken some exercise you will feel fitter" moves them into a future time, past the event, when they will already have done the exercise. This is different from saying, "*If* you do some exercise you will feel fitter", which leaves it still in the future ahead of them.

You can make this kind of communication even more powerful by taking the listener into the more distant future, to a time well beyond the occurrence you are discussing. So you might say: "*When you look back at* how well you spoke at that meeting", you are inviting them to contemplate a time when they already know they have done something well. This can be tremendously motivating and confidence-boosting, and you can use it yourself also.

A final aspect of indirect language is to suggest options when you are really giving an instruction. For example, by asking "Would you prefer to sit in *this* chair or *that* chair?", you might really be telling the person you want them to sit, rather than stand up. It sounds like an option but is really a direction.

These skills are worth developing and some will be discussed further in Chapter 9.

Metaphor

Metaphor is embedded in many languages, and especially in English. Even the previous sentence is metaphorical, as metaphor is not literally *embedded* in language. "Embedded" means a physical fixing of one thing in another, whereas the intention of the word "embedded" in this context is simply to indicate that metaphor is used a good deal in some languages.

Metaphor has many uses. One use of metaphor is to draw parallels between things (often referred to as analogy). Another use of metaphor is to enable people to think creatively. Another use of metaphor is to help people overcome problems. Often people (and organisations) have metaphors which they use frequently so that they become part and parcel of their thinking. Do any of the following sound familiar?

- This team all needs to *pull together*

- This problem is really *weighty*

- I need this extra work *like a hole in the head*

- The water looks *like a mirror*

- That *rings a bell*

- I'm having *a running battle* with my accounts

- I'm *going round in circles*

- He threw down the gauntlet.

All these statements use metaphor, which can lend colour to conversation, allow things to be seen in a new light and help people understand what is being discussed through making connections to other situations which can parallel those in question.

To use metaphor effectively in social interactions, you can select things to say in which the other person can find parallels.

Metaphors may be simple or complex. A simple metaphor is like some of those above: "The water is *like a mirror*" or "This problem is really *weighty*". Alternatively, a metaphor can parallel all aspects of a situation and be more like a story (this is sometimes referred to as an isomorphic metaphor, where the form of the metaphor and the form of the situation it describes are similar; see *Therapeutic Metaphors* by David Gordon). A more complex metaphor of this sort would be as follows:

The office was just like a battle zone. The desk was like a line of defence against intruders. As you came in you felt you were in the firing line. Everything that was said provided ammunition for a response. The only thing to do was beat a hasty retreat. . . .

Understanding people's metaphors as they speak will give you useful information about them; I will be returning to the topic of understanding in Chapter 9.

Sensory Language

The principle behind sensory language is that people not only use their senses (sight, hearing, touch, taste, smell) directly, but also use language which relates to each of the senses. For example, suppose a person describes their house to you as follows: *"It looks quite modern. The rooms are very bright and decorated in pale shades. There are lots of mirrors and pictures on the walls. It has a really colourful garden with shady borders and a sunny patio. And when it's sunny, the light reflects on the greenhouse and makes it look really luminous."* It would be pointless to say to that person: "You must feel really good about living there", because they have been describing *image*, by using visual words such as "looks", "bright", "pale", "mirrors", "pictures", "colourful", "shady", sunny", "light", "reflects", "luminous". Your statement about feelings would not "fit" with the visual emphasis of the description. A better response would be to say: "I can just *picture* you living there; it must *look* really good; I can *see* you being really happy there."

So noticing how people use sensory language is important and I will be returning to this principle in the next chapter. For now, here is a list of some sensory words, which you might like to notice in your own, and other people's, conversations:

- *Words to do with the sense of sight (Visual)*: see, picture, clear, bright, colourful, view;

- *Words to do with the sense of hearing (Auditory)*: hear, listen, buzz, rustle, ring;

- *Words to do with internal dialogue ("Self-talk")*: I'm minded to do, I say to myself, When I talked it through;

- *Words to do with the sense of touch and feeling (Kinaesthetic)*: feel, grasp, pressure, hassle, heavy, weighty;

- *Words to do with the sense of smell (Olfactory)*: smell, scent, acrid;

- *Words to do with the sense of taste (Gustatory)*: taste, chew, swallow;

- *Words to do with the sense of balance (which some people believe is a separate sense)*: balance, wobble, kilter, spin.

There are many ways of using sensory language to good effect; for example, using appropriate sensory words to describe an experience. So, if you were describing a day at the seaside you could say:

*"The sun was very **bright** and the sky a deep **blue**. The waves **rolled** in to the shore making a **lapping** sound as they arrived. Overhead seagulls **cried** as they **circled** round and round. The sand felt **warm** and **soft** and your feet made **patterns** as they moved. There was a **salty scent** from the seaweed. You could almost **taste** the salt in the air. **Far away**, on the **horizon**, there was a small boat, **bobbing** on the waves. Children **shouted** as they played and everyone seemed **relaxed** and **happy**."*

Using words to give sensory descriptions makes what you are saying seem more real. If you want someone to really imagine things you are describing, or you want to motivate someone, sensory language can be very effective. I will refer to this again in Chapter 9.

Motivational Language

It is possible to do psychological (psychometric) tests, which assess various aspects of people's personalities. It is also possible, however, to find out things about how people function simply by listening carefully to their language patterns and then to influence them accordingly. I will be covering this in Chapter 9.

Familiarity

Finally, there is the question of the language patterns you use when with people you know, or strangers; in formal situations or informal ones. Most people use slightly different ways of speaking in different situations (and in some languages there are different word forms for use with family and friends and with more distant contacts). For example:

- Shortening phrases ("Would you like a cup of tea?" to "Like some tea?");

- Using familiar terms ("Love", "Mate", etc.) to show familiarity (and be careful, as such terms can give offence to certain people);

- Using formal language ("position" rather than "job", or "refreshments" rather than "snacks").

Paying attention to your language in this way will help you communicate in ways which are appropriate to the situation and to your listeners.

This chapter has given you some ways of using speech and language effectively. It is worth taking time to practise the skills described, as they are the basic foundation for effective communications, whether face-to-face or at a distance.

The next chapter deals with conversational techniques.

Chapter Eight

Communication Skills — Conversation

In the last chapter, I discussed speech and language and this chapter continues the topic into conversation. When we converse with others, a range of processes goes on and three of these are particularly important to the networker:

- Listening
- Questioning
- Feedback.

Before moving on to consider these, take a few moments to answer the following questions:

- Do you think you are a good listener?
- Do you find it easy to listen when others are speaking?
- Do you think other people think you are a good listener?
- Do you ask many questions in conversations?
- Do you find it easy to formulate questions?
- Do you ask many questions in a group situation?
- Do you find it easy to tell people what you think of their behaviour, ideas and opinions?
- Do you find it easy to accept feedback on your own behaviour, ideas or opinions?
- Do you find it easy to keep conversations going?

- Do you know any people who you think are really good conversa-
  tionalists?

Recognising your own capabilities in these areas will be a good start
in the process of enhancing your skills.

Listening

Listening is a basic skill in networking. How do you feel when you
know someone is really paying attention to you? You probably find it
encouraging or even flattering. Conversely, if someone doesn't seem
to be listening, you may feel ignored or wonder if you are boring
them. If you listen well to others, they will enjoy talking to you and
feel they are being taken seriously. You will also have the advantage
of gaining useful information, which you might miss if your attention
was not truly on the conversation.

So, how do you listen well? There is a concept called "Active
Listening" which means really showing the person you are with that
you are listening to them and engaged in the conversation. There are
five stages involved in conversations, as follows:

1. Hearing (this is just taking in sound, without becoming too aware
   of its significance);

2. Listening (really paying attention and trying to make sense of
   what you hear);

3. Understanding (checking with the other person to make sure you
   have taken in what they said);

4. Acknowledging (letting the other person know you have heard
   and understood what they have said);

5. Responding (reacting in some way to what has been discussed).

Unfortunately, many people move from stage one to stage five
without going through the other three stages, so they often jump to
conclusions, miss information or leave the other person feeling
misunderstood or ignored.

Active listening aims to avoid negative responses by showing you
are involved. Before I explain active listening, let's revisit Jeremy and
Janice from Chapter 1:

When discussing things with others, Jeremy often looks at the floor or into the distance to collect his thoughts. He sometimes speaks while looking away and seems very engaged with his own ideas and imagination. He tends to assume that both he and the other person have the same understanding of the subject unless he is told anything to the contrary.

Janice looks at the person she is speaking to and gives them her full attention. Her conversation is animated; she smiles and nods and often repeats back points which have been made and confirms things which have been agreed. She uses her hands quite a lot and leans towards the other person slightly to take in what they are saying.

The differences between Jeremy and Janice illustrate nicely the elements of active listening. All the elements may be used independently, or they may be used together and the other person is likely to respond to you according to the total pattern of listening behaviour you display. I will discuss each of the elements in turn.

Looking at the Other Person

When you look at the other person, they are more likely to feel you are engaged in the conversation and paying attention to what they are saying. You don't have to stare them directly in the eyes; simply look at their face while they are speaking. Direct eye contact (staring at someone's eyes) can come across as intimidating, although when there is a point you really want to emphasise, it can be a useful technique.

To check a person's tolerance for "direct" eye contact, you can look at their eyes for a few seconds and notice if they have looked away; if they have, reduce the eye contact to a level with which they feel comfortable.

Avoid looking away from a person while either of you are talking. It is all right to look away to collect your thoughts before speaking, but avoid speaking until you are looking at the person again. When someone else is speaking, if you look away from them they may well feel you are not paying attention. And do remember to pay attention: just "seeming" to do so isn't enough.

Smiling

As long as the topic of conversation makes it appropriate, smiling indicates a friendly response and encourages the other person to speak more. It makes you look comfortable with the conversation and as if you are enjoying it.

Nodding

As with smiling, nodding is a direct encouragement to continue the conversation. The more you nod, the more the other person is likely to continue speaking. So nodding is an excellent way of maintaining a discussion; conversely, nodding is also likely to encourage a person who is talking endlessly to continue.

Using Gestures

Gestures such as moving your hands, shoulders or head are also likely to help a conversation along. People from some cultures tend to use gestures more expressively, especially hand gestures, but anyone can learn to use such movements as a real aid to communicating. When you add gestures to speech, you support the content of the conversation with relevant movements. For example, shrugging your shoulders if you want to express uncertainly or waving your hand towards yourself if you want someone to come forward. Gestures can show you are following the meaning of the conversation and are willing for the person to continue speaking.

Making Sounds

Useful face-to-face, and vital in telephone conversations, making some vocal response to a person's speech helps them know you are taking in what they say. Simple sounds such as "Mmm" or "I see" will let the other person know you are following what they mean. On the phone it is almost the only thing that tells someone you are still at the other end of the line.

Leaning Forward

Leaning forward can also indicate interest. You might simply incline your head in the direction of the other person, or move your whole body forward, or step forward if you are both standing. In each case, you are likely to send the message that the conversation is of interest to you, providing you don't move forward in an apparently threatening way (see more on this in Chapter 9 under assertiveness).

Reflecting

This is a term used for the process of repeating, or rephrasing, what the other person is saying. For example, if a person says: "I've enjoyed the talk" you might say: "You found it interesting?" If the person says "Yes" you have reflected correctly; if the person says "No, not interesting, but amusing" then you have checked exactly what they mean by giving them an opportunity to correct you. Either way, reflecting is likely to lead to a better understanding of what the person actually means.

Summarising

This is about going over, from time to time, what the conversation has been. So, you might say: "So, we've agreed that we will start the meeting at 11.00 a.m. and we will invite everyone who has given us their contact details, now we can move on to drawing up a schedule for what will be covered." Such a summary ensures both parties agree on what they have discussed before moving on to another aspect of the conversation. Summarising helps keep everyone in tune with each other and on the same track, although it is probably not needed in every conversation.

So, listening actively involves taking a real part in the process, not simply keeping still and keeping quiet while the other person is speaking. Becoming an active listener will help your networking success immensely, as people are more likely to respond well to you and want to continue the relationship.

Using Listening in Networking Conversations

In networking, it helps to give the people you are with an opportunity to express themselves. Good listening involves you taking a "back seat" for part of the time so that the other person can speak. So think about the balance between how much you speak and how much you listen. (Remember the old saying: "You have two eyes, two ears and one mouth — use them in that proportion.")

When you meet new people, it is useful to tell them things about yourself, so they can think of you if they have opportunities which might be relevant. But if you also listen to them you are likely to pick up many useful items of information. So, remember the balance and aim to take in at least as much as you give out.

Questioning

Being able to ask good questions, and being able to deal with questions well, is also important in networking. When you contact people, it is useful to be able to find out things about them in a sensitive and acceptable manner. It is also useful to know that the information you obtain is accurate; if your questioning is poor, the information you gain is likely to be poor too.

Similarly, when people ask you questions, it helps if you can answer clearly and interestingly, rather than being vague, or tedious or irrelevant in your answers. So the following information should be useful in your networking activities.

Let's think for a moment of the different types of question there can be. I will cover five here.

Closed Questions

A closed question is one to which the answer is very short. For example: "What is your name?", "Did you come by car?", "Do you enjoy making presentations?". Closed questions are useful for getting facts, especially when you need the information in a short time frame. However, using closed questions is hard work for the questioner, because once the answer has been given, the questioner then has to continue the conversation or ask another question. Closed questions are also not very helpful in talking to rather shy or uncommunicative people, as they are not encouraged to expand on their ideas.

Open Questions

Open questions, in comparison, encourage the other person to speak more. An open question is one where the person has to think about what to say. For example: "What do you think of the speaker?"; "How do you make new contacts for your business?"; "Can you tell me about your approach to marketing?" Such questions generally lead to more in-depth discussions and make it easier for the questioner because the conversation tends to be shared more equally between the people involved.

Leading Questions

Leading questions are those which imply the answer in the question. For example, "You would like to come to the meeting, wouldn't you?" implies you want the person to agree, or "You will be able to look after the speaker, won't you?" implies that the person is going to agree with you. Leading questions really aren't questions, but are more of a way of indicating the questioner's interests or preferences. Avoid leading questions, unless you are using them for a deliberate purpose.

Multiple Questions

Asking several questions together can be confusing for the other person and might mean that one or more of them never get answered. If you really want to ask several questions, you could do it by giving the other person advance notice and focusing them on which to answer first. For example, "I'm interested in how you got into sales, where you started and what particular approaches you use; perhaps I could ask first how you got into the function in the first place." In this way you can indicate that there are three questions and tell the other person which one to answer first.

Hypothetical Questions

Finally, hypothetical questions. Such questions, where the person has to imagine a response, are useful in discussion, but may be misleading in reality, as what the person would actually do might differ. For example, a question such as, "If we invited you to become a member of the group, would you join?" might result in a person saying "Yes" but if it came to it they might actually decline. You never can know with a hypothetical question if the outcome will be the same as the answer given at the time.

Using Questioning in Networking Conversations

Being a good questioner will help you elicit useful information and handling questions well will create an impression of competence and helpfulness. Although all the question types I have mentioned have their uses and can be effective, there is one technique for starting conversations which is particularly useful. The technique is to ask a closed question followed by an open one. For example you could ask, "Did you enjoy the talk?" If the answer is "Yes" you could go on to ask, "What did you think of the ideas it raised?" If the answer is "No", you could go on to ask, "Why was that"? This is an easy way to begin a conversation and also to maintain the discussion subsequently.

So far I have discussed types of question; I would now like to cover a questioning technique which enables you to get different quality information from people.

Three-level Questioning

You can think of this technique rather like an iceberg. Icebergs project out of the water, but most of their bulk is hidden beneath the surface. People are rather like that too; you can see the surface, but what lies underneath is often concealed from others (and sometimes concealed from the individuals themselves also).

So, when you question people in normal conversation, you generally obtain information at a surface level. We call this "level-one" questioning. Level one is questioning about *facts*. Typical level-one questions are: "When did you start your business?"; "Do you have a car?"; "Where do you live?" Level-one questions tend to be easier to ask and to respond to because they usually deal only with factual data. Of course, a person might not wish to answer a particular question but, in general, level-one questions are usually fairly non-threatening.

"Level-two" questions go a little deeper. Level two is about *feelings*. Often you do not need to ask a level-two question, as the answer may already be apparent in the person's behaviour. For example, if someone is angry, upset or excited, it will probably show in their facial expressions, in their voice and in their "body language". However, there can be times when a level-two question is needed; for example: "How do you feel about joining the group?"; "What are your feelings about the viability of this project?" In these cases, asking a level-two question is likely to give you information about a person's inner reactions to an issue. Because these inner feelings can be sensitive, you need to be careful about the appropriateness of asking such questions.

"Level-three" questions go even deeper; they deal with what we term *values*. Values are those things which are of core significance to a person. Sometimes people are very willing to share their values with others, and sometimes they could feel it is an intrusion to discuss them so, again, you need to be careful about when and how you use level-three questions. The simple way to find out about someone's values is to ask them the question, "What is the most important thing to you about . . . " For example: "What is the most important thing to you about changing your job?" or "What is the most important thing to you in a business partner?" You don't have to use those exact words, but this kind of question will get to what really matters to people.

Using this questioning technique in networking can help you gain useful and in-depth information about people. One of the most valuable things about questioning at level three (values) is that it is likely to help you identify those people who share your own approach to things. Having shared values is the basis for most real friendships and relationships, so being able to find out what truly is important to people will help you distinguish between those who are on a similar "wavelength" to you and those who are not.

This technique is also useful in helping others focus on their own activities, ideas and principles. It is also a good process to use on yourself, especially the second and third levels. So you could ask yourself the following questions, as an example:

Level-two Questions

- How do I feel about networking as a process?

- How do I feel about meeting new people?

- How do I feel about promoting my activities?

- How do I feel when other people approach me for information or advice?

Level-three Questions

- What is the most important thing to me in networking?

- What is the most important thing to me in attending social events?

- What is the most important thing to me in making business contacts?

- What is the most important thing to me in helping others?

Feedback

Feedback is a vital element in networking. Being aware of how you come across, how successful you are, the impact you make and how far you have gone to achieving your goals are important to know. Equally, it can be useful to give feedback to others so they are better informed about their own effectiveness. I will be covering feedback to you in Chapter 14, under evaluation of effectiveness.

I will be covering the second element, feedback to others, here. There are two parts to this process: giving people unsolicited feedback and responding to requests for feedback from others.

Giving Others Unsolicited Feedback

Giving others feedback when it has not been asked for can be a sensitive issue. Let's take some examples. Suppose you are at a meeting and one person is dominating the conversation in a group. Or, suppose you are speaking to someone on the telephone and their voice is very hesitant. Would you tell the person what your perception of them is?

This is a very important issue, because my definition of networking includes the words "for mutual benefit". If you believe it would be of benefit to the other person to have the information about themselves, you might want to go ahead and give it to them. I cannot tell you when to do this, you have to use your own judgment, but if you do decide to give feedback, here are a few points you might like to be aware of.

Talk about the person's behaviour, not their personality

People will generally respond better to comments on what they are *doing* than about who they *are*. It is also helpful to frame your comments in a positive manner. For example, you could say, "I thought the point you made to Jennifer was a good one and I felt it would have been even better if you had looked at her directly as you spoke." In this case you are making one positive point, then using the word *and* (not "but", which can sound more negative) to give a small point of critical feedback. You concentrated just on what the person *did*, rather than criticising them as a person and saying they were stupid for not looking at Jennifer.

Sometimes people talk of feedback "sandwiches", where you give one item of positive feedback, then one of negative feedback, then another of positive. This can be useful at times, but the most important thing is to use words and body language which create a positive reception, whatever the content of your message.

Give specific information

Telling the person about the specific behaviour you noticed helps them understand the points you are making. The more precise you can be about what you have observed, the more the person is helped to understand what they have done. So if you say, "You actually looked away from Jennifer when you spoke and focused your eyes a few feet beyond her", this tells the person exactly what you noticed.

Explain the consequences

Telling the person what resulted from their behaviour helps them to make changes. You might say, "When you looked away, Jennifer slowed down what she was saying and paused until you had looked back again; this meant there was a break in the conversation when you took your attention away from her. If this keeps on happening you could find she loses interest in speaking to you and you could miss out on the useful things she could tell you."

Separate facts from opinions

Although your opinions can be valuable to the person, it is generally more acceptable to concentrate on facts which cannot be disputed. Saying, "When you spoke to Jennifer, you looked away from her", is a matter of fact, but saying, "I thought you looked uninterested because you looked away", is a matter of personal interpretation. Although you could say that, because you thought the person looked uninterested, another person could have come to the same conclusion too; this is, however, still your opinion and someone else might not have reacted in the same way, even though you personally think they might.

Avoid over-dramatising

Keeping your own emotions out of feedback is generally useful. You may have found the person's behaviour irritating or upsetting, or you may feel frustrated by what they did, but if you can present what you say in an objective and calm manner you are much more likely to be listened to.

Responding to Requests for Feedback from Others

If you are asked to give feedback to others, the same principles generally apply as I have just outlined; keep to the facts, make your comments objective, and leave your personal emotions out of it.

However, in the case of requested feedback, you can ask the person specifically what they would like from you and it may be that they actually do want to know what your personal opinions are about their behaviour or how their behaviour actually made you feel. In this case, you can well give a more personal reaction to what they have done. Check, however, that they do actually want you to be really honest and are not just seeking a positive response to their behaviour.

Giving Feedback in Networking Conversations

If you are in a group of people, be careful about giving any kind of feedback unless a person directly asks for it there and then, or unless you can be sure you will not be overheard.

It may be useful, however, if you are in a group which has been set up with the purpose of providing some kind of personal development, that a time could be set aside for everyone to give and receive feedback. If this happens, everyone could well benefit from some detached, objective comments on their performance.

So I have described three conversational techniques: listening, questioning and feedback. To conclude this chapter, I would like to give you some ideas about how to make your conversations interesting and lively, while considering networking techniques. Let's do this through some examples.

Simon

At meetings, Simon looks around to see who he knows and acknowledges acquaintances with a smile and a brief greeting. He then goes up to someone new. He says, "Hello, I'm Simon; I haven't seen you here before, is this your first meeting?" (a closed question). If the person says: "Yes, it's the first time I've come", he may ask if they would like to meet the organiser, who could tell them about future events. When Simon goes to a new group himself, he makes a point of asking who the organiser is and then introducing himself so he has a way in to meeting others in the group.

Adele

At conferences, Adele talks to many people. She starts with a reference to something which has happened to her during the day, and follows this up with a question about the other person, as she knows that most people like talking about things that affect them. So, she might ask their opinion of a talk, or recommendations for local places to visit.

Paul

Paul makes a point of introducing humour into conversations. He doesn't do this by telling jokes, but by finding odd or incongruous things to comment on. His voice is lively and entertaining and he makes connections between things people are saying and experiences he has had in the past.

Shirley

Shirley makes a point of complimenting people. She says how much she likes someone's scarf or tie; she tells them how well they tell a story; she says how interested she is in the points they were making. She doesn't do this in an artificial way; her compliments arise from a genuine interest in, and appreciation of, the person.

Marcel

Marcel makes a point of looking directly at people and using a clear and audible voice. He makes sure he is heard and seen to be engaged in the conversation. He uses good eye contact and emphasises points or questions with appropriate gestures of his face, head or hands.

Helen

Helen tells people things they can learn from. When they mention a topic, she draws a parallel with something similar, so they can see the connection. For example, if someone is having difficulty with a member of staff, she will tell them how friends of hers handled a situation with a teenage child.

Sam

In groups, Sam notices if anyone is being very quiet. When speaking, he glances at that person on occasion, to include them in the conversation. Later, he makes a point of directing a question to the person who has not been speaking. Through his steady building of a relationship, he is able to help the person feel more comfortable about joining in.

Louisa

Louisa listens a lot. She takes in everything people say and just nods, smiles and makes short comments on the conversation. Many people think Louisa is an excellent conversationalist, although she does little but allow others to have their say!

Example 1

I was in the snack bar of a building frequented by people of Middle Eastern origin. The girl behind the counter noticed me and said something in her own language; I smiled at her. She then went on to have a lengthy "conversation" with me. All I did was look at her, make a few movements of my head, smile and nod. She clearly thought I understood everything she said, although I hadn't the faintest idea what she was talking about.

Example 2

My mother was travelling on a train during the Second World War. Two men were seated opposite her, chatting away on a rather technical subject, about which she knew nothing. Occasionally they glanced at her and, when they did, she either nodded or frowned. Soon they began to ask her opinion of every point. She had become an instant expert, simply by appearing interested and responsive.

Chapter Nine

Rapport, Influence and Assertiveness

This chapter deals with building and maintaining effective relationships and being able to persuade, influence and assert your opinions and needs. Let's start with some definitions.

Definitions

Rapport

Rapport is the state which exists between people when they feel comfortable together and are "on the same wavelength". Rapport often happens naturally and it is interesting that sometimes we meet people with whom we feel an instant familiarity while on other occasions we come across people with whom we seem unable ever to have an affinity.

You will almost certainly have rapport for much of the time with your close friends and partners, as this is the foundation for good relationships. This chapter will give you ways of *creating* rapport with others and *enhancing* rapport with those already close to you.

Influence

Influence may be defined in many ways. I am defining it here as the process of leading someone towards a particular destination which they will perceive as beneficial.

Persuasion

Persuasion is a little stronger than influence, as it pre-supposes a degree of resistance or indifference which has to be overcome. Persuasion can be ethical (when you persuade someone to do something which they will believe benefits them) or unethical (when you persuade them to do something which is against their interests — manipulation).

Assertiveness

Assertiveness is about being able to relate to others on an equal basis, so you can be comfortable with expressing your own opinions and needs and also with acknowledging the opinions and needs of others.

Let's take rapport first. Before starting, I would like you to take time to answer the following questions about rapport:

- Do you feel you get on fairly well with most people?

- Do you find it easy to strike up conversations with people you don't know?

- Do you feel comfortable in situations where you don't know anyone?

- Do you often find you have things in common with people you meet?

- If someone you are with is feeling excited, or upset, do you find it easy or difficult to be with them?

If you are generally able to get on well with others, including new people, and can be comfortable around others no matter how they are feeling, you probably already have well-developed rapport skills. If, on the other hand, you find meeting new people a little daunting and aren't easily able to start up conversations, you may need a little more help in developing your skills in this area.

Rapport

Think for a moment of situations you have experienced where people have been getting on well together. You will probably find that the people concerned have been similar in some way. Perhaps they had similar interests or dressed in a similar manner or lived in the same geographical area.

Similarity underlies rapport. We tend to gravitate towards people who are like us in some way. So, to create rapport, it helps if you make yourself like the person to whom you are relating.

Of course, it helps if you already have similar interests or activities, which you can establish through conversation. However, if there are no apparent areas of similarity you can still generate rapport through the five performance elements I mentioned in the introduction: objectives, behaviour, thoughts, feelings and beliefs.

You might, for example, share objectives. When you and another person are working towards similar goals, you have something in common. This is vital in a business context; a work team which does not strive for the same goals is not likely to be successful. Even if you don't have exactly the same objectives as another person, if you can show you understand how important their objectives are to them, and can empathise with them, they are likely to respond well.

You could also share behaviour. If you eat similar food, play the same sport, get up at a similar time in the morning, wear similar clothes or do a similar job, you have things in common. Again, if you don't exactly share the behaviour, but can understand why the other person behaves as they do, it is easier to get into a state of rapport.

Another way in which you can have things in common is to think in similar ways. Some people have a positive outlook on life while others have a more negative one; some people think long term while others think short term. There are many thinking processes which produce parallels in different people.

A further way of being similar to another person is to share their feelings. It is interesting in a work situation to see alliances develop between people who feel similarly about issues or events; sometimes the most unlikely people can develop an affinity during times of change and uncertainty.

The last area of similarity I will mention here is that of beliefs and values. Shared beliefs and values are very powerful. If you take the examples of beliefs about religion, nationality, freedom of speech, property rights, blood sports, education, morality and unemployment, it is easy to see how people differ and how similar views can unite people for or against a particular cause. So sharing beliefs and values makes for strong bonds — sometimes in a positive way and, unfortunately, often in a negative one.

So how can you create rapport, or enhance it, when it does not occur spontaneously? You could mimic the person, which is likely to cause embarrassment or offence. You could "mirror" them, which is probably too exaggerated. Or you could "match" them.

Matching is the process which is most likely to be of practical use to you and it is an easy one to follow. It simply involves copying the minimum necessary to create a sense of similarity. Let's see how this can work.

Matching Objectives

If you think back to situations you have been in, how easy has it been to relate to a person who shares your objectives and how hard has it been to relate to someone who does not share them? On the whole, sharing objectives enhances rapport. You will need to think carefully about the extent you can go to in matching someone's objectives if you do not fully share them; it is perhaps better to show you understand their objectives, rather than adopt them yourself, if they are not in line with your own outlook.

Example

I was listening to a radio programme recently, and there was an item on childbirth. A midwife was helping a woman who was in labour and she commented that, when a new person came to her it was important to ". . . establish immediate rapport". In such a situation, both midwife and mother have a shared objective — a comfortable and problem-free birth. So being able to match someone's objectives is important in establishing good relationships.

Matching Behaviour

To match someone's behaviour, all you need to do is to copy *part* of what they are doing, or to do something *similar* to the other person. For example, if you are with someone who is sitting in a relaxed position, you can also sit in a relaxed position; it should not be identical, just relaxed, rather than stiff and formal.

You could also dress in a similar way to the other people you are meeting; wearing formal clothes if they do and wearing casual clothes if they do; again this is matching rather than mirroring — the clothes don't have to be identical, just broadly similar.

Other things you could match are tone of voice, speed of speaking, nodding and smiling. You can also match behaviour in meetings (arriving on time, having relevant papers with you, joining in discussions) and behaviour at social events (dressing similarly, chatting about topics of mutual interest and leaving when others do rather than outstaying your welcome).

Example

Some years ago I visited an Indian restaurant with some work colleagues. After the meal, several people wanted to have some tea; the waiter said that only coffee was available. A number of attempts were made to get the tea provided, but to no avail. I had a good deal of contact with the Asian community and had picked up many mannerisms, including the very recognisable way of tilting your head from side to side which is commonplace amongst Indian people. I asked the waiter if he would make the tea for us and, as I did so, I used this head movement — he immediately said he would make the tea. So matching behaviour, especially at a minimal level, is really effective.

Matching Thinking

As well as behavioural matching, you can match how another person thinks. If the other person is thinking about the benefits of a situation, you could match this by considering the advantages; if they are thinking about the disadvantages of the situation you could make observations about that. Similarly, if they are contemplating long-term issues you could do the same and if they are thinking short term you could contemplate short-term issues.

Of course, the only way they will know you are matching them is by what you say and do (your behaviour), as your thoughts are invisible to them. Similarity in thinking is a powerful process and it is not surprising that people who think in similar ways find each other interesting or easy to get on with.

Example

Harry, an operations manager, was finding it hard to communicate with his boss, who always seemed hesitant about suggestions Harry made. Working out that his boss was really concerned about how things might go wrong, Harry began to start his conversations with statements such as: "I know we will have to be careful if we adopt this approach, but there are many advantages to doing it this way." By acknowledging his boss's thoughts that things could go wrong, and allowing time to consider this, Harry found his ideas gained much more support and encouragement.

Matching Feelings

People's feelings often match in situations that precipitate strong emotional responses; for example, at a football match, at a funeral or in a traffic jam. On such occasions, people are likely to share emotions and, through this, feel a link with others.

I would not recommend you create feelings you do not have in order to develop rapport with someone else, but it is simple enough to match the behaviour which goes along with their feelings so you can appear to share in their responses. So, for example, if someone is upset, you could speak quietly and move slowly and if they are excited you could raise your voice a little and speak faster. These are simple ways of matching feelings that may well help the other person relate to you better.

Example

Sandra worked as a receptionist for a manufacturing company. One day she had visitor after visitor complaining to her about the time they were kept waiting for appointments. She was becoming exasperated. Two other staff members came over to the reception desk and spoke to Sandra. When she said how irritated she felt, one of them just laughed, while the other one said: "I know what you mean; I've had a dreadful day too — it will be wonderful to go home." Sandra responded much more positively to the second member of staff than the first, who had mismatched her feelings completely.

Matching Beliefs and Values

More controversially, you could match beliefs, values and assumptions. I say more controversially, as you need to consider the ethics involved here. If you do not genuinely share the person's views and opinions, it could cause problems to pretend you do. So matching in this area has its benefits and it also has its limitations. As with feelings, it might be better simply to acknowledge the other person's beliefs and values, so they know you understand why they hold them, rather than actually trying to copy them directly.

Example

Very often I travel by taxi in London. Some taxi drivers are fairly uncommunicative, while others talk non-stop about all kinds of things. I frequently find myself listening to strongly voiced opinions, reflecting underlying beliefs about various things, such as transport policy, tourists and earnings. I find it easiest simply to question the person about their views, rather than agree with things on which I have opposing views, or enter into a debate when I simply want a few minutes' peace and quiet. By questioning, I can acknowledge the opinions and allow the driver to do most of the talking.

Having considered some of the elements of matching, it would be useful for you to practise some of the skills I have presented, so here are a few exercises that you can follow for this purpose.

Exercises

- When travelling in a train, sit in a similar way to the person opposite; don't copy them exactly, but make slight adjustments to your own posture to conform with theirs.

- When on the telephone, slow down, or increase the speed at which you talk to match that of the other person. Don't exaggerate and copy them exactly, just adjust your speed a little to get closer to theirs.

- When watching television, make your facial expressions similar to those of someone on the programme; smile when they do, nod when they do, raise your eyebrows when they do, blink when they do and so on. (Preferably do this on your own; it could seem strange if there are others in the room at the time!)

- During a conversation, when the other person is talking about a subject, try to find examples of when you had experience of that topic and introduce those experiences into the conversation.

- When you are with someone who is obviously experiencing a strong emotion (but avoid anger and aggression), notice their posture, their facial expression, their breathing rate and their voice speed, volume and tone. Copy some of these (remembering to do the minimum, not the maximum) and notice how the person seems to respond to you once you have done this.

- When you are with someone who is talking about a goal they would like to achieve, discuss that goal with them and notice how they respond when you show an interest in their objective.

I have only given examples of a few ways of matching here; you might also like to come up with some others of your own to practise the various rapport skills further.

Developing rapport can help people feel comfortable together; it can also act as a foundation for influencing. Unless you have rapport with someone it is unlikely that you will be able to influence them easily, so the next element I would like to move to in this chapter is influence.

Influence

I would now like you to take a few minutes to consider the following questions:

- How much influence do you think you have in your life?

- Do you feel you easily influence others?

- Are you comfortable with attempting to influence others?

- Do you feel others influence you a great deal?

- Do you feel it is acceptable to influence?

- What do you think of influential people?

Considering these questions will give you some good starting points for our discussions. I have begun with these questions because some people have strong views about influence; possibly believing it is only certain people who can be influential, or feeling that influencing is not always an appropriate thing to do.

Example

*My own view is that we cannot **not** influence and that everything we do influences others. A story I like to tell is about a time, many years ago, when I was asked to video a training session. In those days it wasn't called video, but closed circuit television, and it was unfamiliar to many people — myself included.*

*I was given a few minutes' (!) training before I started and the particular point emphasised was that I should move the camera slowly, as fast movements would be disturbing when replayed. So off we went. The session was part of a marketing course and was a discussion between a group of about ten people. The participants were seated around a long table, with people at each side and a person at either end. At some stage, the person at the end furthest from me made a comment and, at that time, I was pointing the camera at the person at the other end of the table. So, **slowly**, I moved the camera to the other end. By the time I got there that person had stopped speaking and the person at the other end had started to talk. Again, I moved the camera slowly and, again, missed the person, who stopped talking just as I reached him. This continued for a while. On replaying the session there were many shots of silent people!*

The participants reacted in a rather sarcastic way to the video, so I decided to use a different approach next time. For the following session I selected particular things to film; I filmed people fidgeting, people looking down or away, people yawning and so on. The session in fact was a very good one, but my selective filming completely distorted its impact. This experience taught me that there is probably no such thing as total objectivity and that everything we do influences others and influences the outcomes of our actions.

So, given that influence is probably inevitable, how can you use it in a positive and ethical manner? One way is through the use of language and I will be covering two aspects of this here. The first is recognition of, and matching people's language patterns and the second is recognition of, and responding to people's values.

Language Patterns

Those of you who work in the business sector may be familiar with the use of psychometric (personality and aptitude) tests, which measure sociability, motivation, stress, sensitivity, energy and so forth. It is also possible to assess much of this conversationally. What follows relates to the NLP "Meta Programme" language model, referred to briefly at the end of Chapter 7.

By matching people's Meta Programmes, or motivational and other traits, you are likely to be more easily accepted and enhance your communications with them. I will cover five Meta Programmes here; just to remind you, they are:

- Towards and away from (carrot and stick);

- Internal and external (me and you);

- Procedures and options (what about the rule book?);

- Detail and general (depth of information);

- Sameness and difference (what do you notice?).

In the examples that follow, I will show how people act if they are demonstrating specific Meta Programmes. Once you can deduce motivational and other traits from people's language and behaviour, you will find it easier to gain rapport with them (by matching their own patterns), and then influence them once they are comfortable with you. See how easy you find it to work out the examples.

Please remember as you read the following that Meta Programmes are context- and time-dependent; i.e. they can change over time and people can demonstrate one approach in one situation and something different in another. In the case studies, however, I have talked about the people "as if" they always demonstrate one or other of the categories.

Sally

Sally works in an advertising agency. She is very lively and enthusiastic and always talking about things she has planned. Her conversations are peppered with statements such as: "I want to really make an impact on this new account" and "I am really looking forward to achieving some results with my new client." Sally always looks on the bright side and counters any ideas of drawbacks with ways in which she could move ahead and reach her objectives. She finds it easy to express her ideas clearly and tell people exactly what she has in mind for her next project.

To establish rapport with Sally, would you:

a) *Talk to her about her plans for the future?*

b) *Point out some possible obstacles to her achieving her goals?*

c) *Show her that there could be advantages in keeping things as they are?*

Nigel

Nigel works for an insurance company. He is thoughtful and takes care that his work is error-free. He can easily see what needs to be done to solve a problem or difficulty and talks a good deal about how he has overcome some of the awkward features of his computer system. Nigel is good at spotting mistakes in documents and people often come to him to check their work before presenting it to others.

   To establish rapport with Nigel, would you:

a) *Share with him some of your own work problems?*

b) *Tell him how he could achieve even better results if he concentrated on specific target areas?*

c) *Show him how to speed up his activities by taking short cuts?*

Jan

Jan works for a health authority. She knows she does a good job and always seeks high standards for herself. She makes decisions easily and can be relied upon to have an opinion on any matters that arise. Jan is very self-motivated and doesn't need telling what to do or how to do it; she is often in the forefront when someone needs to take the lead and show what can be done.

   To establish rapport with Jan would you:

a) *Ask her views on a topic of current interest?*

b) *Suggest ways in which she could improve her performance?*

c) *Talk to her about your own problems?*

Winston

Winston works for a housing association. He likes to get team members' views on how things are going and will usually check with others what their preferences are when decisions need to be made. Winston is good at listening to people and likes to make decisions based on what the majority view is.

   To establish rapport with Winston, would you:

a) *Tell him about a new approach that people seem impressed by?*

b) *Ask him to prepare an agenda for a meeting on his own?*

c) *Ask him for suggestions on how you might do your job better?*

Naseem

Naseem works for a travel agency. She always follows the systems set out in the agency, so that she is certain to get things right. She likes to know how things have been done in the past so she has a good idea of what happens in each area of her work.

   To establish rapport with Naseem, would you:

a) Ask her what is the best way to handle complaints?

b) Suggest a new way for her to deal with her customers?

c) Ask her for new ideas on developing her filing system?

George

George works for a car dealer. He likes to try out new approaches to selling and sees each customer as a fresh challenge. He prefers his day to be varied, so he can move from one task to another. He enjoys collecting ideas on how to enhance his performance.

   To establish rapport with George, would you:

a) Suggest a new way of starting a conversation with a customer?

b) Tell him about your daily routine?

c) Suggest that tried and tested ways of working are best?

Frankie

Frankie works as a bookkeeper. She is very accurate and likes to keep all her work neat and correct. She easily spots any tiny mistakes and when she explains things to people she is precise about giving them all the information they need on the subject.

   To establish rapport with Frankie, would you:

a) Tell her about your recent holiday, including lots of information about the place and the activities

b) Ask her for a rough idea of your budget for next year?

c) Suggest she cut down on the checking she does to save time?

Isohel

Isohel is a senior manager in an IT firm. She spends a good deal of time thinking about strategic planning and likes to have as broad a view as possible of the company's markets and resources. Isohel *often talks to people about her thoughts on development of the organisation as a whole.*

To establish rapport with Isohel, would you:

a) *Give her an overview of how her company's competitors are doing?*

b) *Talk to her about the specific approach she envisages for the following year's marketing?*

c) *Ask her exactly how she carries out her planning activities?*

Robert

Robert works as a men's tailor. He likes to make sure that all the suits he makes are of a high quality and recognisable as his work. He has regular customers who have come to him for many years because they can rely on him to make their clothes in the same reliable manner as he always has. Robert likes to have a predictable working environment, where he can do the tasks he knows he is good at.

To establish rapport with Robert, would you:

a) *Ask him to tell you which features of his suits he always includes?*

b) *Tell him about some new material which he could try?*

c) *Suggest a different way of talking to his customers?*

Renata

Renata is a tour guide. She enjoys working with tourists and always notices the differences between people — their personalities, clothes, interests and opinions. She likes it when they come up with novel questions and has great interest in the unpredictability of the job.

To establish rapport with Renata, would you:

a) *Suggest a novel way of starting conversations with people?*

b) *Ask what procedure she follows if someone doesn't like their accommodation?*

c) *Say you could help her make her job more systematic?*

The "correct" answers to the sets of questions is "a" in each case. To influence someone, it helps first to establish rapport with them and then to use language which will help them understand the benefits of what you are saying. By matching the person's modes of being (their Meta Programmes) you will have a way of "speaking their language", thereby making them relate to you more easily.

Once you have identified a person's own patterns, you can either stay with that pattern to influence them within it, or you can use their patterns as a way of establishing rapport and, once you have done so, then begin to move them into another pattern which could be more beneficial. So, for example, if a person is strongly "away from", you could begin by acknowledging possible problems or discussing ways of handling obstacles and then help them see how they could move *towards* goals in a positive and satisfying way.

Values

Having covered how to recognise people's patterns in language, I would like, briefly, to consider how you can work with values in order to influence.

In the last chapter, on conversation, I mentioned some questioning techniques. One of the techniques was "three-level questioning" (see pages 154–6). Level-three questions involve finding out about people's values by asking them a question such as, "What's the most important thing to you about . . ."

People are very sensitive to their own values and tend to use very specific words with which to describe them. For example, someone might say that "independence" is important to them in their job, or that" safety" is important to them in a car. These words equate to the values held by the person.

If you listen carefully to people and ask questions directed at eliciting values, you can then match the person by using their exact words when you want to influence them. Actually this is more like mirroring than matching but, in this context, it is a process that works very well. To influence through matching values, you can simply include the person's own words in what you have to offer. So, if you are trying to help them make a decision between two products, by reminding them of which product has the features they value, they will probably be helped to make the decision.

Example

If a friend is looking for a new job and you thought they might make some useful contacts at a particular meeting, but the person was a bit apprehensive about going, you could chat to them about their thoughts on the job and then use some of their words to encourage them to attend the meeting. For example, if the person said they wanted more responsibility at work, you might mention that somebody at the meeting had just moved to a job where they had more responsibility and would probably be prepared to share experiences with your friend. Be careful to use the exact word "responsibility" in such a context, rather than substituting a similar word which means the same thing to you; it may have a totally different impact on your friend.

For more on influencing, I would encourage you to read the book *Words that Change Minds*, which you will find listed in the Bibliography.

Assertiveness

Again, take a few minutes to answer the following questions:

- Do you find it easy to express your opinions to other people?

- Do you often feel your needs are less important than those of others?

- Do you stand up for yourself if you feel you have been treated unfairly?

- Do you sometimes impose your ideas on others?

- Do you often feel that others take advantage of you?

- Do you find it easy to ask for things you want?

Considering these questions will give you some idea of the extent to which you are able to express yourself and state your needs and wishes or, alternatively, the extent to which you subjugate your own ideas and wants to those of others. So what is assertiveness about?

Assertiveness is basically about behaving in a fair manner towards others and expecting the same in return.

The principle underlying assertiveness is that everyone has rights; for example:

- The right to hold opinions and beliefs;
- The right to have feelings, wants and needs;
- The right to be listened to and treated with respect;
- The right to ask for what you want;
- The right to make mistakes;
- The right to say "No".

The aim is to be able to have others acknowledge and respect your rights and to do the same for them.

There are various thoughts about how the concept of assertiveness originated. One way of putting it into context is as follows. The famous psychoanalyst, Sigmund Freud, talked about three "states" which can be simplified as follows; superego (conscience), ego (self) and id (emotional self). Freud's categories were subsequently taken up by a field of psychology called Transactional Analysis, which defined three categories: Parent (dominating), Adult (equitable) and Child (submissive). Later, assertiveness trainers refined these concepts into three further categories — Aggressive, Assertive and Unassertive — and I would like to explain each of these here.

Aggressive

Aggressive people tend to impose themselves on others. They may shout and be physically dominating. They may threaten. They can be actually violent. Aggression can be perceived through postures, gestures, movement, tone of voice and facial expression; it can also be noticed in the language people use.

An aggressive person often speaks loudly, moves close to other people, uses very direct eye contact, takes up a lot of space and uses large gestures. Their face can reflect their manner and they often have a tense muscle tone and their tone of voice can be harsh and imposing.

Unassertive

Unassertive (or submissive) people tend to deny their own feelings and needs and defer to others. They may speak quietly, take up little space — by sitting in postures where their arms and legs are close to their body, move away from others and look timid, avoiding eye contact. Their manner can be apologetic and they may speak very little and avoid situations where they have to express their opinions or take the lead in things.

Assertive

Assertive people find a middle path between the extremes of aggression and unassertiveness. They adopt "open" postures, use direct but non-threatening eye contact, speak in a direct manner, express and stand up for their opinions and needs without being dominating, check they have been understood, use space in a confident manner and allow other people to express their own views and wishes in a fair and respectful way.

In networking, it is generally helpful to adopt an assertive manner, so you are perceived as confident, capable and professional. If you are aggressive, it could mean you are in control in the short term but, long term, it could have a negative effect on your relationships. If you are unassertive, you are unlikely to be able to make the most of opportunities and other people are less likely to remember you and take what you are saying seriously.

Although people all have their own natural tendencies, it is possible to learn to be more assertive and this can be helpful both to people who are very aggressive and those who are very unassertive. So, how can you become more assertive? Here are a few ideas:

- Give yourself some positive thoughts about how you would like to behave. Create mental images of yourself behaving in the way you would like, imagine people responding to you in the way you would like and tell yourself that you are capable of behaving in the way you desire. This will generally increase your confidence levels.

- Start using the word "I" more, expressing your own views and opinions as a matter of fact, without apologising for them or over-defending them. If you already refer to your own opinions a lot, work at doing so a bit less and acknowledging others' views and needs as well.

- Adopt a relaxed posture, using your arms and legs in ways that make the most of your space without invading that of others; for example, resting on arms of chairs (rather than folding your own arms) and leaning forwards to appear engaged in the conversation.

- Work at speaking clearly and at a suitable pace. If your voice is naturally very high, work at lowering it; if it is naturally very soft, work at speaking more loudly. Conversely, if you normally speak very loudly, you can work to tone your voice down a little. The key is to have some flexibility in how you speak, rather than having to speak just one way all the time.

- Use direct language, saying what you mean, being specific and repeating what you say if you do not get a response. Avoid imposing your own thoughts on others.

- Explain to people how you feel about their behaviour if you do not like what they are doing (as long as it is safe for you to do this — I used to ask people to turn down noisy music in trains until I realised that it could be potentially dangerous, depending on the person to whom I was speaking).

- Say "No" if that is what you think is right. You don't have to give a reason if you don't want to but, if you wish to give a reason, give the strongest reason you have and don't weaken it by adding lots of other, less relevant reasons.

- Practise disagreeing with others if you find this hard. If you constantly disagree, work at listening to others and finding out what their opinions are and why they hold them.

There are many more things you can do to develop assertive behaviour and if you would like to follow this up there are a wide range of books, tapes and courses on the subject.

So this chapter has given you some ideas on developing effective relationships and influencing others. By working on the activities described, you will enhance your own performance and achieve even better results in how you communicate and persuade.

Chapter Ten

Non-verbal Communications

Non-verbal communications are found throughout the animal kingdom; for many animals, non-verbal signals are their major way of communicating. For example, the displays of peacocks when attracting a mate; the way dogs roll on their backs when threatened by a larger rival, or how they wag their tails when excited; cats arching their backs when alarmed; or bees dancing to show their fellows the direction of the nearest supply of pollen.

All these signals are very effective as shorthand for conversation; you don't need speech when you can make displays of this kind. Humans use non-verbals as much as animals, but there are a range of ways in which this can be done.

It is possible to communicate with "spoken word substitutes" — for example, the sign language used by deaf or dumb people, the "tic-tac" signs used by bookmakers on a racecourse, Morse code, signalling with flags and using very specific gestures such as pointing and beckoning. All these "word substitutes" have the objective of communicating in the absence of the spoken word. What I would like to talk about in this chapter, however, is not these processes of *intentional* communicating, but the ways in which we send signals or messages to each other, sometimes intentionally, but more often unintentionally, through our "body language".

"Body language" involves non-verbal messages, used on their own or accompanying words. Where we can run into trouble is if the words and the non-verbal signals conflict.

This might be for a range of reasons. It could be because we actually have mixed emotions ("putting a brave face" on a situation while feeling anxious). It could be because we are trying to reconcile our words with a differing thought (inviting someone in for tea but wishing they would decline). It could be because we are trying to deceive (hiding something behind our back while pretending to behave as normal). It could also be because we are confused, we don't know any better or we are unaware of social conventions (wearing elegant shoes and flimsy clothes for a weekend in the country in the middle of winter).

Because of the potential for non-verbals to confuse or to communicate inaccurately or to give away things which you might prefer to conceal, it is helpful to be aware of the signals you are giving to others and to manage those signals in accordance with your objectives. It is also helpful to be able to "read" the signals which other people are giving you through their "body language". This chapter will give you ways of doing both these things.

What are Non-verbal Signals?

I have already covered the way we dress in Chapter 6 and I will be covering accessories, artefacts and written communications in the next chapter. In this chapter I will be covering the remaining non-verbal elements: posture, positioning, movement, gesture, mannerisms and facial expression.

In order to introduce you to this topic, I would like to outline an approach to non-verbal communication which is still relatively little known, although it has been in existence for over 20 years. This approach is called "Action Profiling" and its main exponent is Warren Lamb, who introduced the concept in his book *Body Code: The Meaning in Movement*. I will be combining Action Profiling principles with NLP to give you a range of ways to understand, and to use, non-verbal communications.

Action Profiling

Action profiling enables a trained observer to assess people's characteristics, personality, motivation and aptitudes through analysing their body movement ("the secret and mostly silent language"). Once analysed, information about movement can then be used for many purposes including networking.

In his book *Body Code*, Warren Lamb divides body language into three types, known as PMG, which stands for:

- Posture

- Movement

- Gesture.

He says that behaviour is movement and that, by understanding a person's movements, we can both understand their temperament and abilities and make predictions about their future behaviour.

In this chapter, I will discuss the concept of PMG. I will be incorporating positioning with posture, and mannerisms and facial expressions along with gestures. I will also be discussing the NLP ways of "reading" and interpreting non-verbal signals.

Posture and Positioning

Posture

Posture may be defined as movement involving the whole body and positioning defined as one person's position relative to another.

Your posture says a lot about you. You have probably heard people say things like: "He's down in the dumps" or "She's just mooching around" or "He's weighed down with problems" or "She's floating on air". Expressions such as these are not simply metaphorical, but also communicate things about how people actually carry themselves. A "down" posture can indicate depression, overload and withdrawal, while an "up" posture can indicate energy, enthusiasm and participation.

Analysing your own posture, and that of others, can give you ways of interpreting other people's behaviour and modifying your own to more useful ends. In networking, when you meet new people, if you remember the impression your posture can create, you can take steps to come across in the way you feel will best promote your cause.

For good posture, balance is important as it enables you to stand, sit and move effectively. Balance also encompasses many other elements, such as flexibility, alignment and lightness. When you are balanced, you can move freely and function without getting aches and pains or strained muscles. There are many ways to achieve balance and alignment and some you might like to try are the following:

- *Exercise and stretching.* Taking regular exercise and using a range of stretching activities will help you develop good balance and flexibility of movement. It is always useful to do stretching and warm-up exercises before and after taking any kind of strenuous exercise, as this will help loosen up your muscles and avoid strains and aches. Exercise is particularly helpful for the major muscle groups of the body and it can also be targeted particularly to specific parts which need to be strengthened or made more flexible. Again, see the Resource List for useful contacts.

• *Alexander technique, Feldenkrais, Pilates, Yoga and T'ai Chi.* These techniques, some of which I mentioned in Chapter 7, help you get your body into a balanced and aligned way of functioning. In the Alexander Technique, especially, you learn to have your spine as the central focus of your overall posture, with your head comfortably balanced at one end, your shoulders resting in a relaxed manner, your feet spread comfortably on the floor, your knees held in a relaxed manner rather than being locked into position, and so on. Good alignment can contribute to overall balance, posture and wellbeing, enabling you to move freely and come across as poised and confident. In each of the disciplines mentioned here, you learn and practise ways of using your body with economy and ease of movement. You can have sessions on a one-to-one basis or you can attend group sessions with other people. Once you learn the techniques, you will find you look and feel better and can move more comfortably and elegantly, without putting strain on your body. If you would like to find out more, see the Resource List for information.

• *Relaxation and meditation.* This is as much to do with mental balance as physical balance. By taking time out to detach yourself from the impact of day-to-day activities, you will refresh yourself mentally and physically. There are many relaxation techniques available, including listening to calming music or sounds such as water, birdsong, whale sounds and gongs. Other relaxation techniques include guided visualisation (there are many tapes available with this kind of process), the Alexander technique's "lying down process" which I described in Chapter 7, having a warm bath and sitting in the open air. Meditation is a specialised kind of relaxation where, as with all relaxation processes, your pulse rate is likely to reduce and your brain waves slow down so that you achieve a relaxed, but often creative, state of mind. To check on how relaxed you are, there are "biofeedback" products available which help you monitor your pulse rate and other physiological functions and so make it easier to be aware of when you are tense and when you are relaxed. See the Resource List again for information.

Positioning

As well as posture, it is useful to think about positioning, or the distances and angles between ourselves and others. It is important to remember that each person has what may be termed "personal space" around themselves. This space varies from person to person and also between cultures. For example, in western society, personal space generally extends about three feet around a person, which is a good distance for social conversation. Closer than this is all right for more intimate contact and more than three feet is more appropriate for more formal interactions, such as presentations. If you ignore this general rule, you may find you upset people by getting too close to them or too far away. Other cultures have different norms for personal space and you may need to move closer or get farther away from people as you speak to them if you are to be socially "correct".

You can generally tell if you are getting too close to someone, as they are likely to move backwards if they feel their personal space is being disturbed. If someone keeps getting closer to you than you would like, you may find yourself moving backwards. Unless you tell the person however, or break the pattern by moving closer to them rather than stepping back, you may find they don't get the message and you end up crossing the room with them in hot pursuit; the other person trying to make contact and you trying to avoid it!

Example

On a training course, one participant, a young man, said his female boss intimidated him. When asked why, he said she moved very close to him, raised her voice, waved her arms around and spoke in an aggressive manner to him. When asked what he did in response, he said he backed off and looked away from her. Now, faced with someone backing away and avoiding eye contact, it is not surprising that a person would move forward and speak more loudly. If the young man had adopted a different strategy, and perhaps taken a step forward rather than back, the outcome could have been different. He felt that his personal space was being invaded, but his actions in fact perpetuated the very behaviour he did not like.

So, being aware of what is going on with positioning, and being able to analyse and respond to it appropriately, is a useful social skill.

As well as distance, the angle between people also matters. For example, if you sit the other side of a desk or table, say at an interview or in a negotiation, you create a different impression and expectation than if you sit beside the other person, or at an angle rather than opposite them. Thinking about where to position yourself, as well as how far away, also affects the impact you make in social and business situations.

In networking, this is important and when you meet people it is worth thinking about how you position yourself in relation to them. Do you stand facing someone or at an angle to them? Do you get close to two people engaged in discussion or do you stand a little to the side until you are certain you are welcome to join in? Thinking about such situations will help you select suitable behaviour and be perceived as socially aware.

Movement

Movement is comprised of many elements, including speed, direction, plane, rhythm and fluidity. You can also include breathing as an element.

So, movement is a complex function. By considering the specific elements of your movement, you will be better able to choose and maintain the image you create. One particular aspect of movement that you might like to think about is fluidity — the degree of ease and gracefulness with which you can move. The more flexible you are, and the more lightly you hold yourself, the easier movement will be for you.

There are many common activities which can enhance flexibility and you might like to use some of the following to improve your overall flexibility in movement:

- Using graceful movements, rather than jerky or awkward ones, when carrying out everyday tasks such as cleaning the house or gardening;

- Doing stretches while sitting at a computer screen or while waiting at traffic lights in your car;

- Using balanced, easy movements when lifting objects.

If in doubt about how to do any of the movements, do consult a trained practitioner who can give you specific advice.

Exercises

1. Imagine being the following creatures. Have a go at moving like each one on the list.

    - An elephant
    - A gazelle
    - A cat
    - A snail
    - A chicken.

2. Select a few people, either ones you see in "real life" or ones you view on television. Now, copy their posture and gestures yourself.

3. Find two friends or colleagues who are prepared to help you, and learn something of benefit to themselves also. Ask one of the people to sit or stand or move in a way that is typical of them. Now ask the second person to help you adopt as close as possible a copy of the first person's posture, gesture and movement. This will include overall body position, movements of hands and feet, facial expression, breathing, eye focus and so on. Once you have adopted the behaviour, notice how it feels. Often you will be able to understand the person much better by "being in their shoes" and you will certainly have a better idea of how it feels to be in their body.

Doing such exercises is helpful in networking, as they will both help you manage how you come across and enable you to see someone and imagine being them, "as if" you were that person. This can give you some useful insights. Of course, you cannot really be that person, but the exercise will help with shifting your perspective and understanding more about how they function in the world.

Gesture, Mannerisms and Facial Expressions

Gestures

Warren Lamb says that gestures only have meaning in a context. So, to understand what a particular gesture means, we have to consider the body posture in which the gesture takes place. We *make* a gesture but we *have* a posture. Lamb gives a nice description of posture: "A dog may walk on his hind legs, but he cannot lose his 'dogginess'; you do not catch him balancing on his forepaws." (Although I once had a dog which did a forward somersault after tripping on a step!)

Gestures can include movements of the head, shoulders, arms, hands, legs and feet, some unique to an individual and others more culturally determined.

Knowing about the cultural elements of gesture is vital if you are networking internationally or with diverse cultural groups and knowing about individual gesture is helpful in understanding other people's individual patterns of communication. It is also helpful to be aware of the gestures you use yourself, so you can be in control of them and not find you are making repetitive or irritating movements.

Let's take a few common elements of gesture and see how they might be interpreted in social and business interactions.

Pointing your finger

Pointing is a natural gesture which is commonly used to draw attention towards something. You can use pointing in a neutral way or you can invest it with particular meaning; for example, pointing at someone aggressively as you accuse them of making a mistake.

You may think that pointing is neutral, but someone else could consider it offensive; and in certain cultures pointing is regarded as a distinct insult. So be careful about how you use pointing and make sure you don't give offence through this kind of gesture.

Waving your hands

Hand waving can be interpreted in a variety of ways; it may simply be an accompaniment to a state of excitement or a way of "painting pictures in the air". So your hand movements may be fascinating to someone or simply irritating. They could also be offensive if you move your hands too close to a person's face. So, again, be careful how you use gestures of this sort.

Nodding or shaking your head

Nodding can indicate approval or interest and shaking can indicate the opposite. In some cultures, however, the reverse can be the case; it may also be that a nod simply indicates that the person is acknowledging what you are saying, but not actually agreeing with you. So you do need to know how these movements are likely to be interpreted if you are operating in an international context. Nodding is likely to encourage other people to speak longer; this is good if you want to draw somebody out, but not so good if you are with someone who is talking for longer than you have the time or patience to endure. Not nodding is likely to curtail conversation and is likely to make you seem less interested in the other person.

Exercise

Take some time to watch interviews or chat shows on the television, or listen to them on the radio. As you listen, imagine you are the interviewer or host and practise responding to the interviewee, or participants, by a) nodding a good deal as they speak; and b) not nodding at all as they speak. Notice how it feels when you do each of these. In future, you can be aware of the extent to which you nod in conversations and adjust it if appropriate.

Mannerisms

I have given this a separate heading, as it is useful for you to be aware of any mannerisms you have which may affect people in networking situations. I am thinking here of such things as jingling coins in your pocket, clearing your throat, twisting your hair, stepping from side to side and other similar patterns of behaviour which have become so ingrained that you do not notice them, although others often do.

You may need to have someone else help you identify your own mannerisms and then you can decide whether you wish to work on them to make any changes. Certainly some mannerisms are irritating to others and can seriously affect your success in relating to people.

Facial Expression

This can include eye movements and also mouth and nose movements and general muscle tone of the face. There are other elements of facial expression which can be analysed, but these are beyond the scope of this book.

Eye Movements

Eye movements communicate a good deal to others. To start with, let's take some of the things that could seem off-putting.

Negative Impressions

If you are speaking to someone and you constantly look beyond them, over their shoulders, or to one side, they may think you are not paying attention and are more interested in other things.

If your eyes constantly dart around, always on the move, it could seem that you are lacking in concentration or are searching for something beyond your field of vision.

If you defocus your eyes while listening to someone, it can appear that you aren't "with them" and if you focus beyond them they will also get the impression that you are not really listening.

If you stare without blinking it can come across as challenging and if you blink constantly it can seem affected.

Positive Impressions

If you are going to maintain a conversation and appear interesting and interested, there are a range of things you can do, just with your eyes, which will help.

If you maintain good eye contact, by looking at the person, it will seem that you are interested in what they are saying. People sometimes think that eye contact means "eyeballing" the other person; staring directly into their own eyes. This can work but, more often than not, can appear intimidating. To use eye contact effectively, the simplest thing is to look at the person's mouth, or at their forehead, not at their eyes directly. If you are going to look into someone's eyes, it is best to test their tolerance for eye contact by counting to five as you do this. If they have looked away, count to four the next time you look at them, if they still look away reduce the time even more. Only if someone seems unable to maintain eye contact with you at all should you look away from them while the conversation is going on. It may be tempting to keep looking at other things while someone is talking, but it will seem inattentive and possibly rude.

It is all right to look away if you need to collect your thoughts. Many people find it is easier to think when looking down or into the distance. If this is the case for you, look away by all means, but only for short periods and make sure you don't start talking while looking away, or it will seem that you are talking to the floor or ceiling rather than the other person.

So far I have talked about what *you* can do to improve your eye contact with others. Now, what can you tell about other people's eye movements? Although I have said that looking away and defocusing your eyes can give the impression that you aren't listening, when you find that someone you are with does these things, it may not be that they aren't listening, but simply that they have a habit of moving their eyes in those particular ways. So, give people the benefit of the doubt and *check* why they are appearing not to pay attention.

You can do this by changing the subject and seeing if they appear to concentrate more, asking them questions instead of talking, or actually asking them if there is something else they are watching or thinking about. If none of these produce a positive result, you could examine your own behaviour to see if you are making them lose concentration. Are you boring them by being repetitive, or talking about something that doesn't interest them, or are you taking over the conversation? If this is the case, by changing your own behaviour you could get a better response.

Finally, it is useful to know that often people move their eyes in particular ways to fit in with how their mind is processing information. The following comes from NLP and, while true for many people, will not necessarily hold true for everyone.

In general, people will look up when they are visualising things. This is helpful to know, as it means that, if you describe something graphically, you are likely to be able to tell whether the other person is picturing it too.

People often look down when they are immersed in strong emotions, so if you are discussing an emotive issue and the person looks down a lot (accompanied by other signs of emotional strengths such as a deep breath, lowered shoulders and a low voice) you may become aware of the sensitivity of the topic.

People also often look down (or defocus their eyes) when they are using "internal dialogue" or self-talk. Again, this is useful information to indicate they are working through what is being discussed.

Finally, eyes turned to the side could indicate that a person is "hearing" sounds; maybe a previous discussion or an imagined future conversation.

It is possible that people use one side for memory and imagination, so that if you ask a question of fact (what colour is your front door?) the person may look to one side but if you ask a question to which they have to construct an answer (what would it be like if you painted your front door purple with orange spots?) they may look to the other side. Again, this can be useful information, but remember it is only a guide as to how the person is thinking.

Movements of the Mouth, Nose, Forehead and General Muscle Tone in the Face

What you do with your mouth, nose and forehead affects your general expression and, thereby, the impression you create. Pursing your lips, turning the corners of your mouth up or down, wrinkling your nose or forehead and similar movements can all be picked up and interpreted in different ways.

Muscle tone is an interesting aspect. When someone is tense, the muscles of their face and neck tend to contract and tighten, forming lines and furrows. In a relaxed state, lines decrease and muscles become flatter, leaving the face smoother and calm in appearance. It is useful to practise relaxing your own face muscles, which can make you look relaxed and more youthful, as well as making you feel better. As you become more experienced at reading faces, you can notice when other people's facial muscles become relaxed, which will give you clues about their mental and emotional states and make it easier to assess how to speak to them.

Having covered the separate elements of posture, movement and gesture (PMG), I would not like to move to how Action Profiling combines these to form overall impressions about a person from their PMG patterns.

Posture, Movement and Gesture Combined

Action Profiling describes movement as sequences, taking place inside an individual's personal space, sometimes referred to as their "kinesphere", or a bubble-like area surrounding the person. By observing the shapes which people make, you can assess various things about them. To analyse people's patterns, three elements are taken:

- Shape

- Effort

- Action style.

Shape

This consists of four kinds of movement:

- Movement in a horizontal plane, where the body moves from side to side. This is called *enclosing* or *spreading* movement.

- Movement in a vertical plane, where the body moves up or down. This is described as *descending* or *rising* movement.

- Movement in a "sagittal" plane, where the body moves forward or back. This is described as *retiring* or *advancing*.

- Movement described as "Shape Flow", where the body takes up *more or less space*.

Each of these elements gives different "messages". For example, "Shape Flow" can be related to assertiveness. In assertiveness training, people are shown that if they wish to appear energetic, powerful and in control, they need to be comfortable with taking up space and moving comfortably within it, using their hands and arms freely and sitting in open postures.

Effort

There are four elements involved in effort:

- *Focus*: This is about direction and involves movements that go straight to a point or movements that meander (*directing* or *indirecting*);

- *Timing*: This is about speed and involves movements that speed up or slow down (*accelerating* or *decelerating*);

- *Pressure*: This is about intensity of pressure; exerting a light or a firm touch (*increasing* or *decreasing*);

- *Flow*: This is about the degree of control involved in a movement, either being controlled or being free (*binding* or *freeing*).

You can ally these elements of movement with the shaping elements so there can be either an affinity or a lack of harmony between them.

Action Style

Finally, people can have different "communication styles"; these have three areas of focus:

- *Attention*: to do with investigating and exploring;

- *Intention*: to do with persistence and challenge;

- *Commitment*: to do with decision-making and looking ahead.

These styles can be recognised through different patterns of movement, which can be represented pictorially.

Altogether, the three elements — shape, effort and action style — combine to give each person a personal "profile", which is unique and seems to be relatively unchanging once that person is an adult. It is also believed that there is a cultural determinant to movement, so that a person is likely to fit in with society norms. For example, if people are expected to be assertive, they will probably adopt assertive postures, movements and gestures, whereas if they are expected to be submissive, their patterns will be different.

In addition to shape, effort and action style, PMG can be *merged* or *segregated*. "Segregated" is what NLP refers to as "incongruity"; for example, shaking your head while saying you had a good time. It appears that if people have highly segregated PMG, they may be trying to create a false impression.

So, in observing people's non-verbal signals, it is possible to pick up a good deal about them as individuals. As examples of individual patterns, Lamb describes:

- A person who goes indirectly to an objective, circling around it;

- A person who goes straight to the point, as directly as possible.

Action Profiling practitioners also believe that the individual combination of elements give rise to individual behaviour and motivation patterns. In this there seems to be an interesting comparison between NLP and Action Profiling. In NLP, behaviour is generally considered to derive from the "internal" states involved in thinking, feeling and believing (although it can work in reverse also). In Action Profiling, it appears that people are considered to have innate characteristics of movement patterns, which influence the direction they take in life — thus implying that behavioural elements strongly influence motivational ones.

NLP and Action Profiling help us understand more about the "silent language" of non-verbal communications. Naturally good observers of people, with an "in-built" sensitivity to others, will do a good deal of observation instinctively. Their observations may be unconscious and they may say, "I just had a gut feel about him" or "There's something about her; I can't quite put a finger on it"; but, at some level, they are very perceptive. People who are less naturally sensitive can still be trained to observe, and utilise, "body language" and its use is an invaluable aid to face-to-face networking.

Lamb explains perception by saying that some people have a photographic mind and others a cinematic one; some recall events as "stills" while others recall movement. Awareness of the movement is what Lamb says differentiates the sensitive observer of behaviour, and good "perceivers" will often use "movement words" such as "flighty", "gadabout" and "smooth operator" to describe what they see. This approach parallels the NLP analysis of mental processing of events and it is worth reading more on both — see the Bibliography.

To summarise, Action Profiling teaches that PMG patterns express the individual's true self, are relatively unchanging in adulthood and have a compulsive nature, in that people express their personality through repeating their PMG patterns. NLP, too, takes this view, that people cannot help representing their inherent behaviour patterns, however hard they try. This means that, in networking, once you become aware of people's patterns, you have a sample of their "true self" and can then act on this information accordingly.

In networking, if you use the concepts I have described in this chapter, you will have a range of tools for observing and assessing other people's behaviour and for monitoring and managing your own. Do remember, however, what I referred to earlier about cultural differences. Some non-verbal behaviour may be unacceptable in certain cultures: for example, sitting so that the sole of your shoe faces the other person; blowing your nose in public; standing very close to or very far away from the person with whom you are talking; touching someone's shoulder, arm or hand; looking directly into the other person's eyes; not covering your head or arms; not taking your shoes off indoors. These, and many others, are examples of cultural differences in acceptable behaviour. You may not always know what is acceptable or not, but checking the other person's response and changing your behaviour if you get the impression that what you are doing is not being well received, can be useful, especially in business situations.

I would like to end this chapter with another quote from Warren Lamb (*The Body Code*, page 179):

> "In our culture, we give far too much importance to intelligence and to the spoken word. What really shapes our lives is not so much what happens on the intellectual and verbal level, but the underlying motivations by which skills, knowledge, and intellectual ability are deployed in uniquely individual ways. The secret of motivation is in behaviour, and behaviour is expressed in movement, which has no tongue, but can tell us in silence how we can make the best use of our abilities, and relate to others."

This chapter has introduced you to the concept of non-verbal communications. This is a fascinating topic and one that will repay serious study. You will find several books mentioned in the Bibliography which you might like to explore.

Chapter Eleven

Networking at a Distance

There are many times when you can benefit from networking at a distance. The aspects I will be covering in this chapter are:

- Written/printed material

- Telephone and fax

- E-mail and the Internet.

Before discussing these, I would like you to think about your purposes in communicating at a distance. These purposes are not unique to distance communications, but are important when considering how you will communicate in this way.

Exercise

Consider how relevant each of the following functions is to your own networking. You might also like to add other purposes in the blank spaces at the end of the list.

- Persuasion

- Influencing

- Motivation

- Information providing

- Rewarding

- Gaining support

- Winning new business

- Attracting like-minded people

- Entertaining

- Provoking

- Generating debate

- Selling

- Explaining

- Generating ideas

- Rectifying misunderstandings

- Updating

- Introducing

- Amusing.

Knowing your purpose is important in selecting communications media and techniques.

Example

I recently had a business card rejected; the person asked me to e-mail her instead with information. She certainly knew which medium she preferred, but rejecting people's cards is not to be recommended as a means of establishing a good relationship!

Written/Printed Material

Often, the first contact you make with someone is through the written word. As presentation influences readers, it is worth thinking about both the content (*what* you communicate) and the process (*how* you communicate) of your written communications.

Exercise

There is a wide range of material which can be used to communicate at a distance. Which of the following do you use?

• Letterheadings	• Calendars
• Compliments slips	• Newsletters/bulletins
• Business cards	• Manuals

- Brochures
- Invoices
- Receipts
- Memo forms
- Order forms
- Fax paper
- Post-it notes
- Notelets
- Folders
- Inked stamps
- Stickers
- Labels
- Christmas, New Year and other holiday cards
- Notepads
- Binders
- Mouse mats
- Glass mats
- Briefcases
- Badges
- Envelopes
- T-shirts
- Key rings
- Mugs
- Ties
- Scarves
- Advertisements

This is not an exhaustive list, but will give you an idea of media available. You might also like to compare notes with colleagues to see how your own practices relate to theirs.

Let's take a few minutes to think about the items on the list; I will group them into three categories for convenience:

- Business stationery
- Promotional items
- Items useful in meetings, workshop or other events.

Business Stationery

Business stationery includes the following:

- Letterheadings
- Envelopes
- Compliments slips
- Business cards

- Notelets

- Invoices

- Memos

- Receipts

- Order forms

- Fax paper

- Inked stamps.

All these items can be used to create an impression of you and your business. If they are considered, and designed, as a package, they tend to be referred to as your "corporate identity" — in other words, they add up to the business image you project to others.

Exercise

You have many choices concerning the image you create. Have a look at the following list and tick those which are closest to the image you would like to convey:

• Professional	• Technical
• Up-to-date	• Accessible
• Caring	• Young
• Friendly	• Mature
• Slick	• Go-ahead
• Sophisticated	• Traditional
• Down to earth	• Organised
• Competent	• Positive
• Flexible	• Creative
• Straightforward	• Anything else?

Before you begin to work on your corporate image, you need to know what impression you wish to give. Once you have done this you can make a start — either by yourself if you have the ideas and technical ability to carry it off, or with the help of a professional designer if you do not.

If you go to a designer, check the person's attitude and approach and ask to see examples of their previous work to check that you would be comfortable working with them and using their designs.

If you can't decide what would be right for you, then it could help to speak to others, including friends, colleagues and customers/clients in order to find out what they think your strengths are and what your marketplace would like to know about you.

Having chosen your basic approach, you can now think about how your material is presented; for example:

Paper type and quality

- What will best reflect your features (glossy, weighty, textured, etc.)?

- What can you afford (quality needs to be paid for)?

- What is available (can you get exactly what you want?)?

- What is attractive to others (for example, paper weight and texture is particularly important to "kinaesthetic" people; ones who use their sense of touch and feeling a lot)?

Colour

- What image does it create (plain white for simplicity and elegance, bright colours for impact, subtle colours for sophistication and so on)?

- What needs does it serve (for example, colour is particularly important to "visual" people)?

Typefaces and sizes

- What image do they convey (modern, traditional, quirky, etc.)?

- What purpose do they serve (condensed to get more in; large for impact and easy reading)?

Format and layout

- What size works best (small and easy to handle or large and impressive)?

- What shape works best ("landscape" — horizontal shape, or "portrait"— vertical shape)?

- What image is conveyed (e.g. conventional A4 or A5 size, or unusual sizes and shapes)?

- How is information displayed (placing of material within the document to maximise its impact or its accessibility)?

Materials

- Conventional (standard paper)

- Something different (plastics, foils, etc)?

Graphics

- Illustrations, photographs, diagrams, cartoons, etc.

All these things will combine to create an individual image for you; to say specific things to your contacts and to give a feel for the kind of person you are and the kind of organisation you run or represent.

Business Letters

For networking, letters are a useful way of keeping in touch and making or responding to enquiries. A few simple pointers should help make your letters effective:

A good business letter should be on pre-printed letterheads, giving your contact details. You should include a subject heading to clarify the topic of the communication. You should then include three elements:

- *Statement of purpose*: why you are writing;

- *Statement of fact*: what you wish to convey;

- *Statement of action*: if any follow-up is needed by you or the recipient.

You should also include your title (Mr, Mrs, Ms, etc.) and any position or job title, so the recipient knows how to address you in a reply.

Promotional Items

Having considered business stationery, I would now like to move to items with more of a direct marketing purpose. There are many kinds of promotional items and you might like to consider which you already use.

Exercise

Tick which of the following you use currently, adding to the list any which you feel have been missed out:

- Brochures
- Newsletters
- Bulletins
- Press releases
- Newspaper advertisements
- Posters
- Gifts (calendars, mats, pens, mugs, T shirts, ties, scarves, key rings, etc.)
- Stickers
- Christmas, New Year or other holiday cards.

You can divide promotional items into three categories, as follows:

- Printed material, e.g. brochures, newsletters and bulletins
- Advertising
- Gifts and publicity material.

Let's take each in turn and see how they can benefit your activities.

Brochures, Newsletters and Bulletins

These items are intended to inform people about you and to keep them up-to-date with what you are doing. They can be very sophisticated and expensive, or very simple and inexpensive, depending on your purpose and the impression you wish to create.

To be effective, these communications need to draw the reader's attention. Some people may simply file away your brochures, keeping them on tap until needed. For most people, however, they are likely to be treated as disposable items. If they meet an immediate need they will be used, if not they may well be discarded. These items therefore need to have a fast impact in order to serve their purpose.

So, all the points we discussed earlier under business stationery apply — the style, the appearance, the layout and so on. In addition, there are a number of other elements which will help your documents be appealing and useful.

Writing style

To work on this, go back to your list of attributes, e.g. professional, friendly, accessible, etc.) and make sure your writing style matches what you want to convey.

Think about whether to write in the first person ("I have experience in . . ."; "We offer the following . . ."), second person ("You can be reassured that . . .") or third person ("The XXX organisation provides an excellent service in the field of . . ."). The first person tends to create a friendlier, but less formal impression; the second person focuses on the requirements of the customer and the third person is more detached and formal. There is no right or wrong style; which you select depends on your objectives and your market.

Signposting

This is about making your documents accessible to your readers. It includes page numbers, section headings, contents pages and so on, to help people know where they are in your printed material.

These elements are particularly useful to people who use their visual sense a lot, as they really need to *see* where they are in a document.

Structuring

This is another vital element in readable documents. Having an effective structure both looks professional and helps your readers to find their way through what you are communicating. The simplest structure to consider has three parts:

- A beginning
- A middle
- An end.

This may sound obvious, but often people do not introduce their subject well, or tail off without a good conclusion. A saying which is commonly used in training goes as follows: "Tell them what you're going to tell them; tell them; tell them what you've told them." This can be a useful concept in writing also; in other words, lead into your topic, present your topic and round off your topic. Your readers will then know what they are coming to, what they are reading and how it is concluding — all useful information to them.

Another thing to think about regarding structure is how you progress from general points to detail. The mind-mapping process I mentioned in Chapter 4, where you think of a tree, is useful here in structuring documents (and it is also useful for planning talks, speeches and presentations). You can start with your main subject area (the trunk); then go on to discuss the sub-elements of it (the branches); and then go into more detail on the smaller elements (the twigs). Alternatively, you could start with the main topic (trunk) then go to one sub-topic (one branch) then the sub-areas of that (its twigs) then move to another branch and twigs and then another. In either case, by signposting the system you are using, the reader will be helped to work through the document.

Grammar, punctuation, spelling and word usage

These elements are important for a number of reasons. Firstly, "good" use of language is more professional and creates an image of competence and proficiency. Secondly, language can be confusing or ambiguous if not "correct". For example, think about what the following sentence means: "I went into town and saw a friend on my bicycle". It could mean I went into town — on my bicycle — and saw a friend. Or it could mean I went into town and saw a friend who was on my bicycle. Written like this: "I went into town, on my bicycle, and saw a friend" — the meaning becomes clear.

Another example, showing the importance of punctuation, is this: "My friends bicycle" is ambiguous and could be interpreted as implying that the bicycle belonged to one friend or more than one friend. "My friend's bicycle" makes it clear there is one friend, whereas "My friends' bicycle" denotes that the bicycle belongs to more than one person.

Similarly, spelling is important. I received an article from a journalist a while ago. The accompanying note read, "Here is the draught of my article". This is just incorrect (the word should have been "draft"). There can be times, however, when the actual word usage can completely change the sense of a message. For example, there are many words which sound the same but are spelled differently, as in "draught" and "draft". There are also words which can be interpreted differently, even though they have the same spelling (for example, "heavy" could refer to weight or it could mean that something is difficult to read or make sense of — so the word is ambiguous). And of course there are many words which are different although they have the same meaning (synonyms). So word use and spelling are important and can have a major impact on the effectiveness of your communications.

If you know you find it hard to spell correctly, or your grammar is not always good, do get a friend or colleague to check what you have written before sending it out. (There is an excellent NLP technique for learning to spell well.) And do remember to spell people's names properly when writing or e-mailing; as well as being courteous, it is more likely to reach the right person.

Sentence length

This also is related to the overall image you wish to create. Longer sentences can sound more authoritative, but can be complex and difficult to read. Shorter sentences can seem chatty and straightforward but could also seem to talk down to your readers. Selecting which is most appropriate for your purpose is another task for you.

You might, in this context, like to consider the "fog index". There are different ways of working this out; the one I like is this: You take a sample sentence from a piece of printed material and count the number of words in it, then count the number of words in that sentence which contain three or more syllables. You then multiply the first number by the second. So if your sentence had 15 words and five of them had three or more syllables, your figure would be 15 x 5 which equals 75. If your sentence had only ten words in, with only one of these having three or more syllables, the figure would be ten. The higher the figure, the more complex your writing, and the lower the figure, the simpler the writing. This is worth remembering when you compose documents, so you can decide how "accessible" you wish your writing to be.

Tense

This relates to the extent to which you wish your readers to focus on the past, present or future. A document which contains a lot of past tense writing ("We worked hard last year on . . ."; "Our customers have complimented us on . . .") can seem backward looking. Present tense writing ("We have clients in the following fields . . ."; "We are expanding our activities in . . .") can sound more immediate. Future tense writing could create an impression of forward thinking and activity ("We will be presenting courses on . . ."; "We look forward to introducing . . ."). Again, which you choose depends on your purpose and a mixture of all three can be as effective as concentration on one only.

Precision

This is to do with the clarity of your language. Sometimes you may want to be very precise, in order to give specific information. This is important where you have a particular product or service to offer which needs describing accurately. At other times, however, you may wish to encourage your readers to use their imagination and just create a mental impression for them of what you have on offer. For example, if you are selling a holiday, you may wish to create a feel for the atmosphere they will encounter, or if you are promoting a product such as an exercise machine, you may wish to give an idea of the healthy state it could produce. In these cases, your language will need to be more indirect, so readers can create their own image in their mind, rather than having only your specific words to create a response. You will find more on language pattern uses in Chapter 7.

Content

While your documents should reflect your own particular purposes and image, there are general points you might wish to include; for example:

Brochures

- Information about you;

- Information about your business purpose/aims/vision/goals/etc.;

- Information about your business activities;

- Benefits to your customers/clients of using your services or buying your products;

- Comments from past or current customers/clients;

- Contact details;

- Guarantee of service and quality (possibly money-back guarantees if not satisfied).

Newsletters

- Current activities;

- Current or recent clients or customers;

- New products or services;

- News items about you or your business;

- Forthcoming dates for events.

Bulletins

- Brief, concise information on current issues.

Press releases

- Brief statement of purpose;

- Main features;

- Contact details.

Advertising

There are many ways to make advertising effective, including:

Medium

Where should you advertise? There is a choice of local, national and international publications; general or specialist publications; freesheets or publications for which the reader has to pay a purchase price. There are in-house publications aimed at employees or members of specialist organisations and associations. There is also a range of other processes for advertising including radio, e-mail, Internet, direct mail, flyers through letterboxes or on car windscreens, cards in shop windows and so on. You will find more on this in Chapter Seven on setting up your own networking group.

Frequency

How often should you advertise? Repeated advertisements keep your name in people's minds (although over-exposure could mean the advertisements stop being read). In many publications there can be cost benefits to repeated advertisements.

Format

You can consider classified or display advertising, size, layout and position in the publication.

Style

You will need to link the style of your advertisements with their purpose and with the image of yourself or your organisation.

Content

Including few words can create a good impact, but provides less information; including many words can be informative but can be off-putting or time-consuming to read. The minimum facts need to be there to gain interest and you need to include elements which will tell your readers of the benefits to them. Sales experts say that purchasers buy feelings not products, so thinking about what feeling you wish to create will be useful. Remember the suggestions in Chapter 5 for creating feelings.

Gifts and Publicity Material

Small gifts and items of publicity can be useful if used appropriately. Sending Christmas and other holiday cards and calendars containing your details is a common practice. There are many organisations which provide ranges of promotional items; but be careful not to send items that the recipients will find boring or useless.

Example

Some years ago I commissioned a local pottery to make me some mugs with my organisation's name and logo on. I had seen an existing range of products I liked and asked if they could make some "specials" for me. They were pleased to do so and I obtained some excellent items at very reasonable cost. I filled the mugs with rather good dried dates and sent them to current clients with a Christmas card and a label saying "Dates for next year". I was told the mugs were appreciated and made a very pleasant change from the mass-produced giftware generally in circulation.

Items Useful in Meetings, Workshops or Other Events

There are many ways of developing your networking activities through presentations; some things that can make you and your activities memorable are:

Folders, binders and manuals

Document holders containing your name, address, contact details, logo or message give a lasting reminder of who you are and what you can offer. There are many commercial organisations which print such details onto mass-produced or individually tailored items; you can create whatever image you wish to leave with your audience, budget allowing.

Badges and name cards

Name badges and cards which sit in front of participants can be produced with your logo and other details. Do remember with name badges that pins could leave marks on clothes and clips may be suitable for the pockets of men's suits but may be hard for women to place appropriately. The simple peel-off adhesive label, which can be stuck temporarily to clothing, may be the best option, unless very sensitive fabrics are being worn.

Post-it notes, note blocks and notepads

It is possible to have your details printed on each of these; it is also possible to have post-it notes which you can print on yourself to add personalised messages.

Brief cases, pens, calculators, etc.

Some items are very expensive to produce while others are inexpensive and readily accessible. The more unusual, amusing or elegant your items are, the more likely it is that they will be retained and talked about or shown to others. Regarding these items as marketing tools will give you a competitive edge, as long as you produce them in a cost-effective manner and use them appropriately.

Telephone and Fax

Many of the factors I have already discussed also apply to networking by telephone and fax. Because face-to-face elements are missing, so the person you are talking to does not have any visual cues, the vocal elements are emphasised, with tone of voice, pauses, breathing, speed and volume of speech taking more prominence.

The telephone can be a vital took for networking, as it enables you to make contact using your own voice, rather than the written word. Telephone also allows you to contact people at a distance in a simple and personal way and allows others to contact you directly. There are, however, some points to consider when using the phone for networking; they include the following:

- Timing

- Manner

- Follow-up

- "Gatekeeping"

- Messages.

Let's take these points in turn.

Timing

When you contact someone, you may be calling at a time when they are busy, tired, annoyed, with other people or in other situations when a telephone conversation is inappropriate for them. So do think before you call. Work out the best time to ring and, if you are not sure what that is, at least ask the person, when they answer, whether it is a convenient time to speak.

Good times for business calls vary. Early morning may be good because people may not yet have started on daily business, but could be bad because they may be busy planning their day and dealing with outstanding items. The end of the day may be good because urgent business is completed, but may be bad because people are getting ready to leave. Monday morning and Friday afternoon are best avoided for many people, and lunchtime is difficult, as you may not know people's eating patterns.

In some businesses, there are particular times or days which are good or bad and, if it is a sufficiently important call, you would do well to research this in advance. And do remember cost; phoning can be expensive, especially if you are calling long-distance.

Manner

Telephone manner will need to vary from situation to situation, but there are some simple "rules" you might like to follow:

- Say clearly who you are and what the purpose of your call is;

- Ask if it is convenient to speak and, if the answer is no, request an alternative time for you to call back;

- Be polite and friendly, even if the other person is dismissive or distracted;

- Listen well, so you really take in what is being said to you;

- Speak in a clear voice, pausing long enough between statements to allow the other person to take in what you are saying;

- Reflect back what the other person is saying, so you can be sure you have understood what they say to you (reflecting means using your own words to paraphrase the conversation);

- Summarise key points, again so that there is mutual understanding of what has been discussed and what action may need to follow;

- Use sounds such as "*mmm . . . I see . . .*" and so on to indicate that you are still listening;

- Smile, as this alters the sound of your voice and makes it seem friendlier.

Follow-up

At the end of your call, remember to let the person know of any action you will be taking following the conversation. Then make sure you take that action. So, if you have said you will send them some information, do so promptly. If you have said you will pass on their details to a third party, do so promptly.

The more efficiently you deal with follow-ups, the better your reputation is likely to be. It is also more efficient to deal with things there and then, if you can, as stockpiling them for later action means handling them more than once, which can be time-consuming and can result in you having to take time to remember what the discussion was about and what action you need to take.

"Gatekeeping"

You may, when phoning someone, get through to a "gatekeeper". A gatekeeper is someone who is there to act as a filter between the person and the outside world; for example, an assistant, a secretary or another colleague. Knowing how to deal with gatekeepers is important in making your networking effective.

When faced with an intermediary, you could:

- Use your rapport skills and "match" the person's voice and language (see Chapter 9);

- Ask when the person will be available and say you will call them back rather than waiting for a call from them;

- Speak to someone else in the same organisation earlier, if you think there may be a gatekeeper present, and then you can say you have been referred by that other person, rather than calling in "cold".

Messages

As well as using the telephone to make calls, you will need to think carefully about how incoming calls are dealt with. If you are the only person answering your phone, you should consider the same elements as with outgoing calls: manner, tone of voice and so forth. Remember that incoming calls can come at unexpected times, so adopt a positive frame of mind when you answer. To do this, remember that your posture, breathing and facial expression all affect how your voice sounds when you speak.

If you have an answering machine (and no serious networker can afford to be without one), then the message you leave, and the facilities available to callers are also important. Your message should be clear, concise, friendly and informative. It helps to keep it short, in case callers are ringing from a mobile phone or call box. It also helps to give an idea of how frequently you pick up messages. Asking callers to leave their telephone numbers is useful as, if you are away from home or office, you may not have their details to hand.

As far as facilities go, it is useful to let callers know how long they have for their call and to know if the machine has no capacity left for more messages. You might like to think about services such as call forwarding and call waiting.

Try to avoid systems which involve callers paying for their waiting time; they may prefer simply to receive an engaged signal than be held in a queue with no idea of how long it will take to get through. And the user-unfriendly systems which ask callers to keep selecting from a range of options can be very off-putting and time wasting.

So do think carefully about how calls are dealt with and make your system as helpful as possible to people ringing in.

Example

On a recent radio programme, I heard an item regarding the difference between how answering machines are used in the UK and in the USA. In the UK, they tend to be used to play "telephone tag", where you leave a message for someone to call you, and they then call and receive your answering machine and leave you a message to call them. In the US, callers are much more likely to use the machine to convey the information they would have given the recipient in person, so the call is more productive and action can be taken immediately.

Fax

Faxes are used — and misused — frequently. Remember that someone else's fax is their property and if you send them messages you are using up their fax paper and ink in order to send them. So, use faxes either when they have been requested, or when you are as sure as you can be that they will be welcomed.

Keep your faxes short. As well as costing the recipient money in paper and ink, you will be tying up their machine and telephone line all the time your message is coming through, so keep it short unless you know the person expects you to send a lengthy message.

If you think the fax machine may be in a private home, avoid sending faxes late at night; there is nothing worse than being woken up at three in the morning to receive "junk mail". If you are sending faxes abroad and they may be going to a private home, check the time difference before starting.

When you send a fax, remember to put your contact details on it, both phone and fax, in case of difficulty.

Also remember to state how many pages you are sending, so that the recipient can check if the whole of your fax has arrived.

It may be useful to have a separate telephone line for your fax, so that it doesn't tie up your phone and, if you do work from home, you can be sent a fax late at night and will not be disturbed.

Do remember that some fax paper is flimsy and the text on it will fade fairly rapidly, so you will not have a permanent record of your messages. Plain paper faxes provide a much more permanent record, so if you buy an old fax machine, or a very inexpensive one, you may find that the documents it produces have a very short "shelf life". If this is the case, you can always photocopy any important faxes to ensure they are stable.

And finally, you should be aware that many organisations now send out faxes like junk mail. These can arrive on your machine at any time of day or night and you pay for the paper they take up. You can't always do much about this (but you can ask for your name to be taken off the "mailing" list).

Faxes are a simple, quick and useful networking tool and many people find them more helpful than phone or e-mail, as they give a tangible record of information and are easily to hand.

E-mail and the Internet

Both these media rely on computers and telephone links. They enable you to communicate with others, at any distance, quickly and inexpensively. The growth in electronic communications is increasingly rapid and it is almost essential now to have access to them if you are to function effectively in the business world.

To use e-mail or to join the Internet you will need to subscribe to an Internet service provider (ISP). When you subscribe, you will receive all the software you need to use the services and can also obtain information from the provider, although often the software is self-explanatory and training can also be obtained from independent trainers. You can also read books on the subject and some local authorities offer inexpensive training in information technology and Internet use. There is generally a charge for subscribing to a provider, although some services are offered free. There can, however, be hidden costs as telephone calls to the help lines run by providers can be expensive. There can also be a possible nuisance caused to you by the advertisements carried by free subscriptions services; this is like junk mail coming through your letterbox, except that it appears on your own computer screen.

When using e-mail and the Internet, it is worth remembering that if you save your messages and send them outside peak periods, you can make savings on the telephone calls involved.

E-mail

E-mail is growing as a medium for networking. You can network via e-mail to individuals or you can link in to existing networks. E-mail provides a fast and effective way of contacting others; it is relatively inexpensive and there are not always the same conventions applied as to letter writing, so messages can be informal in both tone and style.

E-mail is also fast, so you can send your message and receive a reply back within the same day, and often within the same hour. This means it is possible to check information, issue invitations, make enquiries and generate leads quickly and effectively.

To use e-mail you will need a modem to link your computer to your phone line. If you use the facility frequently, you may have a separate line installed, or to link in with your fax line, if this is already separate from your telephone, so your main line is not tied up during periods when you are sending or receiving e-mail messages.

Because you can copy your e-mail messages to others, one message can go to several people at once, saving on time and cost.

Joining an e-mail discussion group is an excellent way of making contacts, promoting your activities, exchanging ideas and opportunities and doing research. Groups can be public or private; public ones are open to anybody and private ones are restricted to members of a defined group. Remember though that discussion groups can give you a substantial volume of unwanted messages to read, as not all topics discussed will interest you.

Finally, beware of computer viruses which are often distributed as e-mail attachments. These can cause damage to your computer and its software. You should purchase virus protection software and if you receive an e-mail from an unknown source, delete the e-mail and never open the attachment. You may miss an occasional opportunity, but you will ensure that you avoid inconvenience and unnecessary expense.

Example 1

The Richmond Group is a consortium of independent management consultants in the UK. With over 100 members, the group is a thriving "virtual" organisation. Members of the group are linked by their e-mail network (joining the network is a condition of new membership) and it is possible to circulate the entire group or selected individuals.

Members of the group have found the network invaluable for exchanging information, advising others of work opportunities, asking for advice and conducting group business.

Example 2

The UK HRD Network is an e-mail network of HR (personnel) specialists. The network acts as a discussion group and there are daily messages posted by its members. This network has been a slight victim of its own success, however. With around 30 separate messages coming in each day, I found that after being away for a while and not picking up my messages for a week or so, I had around 300 separate ones to sort through. The task was defeating and most of them had to be deleted rather than read.

If you use a discussion group regularly, it helps to keep your messages short so that other readers can access them quickly and find out the salient points. Electronic communications is not the same as old-fashioned letter writing or telephone calls; its purpose is fast, brief information exchange and, if treated in this way, it is an invaluable business and social tool.

Internet

The Internet is not really a networking medium, in the sense that you can communicate directly with others through it, but it is important as a source of information and therefore a useful tool in your networking activities.

Using the Internet, you can both find resources yourself and gather information of use to others with whom you interact. Again, you will need a telephone link to your computer and will probably need a separate telephone line installed so you can spend time searching for information without tying up your own line. Do remember that, as Internet searching can take up considerable telephone time, using it out of peak hours will be more economical.

Finally, before leaving this section, a reminder that all the above services can be accessed by portable computers, laptops and, to a degree, by mobile phone. Using these machines, and also pagers, will give you continuing access to your network and to sources of information wherever you are. You could send faxes and e-mails or call up the Internet and immediately be in communication with the people you choose. Please remember one thing though — if you use your portable office equipment in a public place (train, restaurant, waiting room, etc.), you may well annoy other people. Recently, one major train operator in the UK announced the introduction of "quiet carriages" on their trains, so that those who wished to enjoy their journeys in peace and quiet, or to concentrate on their own work, could do so. By all means, use modern technology, but remember the needs of others as you do so.

Chapter Twelve

Networking for Specific Purposes

So far in this book I have covered general principles and skills; in this chapter I will be dealing with how to use those skills in specific situations.

The applications I will be covering here are:

- Job search

- Self-employment/homeworking

- Professional and business development

- Gaining personal support

- "Cultural" networks

- Enhancing social relationships

- Purchasing Networks and LETs

- Expatriate interchange

- Pressure and action groups

- Helping others develop.

First, however, one point of information. In many of the examples that follow, I refer to existing networks of people. Some of these can be easy to track down and others more difficult. You will find listings of groups and networks available in directories at general libraries. If you do not find an appropriate listing, however, there may still be networks in existence, but they could be very local or lack funds to publicise themselves.

Asking around (using your existing personal network) to get such information is a good starting point, as is contacting other formal organisations operating in a similar field or area of interest. If you find no such network exists, you could contemplate setting up your own, in which case see the information in Chapter 13.

Job Search

Networking is a major factor in job search. It is estimated that up to three-quarters of jobs do not come onto the open market, but are filled through either personal contact or internal promotion. Whatever your opinions regarding the fairness of this, it is a fact. This means that, if you are looking for a job, or to change your career, you will stand a better chance if you use informal networks to help, rather than relying solely on advertised vacancies. How can you do this?

Firstly, you need to prepare the ground by getting together as much information as you can about yourself, what you have to offer and what you want in return.

Once you have done this, you are ready to begin the process of job search in earnest. There are many ways of going about this and I will simplify them by suggesting two alternatives: using established networks or developing your own.

Using Established Networks

There are many networks associated with job-seeking and they will vary from country to country. An excellent way of networking is through organisations called outplacement agencies. These organisations are set up to help people find work; often executive and managerial jobs but, increasingly, other kinds of jobs too.

Because these agencies have been established for some time and have excellent links with other bodies, once you sign up with one you will have access to a wide network of services and contacts. In particular, you will be able to network with others in a similar position to you, also seeking employment, and in this way will be able to share experiences and give each other support.

There are also government agency networks for unemployed people, offering a similar, although generally less extensive, range of services, and in some areas there are local "job clubs", formed by people who gather together to support each other in their job search campaigns.

Developing Your Own Network

You will already have many contacts of your own and using them for job search is easy when you know how. What you need to do is contact acquaintances with a simple request. The request is to let you know if they know of anyone who might be able to help you in your job search campaign. They may be in a position to help you directly, or they may be able to give you contact details of others who could. Even if they have no immediate ideas, you can ask them to keep you in mind in the future.

Because so many people are in the same situation, you can find out who else would share their resources with you in return for you doing something similar for them. You may also track down sources of information on job search through the Internet, and this can be a useful way of starting the process. You could also start up a local job club yourself; there are many precedents for this, so there should be a reasonable amount of material available to help you.

You can also identify and approach organisations you think could be potential employers, or in a similar field to potential employers and bring your details to their notice. If they happen to be looking for people at that time, your request might just coincide with a vacancy. If not, they may be able to help with a referral to another organisation.

When you make such approaches, remember to ask if it is convenient to discuss the matter and do not tie people up with lengthy phone calls or letters. It is generally best to speak to someone in the personnel/human resources department if the organisation you are contacting is a large one, and do remember they are likely to get many such contacts, so be brief, concise and pleasant and it is likely that you will at least get a hearing.

Once you have started the process of networking for job search, keep in touch with your network. Don't be over-persistent, but follow up contacts periodically — say at monthly intervals — to find out whether there is any new information which could be useful. Remember to have something to offer in return; maybe a contact of your own which could be useful to the other person.

Job search through networking is a productive process; it may not seem as immediately rewarding as responding to advertisements, but it can be far more useful in the long run.

Example

Liz had worked in marketing for some years, but felt she needed to move on from her present company. She contacted all the people in her personal network and began by chatting about her situation and just asking for a few minutes' time to discuss ideas. Many of the people came up with suggestions and further contacts and one even alerted Liz to a specific job opportunity which sounded just right for her. Liz, however, decided to continue the process of exploration and talked to people about their own situations and what they wanted for themselves. After a good deal of consideration, she decided that she didn't want another employed job, but would prefer to start up on her own. She now offers marketing advice to small businesses, which she finds enjoyable and rewarding. Being self-employed was not initially on Liz's agenda but, the more she talked to people, the more she realised that it was a course of action which could suit her very well.

Self-employment/Homeworking

If you are considering, or in the process of, becoming self-employed, networking will be one of your major tools for success.

Firstly, you can use your existing network to get ideas. This can include choosing a field of activity, marketing, fundraising, assistance and support. By drawing on other people's thoughts and experience, you can save yourself much time and energy.

Secondly, you can use your network to create business. This may be through contacting previous employers for possible assignments or temporary work, or it could be through referrals from friends and colleagues.

Thirdly, you can use your networking skills to promote your activities. Some particularly useful things to do in this context are:

- Talking to local groups about what you offer;

- Writing articles about your field of business, especially if you have a particularly interesting slant on an issue;

- Going to meetings of business and social organisations which could have members of your target market attending.

Fourthly, you can access registers of "Associates". There are many organisations which run lists of people looking for work, either as locums or on a project basis. For example, most professional bodies have such lists, there are others in the public sector and there are also many commercial registers. Some of the registers can be found on the Internet and others appear in published form; usually an annual directory of people and services. An advantage of some of these registers is that the organisations running them organise networking days for people on the register. This can provide excellent opportunities for both personal development and business growth.

Fifthly, you can locate networks established to help self-employed people find, develop and exchange information on opportunities and activities. Many people enjoy being independent, and like the control and freedom they gain; others, however, find they feel somewhat isolated and lacking in support and information. Homeworking networks can provide the social interaction and information base they desire.

Often these networks produce newsletters, giving ideas and contacts, and provide a forum for individual members to advertise their products and services. Sometimes there are meetings for members of the network to come together and exchange ideas. There will frequently be an annual subscription to cover the cost of benefits provided.

Again, information about these groups can be available from listings; other good sources include personal development or business magazines and classified advertising in relevant magazines.

Example 1

In the personnel field in the UK, there are numerous agencies aimed at providing short-term human resource staff to organisations. Sometimes this is to cover for people on maternity leave or off sick, sometimes this results from the fact that the personnel function has been "outsourced" and many activities are handled by independent contractors. Either way, there is plenty of scope for the newly independent person to obtain short- or longer-term assignments.

Example 2

An organisation called Business Opportunities Digest (BOD) has a regular newsletter available on subscription. In the newsletter, which is produced inexpensively, there are ideas sent in by subscribers about business activities they have tried themselves. There is also a back page with advertisements for business opportunities. This is a simple and effective way of exchanging information about work opportunities.

Professional or Business Development

Following on from self-employment, there are additional networking groups which can help those wishing to enhance their professional and business activities, whether or not they are self-employed. There are some distinct types of network within this heading; some of these are discussed in the following examples.

Profession or Function Networks

These groups act to keep people within a particular profession or occupational group in touch with each other and up-to-date with developments in their field. As a by-product, they also act as an informal way of finding out about job opportunities and other matters of joint interest.

Most established professions will already have institutes or bodies to serve their members; however, it can be useful to establish local networks of people within a particular profession if the national body does not already do so.

Example — Mid-Wales Personnel and Training Group

In one mid-Wales area, a group of personnel and training specialists was set up some years ago. There was already a professional body in existence, but it only had one or two members in the geographical area and there were many people in the relevant fields who wanted an opportunity to network with others but did not intend to join the professional body. The group was well attended and provided opportunities for members and guests to meet, listen to speakers and update themselves on developments in their field.

Business Development Networks

These can be set up to help members enhance their business success. Some of the activities of these networks include location of sources of funding, exchange of ideas on business development, joint marketing and sales and so forth. There are many networks for business development and members find them very helpful in promoting and enhancing their businesses.

Example

Business Networking International (BNI) is an organisation set up to facilitate business development through networking. BNI, operating in several countries, has "chapters", organised on a local geographical basis, where business people join together for mutual promotional activities. Those involved tend to meet for breakfast once a week and only one person from any particular occupational category is allowed to join a particular group. So, there can be only one accountant, only one plumber or only one hairdresser. The meetings are solely focused on development of business opportunities, so members may take turns in describing their businesses, exchange cards and pass on leads to each other. At subsequent meetings, checks are made on how successful the leads were and members who do not attend regularly, or fail to pass on leads to others, are likely to be asked to leave. These groups appear to be extremely successful. For more, see the Resources list.

Gaining Personal Support

There can be many reasons for wishing to have support from others. You may have a particularly difficult situation to deal with and need someone to help or you may simply be the kind of person who functions better when other people are around you. Whatever the case, personal support networks can help.

There are many such networks in existence. Recently I telephoned a personal contact, found I had misdialed, and was answered by a voice saying "Victim support . . .". Networks are frequently used by people with physical, mental or emotional needs. Some examples are networks for people who are living with, or caring for, someone with a particular illness or disability, such as Alzheimer's, autism, schizophrenia, cancer, AIDS, blindness, paralysis and so on. Other examples are networks for people who have been bereaved, suffered post-traumatic stress or are victims of crime or abuse. There are also support networks for people with financial difficulties and addiction problems such as eating disorders, alcoholism or gambling. And there are networks for people who are undergoing counselling or therapy for specific personal issues. All these networks have been set up to meet the needs of individuals who wish to share their experiences with others in a similar situation. Often the networks have been set up by someone who has been personally affected.

Example 1

I have an acquaintance who set up a small charity/networking organisation for those who had children born with a particular genetic disorder, which was not being fully acknowledged by the leaders of the particular community involved. The possibility of networking with others helped people deal with their situation and pool information and ideas as well as put pressure on the medical profession and other "establishment" figures to deal with those affected in a more appropriate manner.

Example 2

The oldest established hospice in London, St Joseph's, has a bereavement service for people whose relatives and friends have died in the hospice. They run various activities including support groups, facilitated by a trained counsellor on the staff of the hospice, and one-to-one counselling (at the Hospice or in people's homes) carried out by a team of volunteer bereavement counsellors.

You can find out about such networks through a variety of sources, including libraries and advice bureaux, the Internet and professionals in the field (doctors, counsellors, therapists and so forth). If there is no network for your particular interest, you might consider setting one up (see Chapter 13).

There is one further set of issues to consider if setting up a support group. Often, people who come to such groups have undergone, or are undergoing, sensitive or stressful experiences. If this is the case, you need to make sure a) that the group can provide the kind of support they need; b) that they will not be destructive, over-demanding or hostile within the group (and if they are, that you can handle their behaviour appropriately); and c) that the group does not act as a substitute for things they should be dealing with elsewhere.

If you can deal appropriately with these issues, a support group can be an excellent forum for people to come together and develop. If you join a group for one of the above purposes, try to ensure you use it appropriately, and don't make unreasonable demands on other group members or take over meetings solely for your own ends. The more you can contribute, the more you are likely to benefit overall.

"Cultural" Networks

I am using the word "culture" here in a very broad sense, to mean any group which has shared values, norms or experience. Because of this, cultural networks can appeal to those people who wish to share part of their life with others of a similar ilk.

Some examples of cultural networks are the following:

Gender Groups

Both women and men have network groups of their own, although current legislation is concerned that groups do not discriminate unfairly against one gender. There is an increasingly large number of women's networking groups — for women in business, in the media, in finance and so on. Often, such groups can establish a climate that differs from one where there is a mixed gender membership, and many women feel more comfortable in such an environment. Men's network groups also exist and, while these are often the more traditional "old boys' clubs" (see below), there seems to be a growing movement in the US for men's "bonding" groups, running activities that parallel some of the women's groups.

Religious Groups

Many religions have local groups of people who practise within a particular faith and wish to meet similarly minded people in their community.

Interest or "Affinity" Groups

There are many networks for people with an interest in a particular subject, for example gardening, music, vintage cars and so on.

Example 1

In the UK, a group called simply "Network" was founded by Irene Harris. The group had a programme of meetings at which members could socialise, promote their businesses and engage in development through talks and visits. The group produced a members' directory, listing contact details and areas of activity. I belonged to this group in the 1980s, when it provided a service to many women wishing to take advantage of contact with others.

Example 2

In a London borough, local artists formed the Islington Art Circle. The group catered for both professional and amateur artists and held exhibitions and classes, organised painting trips and ran social events including the successful annual ball. A film was also made of the group, which is interesting archive material. Through the group, artists could meet with like-minded people and exchange ideas and information as well as having a commercial outlet for their work.

Example 3

Afghan Hounds were very popular dogs in the 1960s and 1970s, their long flowing hair fitting well with the hippy culture (although in their original form they were desert animals, suited to hunting wolves in challenging conditions — not a trendy fashion accessory). The Southern Afghan Club promotes the interests of the breed, runs shows, trains judges, has social events, runs a rescue scheme for abandoned and neglected dogs and has a magazine (which I edited for many years) to keep enthusiasts in touch. This club, and others, provides members with an opportunity to network with others in their field of interest.

Enhancing Social Relationships

These groups are set up for members to meet new people and develop their social skills. Networking in this way is simply aimed at creating and developing relationships and extending skills at dealing effectively with other people.

There are many networks in existence for this purpose, such as dinner or luncheon clubs, where people meet to talk to others in a relaxed and friendly setting. Often such groups have membership by invitation only, but it is usually possible to attend one or more meetings through invitation of an existing member, before a decision is made about joining.

With this kind of network, you will probably find that members are interested in events and activities, such as meals out, outings to the theatre, trips to places of historical interest and topical speakers.

Three particular network types which come under this category are "old boys' clubs", dating agencies and retired staff clubs.

Old Boys' Clubs

This term is a little outdated nowadays, but is still sufficiently well known to be used as a shorthand title for such organisations. These groups are often formed with members who have some common past experience; for example, going to the same school, serving in a particular branch of public service and so on.

These groups work on the principle that shared experience gives common ground and that people with similar interests are well placed to come together for mutually beneficial purposes.

Dating Agencies

These exist to make introductions between people wishing to find long-term social partners. Although some function simply as introduction agencies, others do act on a networking basis, running events at which people can meet others and build friendships.

Retired Staff Clubs

These tend to be set up by employers' associations and provide a forum for retired people to continue to meet others who have worked in the same organisation. Such clubs can be for small organisations or for major public bodies, such as the armed forces.

Purchasing Networks and LETs

These are groups set up to benefit their members through the purchase of goods and services at reduced rates, or the exchange of goods and services between members. There are often discounts available for group purchases and, by having such a network, members can often benefit substantially.

One particular form of purchasing network is the LET network, which exists internationally. LETs stand for Local Exchange and Trading schemes and the groups are composed of members whose aim is to exchange goods and services with each other without money changing hands. What happens is that anyone who can offer goods or services does so and anyone wishing to acquire them does so. You can build up credits if you give more than you receive and can go into "debt" if it is the other way around. Groups generally have vouchers with local names (for example, "Olivers" in Bath and "Bennys" in Portsmouth). The vouchers can be exchanged in return for goods or services and often groups can exchange with each other on a regional or national basis.

LET schemes originated in the 1920s (based on traditional methods of barter which go back many centuries). They appeared in Canada in the late 1970s and in the UK began developing substantially in the late 1980s. There are now around 450 local groups in the UK and they are proving very popular and productive. To contact a LET scheme, see the Resources list.

Expatriates

These groups are designed to help people whose country of origin is elsewhere to meet others in a similar situation.

Some of the best way of finding out about these groups is through embassies, newspapers of the particular nationality or clubs frequented by people from the country in question.

Pressure/Action Groups

These groups are for people who wish to come together to act as a focal point when there is a topic of personal, local or professional interest which concerns them. Some examples of such networks are neighbourhood watch schemes, where residents gather together to take a stand against local crime; protest groups against the building of motorways through sites where rare wildlife may be endangered; and groups wishing to encourage local or national government to pass particular kinds of legislation or amend existing provisions.

Such networks can be different from the others mentioned previously, as they often have a fixed life span; they only have a function until their aim has been achieved. Of course, some may need an ongoing presence, but others will be very time-limited. There can also, because of the time elements involved, be an urgency to such groups' activities, which means that the person leading them needs to have both a clear vision and organisational, influencing and leadership skills to make sure the job gets done. Some of this can be delegated to other members of the group, but it is probably better if they are combined within the leadership role.

Pressure groups will need to influence others, so they are likely to require promotional skills plus funds to support such activity. They are also likely to attract adverse publicity, so members need to be prepared for this and able to deal with it. On the plus side, the media are often very good at helping these groups promote their activities, as protest and pressure makes good news and you can find yourself establishing strong and ongoing relationships with journalists and politicians locally, and possibly nationally or internationally.

Example

In London, there is a famous Victorian building called Alexandra Palace. Over time, the building fell into disarray and the Alexandra Palace Action Group (APAG) was formed to put pressure on the then owners of the Palace (the GLC) to do something constructive. APAG held open meetings to promote the cause, produced a magazine, fronted radio programmes and phone-ins, led guided tours round the building and generally acted as a focal point for interest until the building was regenerated.

Helping Others Develop

There is an increasing emphasis nowadays on developmental networks. Their purpose is often educational or informative and the networks often have a particular bias towards particular applications.

If you think you could benefit from enhancing your knowledge and skills in a particular area, or would like to help others to develop similarly, you could find out about networks in the field that interests you.

Example 1

In the NLP community in the UK, there are a number of networks aimed at helping others in various fields. Three of these are the NLP Business Group, the NLP Education Network and the NLP Health Network. All these networks provide a forum for people working in or interested in the field, to meet, exchange ideas and update themselves on new developments. Health and Education are growing rapidly in interest and there are many new developments and links between organisations in these fields. The Association for Neuro-Linguistic Programming, of which I am currently Chair, also acts as a focal point in the UK for informing people of ways in which they can network with each other for personal and professional development.

Example 2

Trainset® is the brainchild of Mike Leibling in the UK. Trainset aims to ". . . help people handle any situation they might find themselves in". Trainset's experience has been that gentle networking, where people decide for themselves if they wish to be associated with the cause, is more beneficial than aggressive networking, where they are press-ganged into involvement. Mike Leibling talks of his networking activities as simply "being there", an approach which he finds works well. Trainset's target is two million people involved in development over five years. Contact details for Trainset can be found in the Resources list.

This chapter has taken a look at some of the particular contexts in which networking can take place. You will find many more examples as you go along and can select those which appeal to you, or those which you feel will be most beneficial to take part in.

Chapter Thirteen

Setting up Your Own Networking Group

Once you have become familiar with the process of networking, you may wish to set up and run your own networking group. There can be many reasons for doing this. For example:

- Living in an area where there are few contacts for social interaction;

- Wanting to exchange information and ideas on a specialised topic for which there is not already an existing networking group, or at least not in your own area;

- Wanting to help others benefit from networking; and so on.

Whatever the reason, if you are contemplating setting up your own group, there are various factors to take into account and this chapter will give you some ideas on a range of these.

Where to Start

Firstly, take time to assess your reasons for wanting to start a group and the resources you have available for doing so. If you are doing it solely to look good on your CV, to impress colleagues, to fill in spare time or to make money through charging for membership, you might find that the activities involved are more demanding than you had anticipated and the personal, business and financial returns smaller than you had envisaged. Running a networking group has many personal benefits, but if you do it for the wrong reasons, it can lose its appeal and you may have both wasted your own time and let others down. If, however, you have analysed things and decided it is for you, there is plenty of help available.

If you have not already ascertained that no similar group exists, it helps to do some research into what is already available. Local libraries and information services can be very useful and you may well find that there is a free information service in your own locality, which can be an invaluable aid.

It could also be, if there is no similar group, that there is no real (or potential) demand for it. So, although it helps to approach your project in a positive frame of mind, it would be wise to allow for the possibility that it may not actually come to fruition.

Once you have found that you are not duplicating existing provision, and that there may well be a reasonable demand for what you have in mind, you can think of how to set about financing, promoting, establishing, publicising and organising your group.

Financing

You can run a group inexpensively, but there are bound to be some administrative costs involved, so you will need to think about such costs in advance. Some of the things you may need to fund are as follows:

- *Publicity*: You will need to let people know about your group and this can cost money. You will find some ideas on publicity in one of the sections that follow.

- *Venue(s)*: A group will need somewhere to meet and, again, this can have financial implications. This is also covered later.

- *Stationery/Phone/E-mail*: Letting people know about the group, communicating with them about meetings and writing to speakers all require writing materials, a telephone, e-mail or other communications media. All have cost implications.

- *Refreshments*: When people come to meetings, it is nice, although not essential, to have refreshments available. Again, this can be costly.

- *Materials and Equipment*: You may need to acquire office equipment to run your group and you may also want to use audio-visual aids at your meetings. These can also be quite expensive unless you can get them donated or purchase them second-hand.

There may also be other costs involved, depending on the nature of your particular group. If you finance the group yourself, you need to be aware of the commitment in advance, because without adequate resources it is unlikely to succeed.

If you cannot finance the group yourself, you could consider funding it through contributions from members or visitors. This will need to be thought out carefully. A high fee for joining or attendance can put people off, unless they know the benefits are worth it, and a low fee may not be sufficient to cover your costs. This is a difficult situation for new groups, as they are unlikely to be able to charge a realistic fee until they can offer things which people value, yet they may not be able to offer those things until they can fund them. So, starting small-scale and working within your resources is important if you are not to over-stretch yourself.

Another way of funding your group is through sponsorship or other forms of fundraising. A local business may be willing to support your group in some way; for example, by letting you hold meetings at their premises. There can be a two-way benefit to such an arrange-ment, as the business can gain additional publicity through attracting visitors to its location. You may also find an organisation willing to do photocopying for you in return for a small advertisement for its products or services on items that you circulate.

Another option is to ask for loans or donations of equipment such as filing cabinets, chairs, typewriters, computers, fax machines, flip charts or cassette players. You may find that organisations are very willing to donate such items if they are surplus to requirements. Another means of support can be through helping you with admini-stration; some local companies may be prepared to get letters typed for you if you cannot do this yourself. Be creative, have something to offer in return, expect success and you can make good progress.

Example

A voluntary organisation was given a large quantity of computers from a manufacturer. It turned out that, although they were donated free, it would have cost a good deal to get them linked with

*their existing equipment and functioning as they wanted. The gift
turned out to be more of a liability than a benefit. So do be careful,
before accepting donations, that they are actually usable and cost-
effective for you.*

Moving from sponsorship to general fundraising, you could consider
holding a raffle (make sure you are aware of any legal requirements
regarding such fundraising), having a stall at a market to sell second-
hand goods, offering services such as walking dogs or taking in
ironing, or having a local auction. A "promise" auction is a simple one
to run; with this, no goods are involved — people bid for promised
items. You might also like to consider donating a proportion of the
money raised from raffles or auctions to an established charity, so
that donors know that some of their contributions are going to an
already established cause.

Finally, as well as membership or attendance fees, you can raise
money from members through sales of refreshments at meetings,
raffle tickets, goods that have been donated to the group and so forth.
Many groups are finding highly creative ways of raising money either
from members or from outside people and organisations.

If you wish to know about fundraising techniques in general, there
are plenty of publications available and there are also directories of
organisations which offer funds or grants, nationally and internationally. You could ask at your local library or information service for
these.

Promotion

For this, you need to consider what your target audience is and then
find ways of reaching it. Some target groups could be:

- *Local or regional groups*: People living in a geographical area;

- *Professional groups*: People with a common business interest;

- *Industry groups*: People working in the same field of activity;

- *Personal characteristics groups*: People with the same, or
  similar, sex, age, family commitments, health issues, etc.;

- *Business promotion groups*: People wishing to develop business
  opportunities;

- *Educational groups*: People wishing to develop their knowledge or skills in a particular subject;

- *Affinity (interest) groups*: People with the same areas of interest.

Publicising your group can be done in a range of ways and I have listed some here under headings that relate to their likely cost.

"Free" Publicity

I have put the word "free" in inverted commas as there is always some cost involved; if not in money, then in time and effort, so do take these points into account when considering promotional activity.

Free publicity can include word of mouth, where you simply talk to people about your group so that you increase the possibility of your target audience finding out about it. It helps to speak to people in a similar context as those you are hoping to attract, but almost any person you speak to could know someone who would be interested, so don't underestimate the value of this process. You could also promote your group through talks to chambers of commerce, women's institutes, parent–teacher groups and so on — a method which can be very productive, as you could "sign up" some potential members on the spot.

Another good way to publicise your group is through free notices on boards in colleges, leisure centres, supermarkets, post offices, waiting rooms, and so on. In many of these places, there are people with time to spare, perhaps while they wait for someone else, and it can be a good source of interest. When putting up notices, think about positioning and, where possible, use coloured card and an interesting design to catch people's attention, and place your cards at eye level.

You can also have some small cards or leaflets printed and leave supplies of them at suitable places. Many libraries and shops will agree to display such items. Remember to replenish your cards from time to time and find out whether there is anything you can offer the organisations who take the cards for you.

Another way of getting free publicity is to put notices through letterboxes or on car windscreens (check that this is legal in your country). This can be time-consuming, but could be done during routine journeys or as a way of getting some exercise, as well as distributing your information. If you do put notices on cars, you may find it easier to go to car parks at supermarkets, colleges, leisure centres and so on, rather than walking along streets.

You could also consider advertising, as many local, and some national, newspapers carry free advertisements as long as you are promoting non-commercial services.

You can publish details of your group on e-mail or the Internet, as this will be relatively inexpensive and can carry your message to large audiences.

And, finally, consider contacting your local newspapers and radio stations to see whether they will interview you or run an item on your group. You can contact them by sending a press release but, for local issues, it is likely to be more effective to contact them in person, either by phone or by dropping in. The more interesting you can make your project sound, the more likely it is that they will follow it up. If you can get a photo in the paper too, it will stand out more than just text. If you do a radio or press interview, you could also make an offer to listeners/readers by inviting them to come to one meeting free, receive a newsletter for a month or have a free or reduced-rate membership subscription. These techniques work and can give your group a good kick-start.

Low-cost Publicity

There are other means of publicity which do have a financial cost attached, although generally a reasonably low one.

One method is to place paid postcards in shop windows. The charge for this is generally very low and your message can be displayed for several weeks at a stretch. Remember to make your message visually appealing as well as including relevant information.

Another method is to use classified advertisements in local news-papers, although this can be expensive unless the paper has a column for non-commercial activities. If you do use this method, it helps to place your advertisement for at least two to three weeks at a time and to make it as appealing as you can within a few words.

Another method is to pay to have your messages delivered by hand locally — to houses, organisations or, again, put on car windscreens. You will need to check that the people you give the task to are reliable and don't simply dump your messages in the nearest bin — something which can occasionally happen.

Higher-cost Advertising

If funds permit, you can use higher-cost publicity, although more expensive methods are not always more effective.

In this context, you can use display advertising in newspapers and magazines, which will make your message stand out more strongly. Again, make sure it is in an appropriate section or your efforts will have been wasted.

You could also use local radio advertising if your group has a local or regional interest, or use mailshots to selected lists of individuals and organisations.

Whatever means your publicity takes, remember the suggestions in Chapter 11 on distance communications; target your messages appropriately, write them clearly, lay them out in an inviting manner and make sure to include details of how and when to contact you.

You may wish to give a post office box number instead of your actual address and phone number if you are concerned to avoid nuisance calls or the risk of unwanted visitors at your private address.

Group Newsletters

Once your group is established, it is helpful to continue publicity to attract new members and keep people informed of what you are doing. A good way of doing this is to have a group newsletter.

A regular newsletter can be a good way of keeping members in touch with each other and publicising the group externally. It can also be useful to send to similar groups with which you want to liaise.

Producing a newsletter takes resources — time, effort and money — and it is important that whoever takes on the responsibility for producing it understands what is involved. A few issues to think of when starting a newsletter follow and you can also refer back to Chapter 11 for some ideas on promotional activities:

- Choose an appropriate title;

- Keep the content relevant;

- Select an appropriate writing style;

- Give people responsibility for sections, so one person doesn't have to do it all;

- Make sure it comes out on time;

- Maintain a two-way process between you and your members; avoid a "top-down" approach;

- Enliven it with anecdotes, news items and so on, plus illustrations if you can.

Administration

To run a successful group, you will need effective systems for organisation and administration. I have already discussed organisation in Chapter 4 and all the same points apply here. You will need to have suitable space for the papers which will accumulate, have a retrieval system which works and acquire stationery for communicating with members. You might also wish to open a bank account for your group and may find your local bank willing to waive charges if you are a non-profit-making organisation.

You will need to set up a system for communicating with members and potential members of your group, for recording who attends and, if you charge a membership or attendance fee, who has paid and when. You could keep a manual system, perhaps with cards for each member, or you could keep your membership records on computer. It is worth keeping attendance sheets for each meeting; it is also helpful to have a process to check on people who have not attended for a while, to find out why this is.

You will also need to organise resources such as venue, refreshments and any support materials needed for your meetings.

Organising Meetings

Once you have a viable membership, you can hold meetings and you may wish to have a preliminary meeting with interested individuals before starting up in earnest. You will need to decide how frequently to meet, whether to meet at weekdays or weekends, during the day or in the evening. Some groups meet for breakfast, before starting work, others at lunchtimes and others in the evenings, rather than during working hours or precious weekend time.

Your venue will also need considering. You can run your group from home, rotate it between members' premises or hire commercial venues. If you are fortunate, you may be able to find free, or very low cost, accommodation, such as village or church halls, office premises or something similar. Alternatives that cost considerably more are hotels, clubs, conference centres and so forth; however, all these are likely to be outside the budget of most fledgling groups.

You will also need to decide whether refreshments are to be provided and, if so, by whom and at what cost. If the group is very informal, it may be that members can take it in turns to provide venues and refreshments, or one person can offer a venue while others bring refreshments. It is also possible, instead of providing refreshments at the meeting, for participants to go for meal together after the meeting; in this way the contact can continue more socially and the cost of eating can be spread between all those present.

Running Meetings

At your meetings, you will need to consider matters such as who will chair or manage the event, how seating is to be arranged, what the agenda will be, what activities will take place and whether visual aids are required. It is often a good idea to rotate the chair, if you have one at all, so that different people take turns to have the responsibility and to gain the experience. An agreed agenda can be useful, so that everyone knows what to expect and, if it is circulated in advance, can plan their contributions. Informal meetings without agendas can also be good if the group is such that the flexibility and lack of structure is preferred by those attending.

It is worth thinking about sessions at the start of meetings where people can introduce themselves to others in an informal and interesting way (perhaps having an "ice-breaking" activity to do so). It can also be worth having a section for exchange of news and information on products or services. You may want to have time for individual members to "showcase" what they do or to lead an activity.

Practical elements such as exercises and group activities can be useful, depending on the function of the group. If you have a large group to start with, or frequent new members, "icebreakers" can help people get to know each other; these can include such activities as:

- Asking each person to speak to someone they have not met before;

- Asking people to talk to the person next to them and find out about them and then introduce each other to the group;

- Asking each person to say a little about themselves to the group.

There are many books available giving ideas for icebreaking sessions and group activities and they are well worth looking at. If your local library does not have such titles available, they can generally be found in libraries of personnel and training institutes.

Visitors and Guest Presenters

You might also like to consider whether to invite guests to your group and whether to invite outside speakers. If you do the former, will you charge for attendance? If you do the latter, will you make any payment for the presentation? Speakers may need expenses, even if they do not charge a fee, and they may also need a map of how to get there, a lift from a local station and accommodation if you expect them to be there late at night or early in the morning.

If you do invite guest speakers, make sure they don't have to sit through long periods of group business before beginning their session. If there are items the group members need to discuss, try to time them for the beginning or end and ask your speaker to arrive at a time when you will not be engaged in group formalities.

Remember to tell your speakers a bit about the group and its members, so they can prepare appropriately for their sessions and let them know whether people dress in a formal or casual way. It helps to publicise outside speakers well, so you get a good attendance.

Finally, remember to thank your speaker and perhaps give them a small gift at the end, or at least a thank-you card as a follow-up.

Liaison with Other Groups

Another point worth remembering is that it can be helpful for your group to network with other similar groups. This can be especially useful where there are a number of networking groups in different areas, all with the same interests or activities; sharing ideas and experience. In some instances, networking groups have set up their own conferences to exchange ideas and information about running groups and making the most of personal contact.

Example

In London, an excellent NLP practice group was set up some years ago. Originally called "The Paddington Group", as that was where they met, they later became the New London Practice Group. The group met weekly (sometimes twice a week) and after some years of successful operation began to organise day conferences for practice group organisers. The conferences were run on an annual basis and provided opportunities for groups throughout the UK to share ideas and experiences and learn new ways of doing things. The group also provided an information pack for people wishing to set up new groups (see Resources list).

Sharing Responsibility

If you started the group on your own, a time may come when it is sensible either to share responsibility with others or to hand over or delegate to other people. Sharing responsibility can be useful, especially if you are very busy and involved in other activities; if someone else can help, you have a ready substitute in case of need.

If you can find others to take over at a later stage you will be able to concentrate your activities on other matters. It can also be quite a burden to take sole responsibility for the starting up and management of a group; sharing the load can help in many ways and can also make others feel more involved and active.

Reviewing Effectiveness

When your group has been running for some time, you may want to think about how it is doing. It can be easy to fall into the habit of complacency, but there may well be elements that could be improved or altered.

A simple way to assess your group is to set aside time for a discussion on how far you are achieving what members of the group want. If you had initial objectives for the group, you may wish to re-visit them at this point and see if they need changing or adding to.

Another way to review effectiveness is to ask members (and visitors, if you want an outside view too), to complete a short questionnaire on the effectiveness of the group and anything they would like to change in the future. Keep the questions short and to the point and avoid leading questions that bias the answers of those responding.

You can either use open questions, where you simply ask for opinions ("What do you think of the length of our meetings?"), or you can use structured questions ("Do you think our meetings are: a) too long; b) about the right length; c) too short?"). The first approach will give you a better feel for the participants' views, but the second will be easier to quantify and analyse.

Whatever you do, find a way to feed back the responses you get. If people have given up time to help with the survey, it is only fair to let them know what the outcome is and to discuss with them what action, if any, needs to be taken as a result.

You may want to use the findings of your survey to promote the group even further. If there is a very good response, you can use this to show how well the group is doing and you can also consider using quotes from respondents in publicity material (with their permission, unless their names are omitted). Such a survey can be a good thing to include in your newsletter, and a press release, so your local paper can consider including an item on it.

Setting up Limited Companies

A final point is that, in some cases, you may find that you want, or need, to set up a limited company through which your network can function. This is outside the scope of this book, but you can get advice on the appropriateness of setting up companies, and advice on how to administer them, from many sources, including banks, accountants, solicitors and tax specialists.

Chapter Fourteen

Monitoring Success and Extending Your Skills into the Future

To assess success in any field, there need to be a number of elements in place. The first is an objective; once you have this, you know what result you are aiming for. The second is some activity, behaviour, or effort that takes you towards your goal. The third is feedback, so you have an idea of what results you are getting. The fourth is a comparison of the objective with the feedback, to see whether there is a match between the two. The fifth is an adjustment, if any is needed, to keep you on track towards achieving your objective.

If feedback matches anticipated results, then you are probably successful. If feedback shows you are falling short of your desired result, you still have some work to do. If feedback exceeds your goal, you have either put in unnecessary effort, or you may simply have done better than expected. You can chart the relationship between the elements described in graphic form. The diagram below, which is known as a feedback loop, shows how this works.

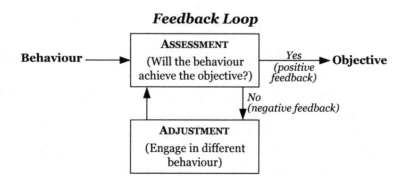

Feedback Loop

So, in assessing your results, you need to be clear about your objectives (which I covered in Chapter 4); you need appropriate behavioural skills (which I covered in many of the succeeding chapters); you need to have a means of getting feedback; and you need to be able to put in place modifying mechanisms if required.

As I have covered objective setting and behavioural skills already, the next section deals with feedback and using it to good effect.

Feedback

There are many ways of getting feedback; the ones I will be covering here are:

- Self-assessment,

- Feedback from others.

Self-assessment

This is about giving yourself feedback on your efforts. With self-assessment, you are relying on your own opinions and information gathering as evidence of your success.

You can give yourself feedback in different ways. Firstly, you can simply match your results to your goals to see whether they are aligned. If you have effective objectives, it becomes easier to assess when they have been achieved. Examples of achieving objectives would be the following:

- Wanting to speak to a particular person and succeeding;

- Wanting to obtain a particular item of information and succeeding;

- Wanting to join a particular organisation and succeeding.

In these cases, it is obvious whether or not your objective has been met (or at least partially met).

There are other ways of giving yourself feedback, however, which do not rely on purely objective facts for evidence. These ways relate to some of the elements of networking mentioned in the Introduction: behaviour, thoughts, feelings and beliefs. When it comes to assessing your success in relation to these, you have to rely on more subjective measures. Let's take each of these in turn and see how you might give yourself feedback on them.

Behaviour

For example, you might wish to assess how you have behaved at a meeting. Behaviour is complex and you may not be able to break down every tiny element of your behaviour so it can be measured in a numerical way. You have, then, to rely on your subjective assessment of how well you have done. So your feedback to yourself could include asking yourself questions such as:

- How did I greet people when they arrived?

- What tone of voice did I use when asking questions?

- How well did I listen to the other people present?

- How much time did I spend talking to each person?

- What space did I take up with my papers at the table?

- How friendly did I seem?

- How interested did I appear?

Your answers to such questions will give you really useful feedback, as long as you are honest with yourself and take as detached a view as you can of how you behaved. Of course, you won't be able to know exactly how you came across to others; only they can know that. You can, however, take a good guess based on self-observation, observation of how people responded to you and assessment of the results of your interactions with others at the meeting.

This kind of feedback is not always quantifiable, but it is worth doing as a review after events.

The following is a feedback sheet, which you could use for self-assessment (you can also use it for assessing others if that is relevant on particular occasions).

You can rate yourself as follows on each of the items:

1 = Excellent   2 = Good   3 = Needs a little improvement
4 = Needs in-depth improvement

Appearance

Clothes	
Posture	
Movement	
Gestures	
Mannerisms	
Facial expressions	
Eye contact	

Voice

Speed	
Volume	
Projection	
Tonality	
Pitch	
Rhythm	
Variety	
Breathing	

Confidence

Self-awareness	
Relaxation	
Confidence	
Authoritativeness	
Enthusiasm	

Language

Clarity	
Precision	
Simplicity	
Logic	
Repetition	
Use of pauses	

Contact with others

Awareness of others	
Rapport development	
Sensitivity	
Flexibility	
Ability to hold interest	
Degree of influence	
Distance communications	

Conversation

Listening	
Questioning	
Giving information	
Dealing with questions	
Giving feedback	
Receiving feedback/criticism	
Maintaining common ground	
Structuring discussion	

Objectives

Extent to which networking objectives are being achieved	

Thoughts

Another thing you can use self-feedback for is your mental state and thought processes. Again, this kind of assessment can be hard to quantify, but you can still gain useful information from the process.

Suppose you wanted to find out how well things had gone at a social event; you might ask yourself the following questions:

- Was I in a positive frame of mind when I went?

- Did I think positively about each of the people I met?

- Was I giving myself ongoing feedback, during the event, by using "self-talk"?

- Did I give myself positive messages about the event before attending?

- Did I picture things going well and see myself interacting with others comfortably and successfully?

Feedback to yourself through such questions will help you work out how you approached the event and your frame of mind during it.

Feelings

The next thing you can give yourself feedback on is your feelings. Suppose you attended a talk at a professional body; you could ask yourself the following questions:

- Did I maintain a state of interest and curiosity doing the talk?

- Did I feel motivated or energised by the speaker?

- Did I feel the speaker was knowledgeable?

- Did I feel comfortable physically with the seating, heating, lighting and room arrangement?

Again, asking yourself these questions will help you monitor your responses to the event.

Beliefs, Values, Assumptions and Attitudes

Finally, you can consider these deeper-seated elements. Suppose you met a fellow passenger on a train with whom you had a conversation. You could ask yourself the following questions about the interaction:

- Did I believe the conversation would be mutually beneficial?

- Did I value the discussion more than having time to relax?

- Did I assume the person would be interested in talking to me?

- Did I have a particular attitude towards what was being said?

Answering such questions will also give you useful feedback, this time at a rather deeper level than with some of the other elements.

Combining all these kinds of questions will give you a reasonable idea of how you think things went in each of the particular situations. You will need to ask yourself questions on each of the elements in any given situation. I have split them between different contexts here to give a little more variety to the questions listed.

I have talked here about giving yourself feedback after the event. With practice you will be able to ask yourself such questions at the time, so you can monitor your behaviour and adjust it accordingly if you feel that is necessary. It may sound difficult at this stage to maintain conversations and also have a running commentary in your head about what is going on, but it is possible and can make it more likely that you will achieve good results.

Example

On a recent course I ran, there was a discussion on "internal dialogue". One of the participants did not know what I meant by internal dialogue. I said that I would demonstrate it by talking to her and, as she spoke, I would say out loud my own internal dialogue. I duly did this and the person was amazed that anyone could have words going on in their head while they were listening to someone else. What I was actually doing was giving her feedback on her own performance, by saying out loud what my internal thoughts were about her behaviour.

Feedback from Others

Having considered self-feedback, it is time to turn to how you can collect and use feedback from other people. Although self-feedback is important, you can never know absolutely how other people perceive and value you. So getting feedback from others is an essential step in effective networking. There are a number of ways in which you can do this and I would like to consider five of them here:

- Noticing how others actually behave towards you;

- Asking others for feedback directly;

- Asking others in advance to observe what you do and then give you feedback later;

- Asking others if they will approach third parties to find out how you came across to them;

- Sending out questionnaires to people to assess your performance.

Let's take these in turn.

Noticing how others actually behave towards you

This requires good observation skills and is worth working at. When you are with other people, or after you have been with others, make a point of noticing exactly how they behave in response to you. For example, in a group, do others:

1. Gravitate towards you?

2. Stay and talk, appearing very interested in the conversation?

3. Stay for a while and then walk away?

4. Rarely come to you without being approached?

After you have been with other people, or when you have spoken to them on the phone, do they tend to:

1. Contact you again quickly just to keep in touch?

2. Only contact you if there is something specific they want or have promised to do?

3. Rarely contact you?

4. Only speak to you if you call them?

Of course, these are generalisations, but you can learn from people's *patterns* of behaviour. If you are always the centre of attention, have many friends and acquaintances and are constantly contacted by others, you are probably an excellent networker. If, on the other hand, you have few contacts and find it hard to attract or maintain relationships, then your networking skills could do with some attention.

Asking Others for Feedback Directly

This is the most direct way, and often the most effective. By asking people directly how you come across, you can get an idea of their reactions to you. Of course, people may not always be absolutely truthful, but the more you can convince them that you are really open to honest feedback, the more likely it is they will be willing to help you.

Asking for feedback may be inappropriate in some situations, but there will be others when it is quite feasible; for example, when you are with close friends, when you are carrying out a new activity or when the people you are with are more experienced than you and you are asking for their "expert" opinion on what you are doing.

Some things you could ask people in this manner include:

- How does my voice come across?

- What impression does my "body language" give?

- What do you think of the way I greet people or shake hands with them?

- What do you think of the way I introduce myself to people?

- What do you think of my business cards?

- How interested do you think I seem in the people here?

Questions such as this will focus the other person's mind on something specific and give you useful feedback on your own performance. Bear in mind that some people may feel uncomfortable giving such feedback, so make it easy for them to refuse if they wish. If you say: "I wonder whether you would be able to help me with . . ." rather than "I don't suppose you could want to . . ." it is also more likely that you will receive a positive response. When approached in a suitable manner, most people are likely to feel flattered that you have asked their opinion and will be only too willing to help.

Asking others in advance to observe what you do and then give you feedback

This requires a little more preparation, but can give you very focused information. With this approach, you need to brief someone in advance to give you feedback on something specific. For example:

- Will you please listen to this telephone call and let me know how I sounded; did I sound helpful, irritated, amused and so on?

- Will you watch how I behave at the meeting and tell me afterwards if I looked at people when they were talking and whether I seemed interested in what they were saying?

- Will you notice how I talk to people at this event and tell me if I seemed to be speaking too much or too little in each conversation?

The more specific your requests, the easier you will make it for others to give you useful feedback.

Asking others if they will approach third parties to find out how you came across to them

This can be useful if you have no direct access to the person concerned, or if someone else is more likely to get a "true" response from them. Do make sure, though, that they know if their comments are going to be fed back to you.

Some examples of this process in action include:

- "Can you ask Fred if he thought my input at the meeting went well?"

- "Can you find out from Jane if she liked my information pack?"

- "Can you tell Sarah I would be interested in knowing how she reacted to my ideas?"

Sending out questionnaires to people to assess your performance

This may sound a little formal, but it doesn't have to be so. You might send a brief note to contacts including a request such as the following:

"I really want to improve my own personal/business performance. I would very much appreciate your help. If you could take just a few moments to answer these questions, and return them in the stamped envelope I have sent, I will send you . . . [mention something which you feel would be of interest to the person; perhaps a report, article or information on sources of information which they might value]".

Here are some examples of questions you could pose:

- What do you think of the services I offer?

- How do you think I could improve them in the future?

- Are there any elements which you think need changing?

- What would be the most useful way in which I could keep in touch with you?

Short, simple questions are likely to receive attention, especially if you can offer the person receiving them some incentive to reply.

With all these approaches, do be prepared to take the bad with the good and to learn from it. All feedback will not be excellent, but any that isn't provides an excellent opportunity for development. If your self-confidence is not always high, positive feedback will give you a real boost and help you do even better in the future.

Remember, the better you brief your helper in advance, the better quality information you are likely to gather. Do ask if you can return the favour; you might be surprised how much other people would welcome objective feedback on their own performance.

Final Observations — Looking Forward

If you have followed the ideas in the book, by now you will have understood the benefits of networking, begun to enhance your skills and thought about the situations in which you could apply what you have learned. Now it is time to think about moving forward into the future and considering how you can continue to develop and use your skills in your own unique way

Let's think, first of all, about planning for the future.

Planning for the Future

In earlier chapters, I discussed how to set objectives and the first thing I would like to encourage you to do here is to continue this process of objective setting into the future.

By having ongoing objectives, and reviewing them periodically, you will be able to ensure that your networking is providing the results you want and is adapting to your own changing circumstances. You might want to set objectives relating to increased networking activity, different kinds of networking, membership of particular organisations and so forth. Whatever you do, reviewing and updating your objectives will pay dividends.

Imagining the Future

Now you have considered what you wish to achieve in the future, you might like to revisit a simple exercise which can help with making your objectives seem more real and which I have already mentioned briefly earlier in the book. The process you will be following involves imagining your future goals and then imagining what it would be like if you had achieved them.

To do the exercise, simply think of one of your objectives, imagine what it would be like to have achieved it, perhaps by making a mental image of it, or by imagining how people would be talking to you if you had achieved it. Now, in your mind, imagine really being in the situation of having achieved the goal. Notice how it feels to do this. By giving yourself this "advance experience" of your goal, you are likely to be more motivated to achieve it and find it easier to imagine it actually happening.

Using Role Models

As I mentioned earlier, finding a role model you can copy is an excellent way of enhancing your success. So, to keep ahead in the future, you can find a succession of role models, each one with the ability to do something you would like to achieve, and then copy each of these, in turn, until you can adopt similar behaviour to each of them. In this way, you will enhance your skills effectively.

Make sure, with your role models, that you observe them carefully before copying, so you are sure what they do works well. So, for example, you might observe how they talk to others, how they write letters, how they circulate between groups at events, how they present their business cards to people and how they describe their activities to others. Once you have observed (and checked with the person, if necessary, to make sure you are truly aware of what they are doing), you can copy these elements of behaviour in appropriate circumstances and check the results you get. This process will enable you to keep developing and increase your range of behaviour.

Incorporating Networking into Your Personal and Professional Development

Continuing professional development is currently a popular process. It involves making sure you keep up-to-date with trends in your field and take opportunities to constantly update your skills and knowledge.

To apply this to networking, you can do some of the following activities:

- Check what articles and books are being written on the subject and read them.

- Share experiences with other networkers, to see whether you can help each other to become aware of, and develop skills in the activity. Listening to people on the radio and television is another way of finding out how others increase their public exposure and raise their personal image.

- Attend courses and meetings which have sessions on networking; this will give you new insights and also give you opportunities to extend your own personal network.

- Keep records of your activities, so you can check what has produced good results and what is worth avoiding in the future.

- Include in your objective setting an indication of what personal and professional value each target will give you — so you are really aware of the benefits of what you are doing.

- Teach other people to network.

It is often through the process of teaching someone else that we develop our own skills. Whether you have practical experience, or have simply read this book, or others, you can impart your own knowledge and ability to other people. You will also find that, by doing this, you gain a better understanding of how others differ from you, which is valuable information to the skilled networker. Even if you think you may not be a natural "teacher", just think of it as coaching and you will find you are able to do it. We all show other people how to do things from time to time; this is just extending the process a little further.

So, we have reached the end of the journey. I hope you found the information and ideas in the book of interest and value and that you will apply them in whichever areas of your life you find most helpful. Networking is not only an essential skill for the future; it is an enjoyable and stimulating way of interacting with others. Have fun!

Bibliography

The following books and tapes have either been mentioned in the text or are additional titles which you should find useful.

Books

General Neuro-Linguistic Programming

The Elements of NLP, Carol Harris, 1998, Element Books.

NLP: New Perspectives, Carol Harris, 1999, Element Books.

Introducing NLP, Joseph O'Connor and John Seymour, 1990, HarperCollins/Mandala.

Unlimited Power, Anthony Robbins, 1988, Simon & Schuster.

Accelerated Learning

Super Teaching, Eric P. Jensen, 1995, Turning Point Publishing.

The Creative Trainer, Michael Lawlor and Peter Handley, 1996, McGraw Hill.

7 Kinds of Smart, Thomas Armstrong, 1999, Plume Books.

Action Profiling

Body Code: The Meaning in Movement, Warren Lamb, 1979, Princeton Book Company.

Action Profiling, Pamela Ramsden and Jody Zacharias, 1993, Gower.

Language

The Structure of Magic, Volume One, Richard Bandler and John
  Grinder, 1975, Science and Behaviour Books Inc.

The Structure of Magic, Volume Two, Richard Bandler and John
  Grinder, 1976, Science and Behaviour Books Inc.

Words that Change Minds, Shelle Rose Charvet, 1997, Kendall Hunt
  Publishing Company.

Therapeutic Metaphors, David Gordon, 1978, Meta Publications.

Precision, Michael D. McMaster and John Grinder, 1980, Precision
  Models.

People Pattern Power, Marilyne Woodsmall and Wyatt Woodsmall,
  1998, Next Step Press.

Voice

The Voice Book, Michael McCallion, 1988, Faber and Faber.

The Breath Book, Stella Weller, 1999, Thorsons.

Confidence

Total Confidence, Philippa Davies, 1994, Piatkus.

Motivation

Finding Flow, Mihaly Csikszentmihalyi, 1998, Basic Books.

Stress Management

The Twenty-Minute Break, Ernest Rossi, 1991, Jeremy P. Tarcher
  Inc.

Stress Check, Stress Check Publications (Berean Place, Beoley,
  Worcestershire, B98 9BH, Tel: 01527 595211).

Impression Management

Your Total Image, Philippa Davies, 1990, Piatkus.

101 Ways to Make a Professional Impact, Eleri Sampson, 1996,
  Kogan Page.

The Image Factor, Eleri Sampson, 1994, Kogan Page.

Communications

Constructive Feedback, Frances Bee and Roland Bee, 1996, IPD Training Extras.

Personal Power, Philippa Davies, 1991, Piatkus.

Assertiveness, Terry Gillen, 1997, IPD Training Extras.

Listening Skills, Ian Mackay, 1984, IPD Training Extras.

Asking Questions, Ian Mackay, 1980, IPD Training Extras.

Handbook of Internal Communication, Eileen Scholes (ed.), 1997, Gower.

Transformational Mentoring, Julie Hay, 1995, McGraw-Hill.

Mind Mapping

The Mind Map Book, Tony Buzan, 1993, BBC Books.

Memory Training

Master Your Memory, Tony Buzan, 1998, BBC Books.

Rapid Reading

The Speed Reading Book, Tony Buzan, 1997, BBC Books.

The PhotoReading Whole Mind System, Paul R. Scheele, 1993, Learning Strategies Corporation.

Time Management

Procrastinator's Success Kit, Alyce Cornyn-Selby, 1986, Beynch Press.

The Complete Time Management System, Christian Godefroy, 1989, Piatkus.

The 80/20 Principle, Richard Koch, 1999, Nicholas Brealey.

Visualisation

Creative Imagery, William Fezler, 1989, Simon and Schuster.

Self-assessment

Build Your Own Rainbow, Barrie Hopson and Mike Scally, 1984, Lifeskills Publishing Group.

NLP Magazines

Rapport, P.O. Box 10, Porthmadog, LL48 6ZB, Wales, UK.

Anchorpoint, 346 South 500 East, Suite 200, Salt Lake City, UT 84102, USA.

NLP World, Les 3 Chasseurs, 1413 Orzens, Switzerland.

MultiMind, Junfermann, Postfach 1840, D-33048, Paderborn, Germany.

Audiotapes
Confidence and Motivation
Super Self, Carol Harris, 1994, Management Magic.

Interpersonal Skills
Handling Social Situations, Carol Harris, 1994, Management Magic.

Appearance
Creating a Good Impression, Carol Harris, 1994, Management Magic.

Voice
The Sound of your Voice, Carol Fleming, 1988, Simon and Schuster.

Card Sets
Feedback
The Feedback Game and *The Feedback Game Manual*, Peter Gerrickens, 1999, Gower (cards and manual).

List of Resources

This list contains a range of organisations and associations, UK and international. Most countries have networking organisations, but they may not all be listed in directories. To find out what exists near you, either try some of the contact details listed below or, alternatively, contact a local library or information bureau, a professional institute or an appropriate government department in your own region.

If the organisation you contact initially is not appropriate for your needs, ask whoever you speak to there if they can suggest anyone else you can contact; in this way, you can use networking to find out about networking!

Professional Bodies in the UK

Institute of Directors,
116 Pall Mall, London, SW1Y 5ED.
Tel: (+44) 020 7839 1233.
Fax: (+44) 020 7930 1949.
E-mail: marketing@iod.co.uk
Web site: www.iod.co.uk

Institute of Management,
Cottingham Road, Corby, Northamptonshire, NN17 1TT.
Tel: (+44) 01536 204 222.
Fax: (+44) 01536 201 651.
E-mail: mic.enquiries@imgt.org.uk
Web site: www.imst-mgt.org.uk

Institute of Management Consultancy,
5th Floor, 32–33 Hatton Garden, London, EC1N 8DL.
Tel: (+44) 020 7242 2140.
Fax: (+44) 020 7831 4597.
E-mail: consult@imc.co.uk
Web site: www.imc.co.uk
Also the IMC Women's Network — e-mail: mary.akpala@lineone.net

Institute of Personnel and Development,
IPD House, Camp Road, Wimbledon, London, SW19 4UX.
Tel: (+44) 020 8971 9000.
Fax: (+44) 020 8263 3366.
E-mail: ipd@ipd.co.uk
Web site: www.ipd.co.uk

Other UK Associations

London Chamber of Commerce and Industry,
33 Queen Street, London, EC4R 1AP.
Tel: (+44) 020 7248 4444.
Fax: (+44) 020 7489 0391.
E-mail: lc@londonchamber.co.uk
Web site: www.londonchamber.co.uk

Forum of Private Business,
Ruskin Chambers, Drury Lane, Knutsford, Cheshire, WA16 6HA.
Tel: (+44) 01565 634467.
Fax: (+44) 01565 650059.

Institute for Independent Business,
Clarendon House, Bridle Path, Watford, Hertfordshire, WD2 4AA.
Tel: (+44) 01923 239543.
Fax: (+44) 01923 239643.

Society of Business Practitioners,
P.O. Box 10, Hazel Grove, Stockport, Cheshire, SK7 4AD (Mail
address).
Rankin House, Haig Road, Parkgrove TE, Knutsford, Cheshire, WA16
8DX.

The Sales Training Organisation). Web site:
freespace.virgin.net/sta.org/

Richmond Group (Consortium of Independent Management
Consultants),
Tel: (+44) 0870 606 0094.
E-mail: rgroup@cix.co.uk
Web site: www.richmond-group.co.uk

Association of MBAs,
15 Duncan Terrace, London, N1 8BZ.
Tel: (+44) 020 7837 3375.
Fax: (+44) 020 7278 3634.
Web site: www.mba.org.uk

Farmers' World Network,
The Arthur Rank Centre, National Agricultural Centre, Stoneleigh,
Warwickshire, CV8 2LZ.
Tel: (+44) 01203 696969.
Fax: (+44) 01203 414808.
E-mail: fwn@ruralnet.org.uk

YHA (Youth Hostels Association),
YHA (England and Wales), Trevelyan House, 8 St. Stephens Hill,
St. Albans, Herts, AL1 2DY.
Tel: (+44) 0870 870 8808.
Fax: (+44) 01727 844126.
E-mail: customerservices@yha.org.uk

Associations in the US

International Women's Forum,
1621 Connecticut Avenue, NW, Suite 300, Washington DC, 20009.
Tel: (+1) 202 775 8917.
Fax: (+1) 202 429 0271.
E-mail: kellyiwf@aol.com
Web site: www.iwforum.org

Society for Human Resource Management,
1800 Duke Street, Alexandria, Virginia, 22314.
Tel: (+1) 703 548 3440.
Fax: (+1) 703 535 6490.
E-mail: shrm@ahrm.org
Web site: www.shrm.org

Junior Chamber International,
World Headquarters, P.O. Box 140577, Coral Gables, Florida, 33114.
Tel: (+1) 305 446 7608.
Fax: (+1) 305 442 0041.
E-mail: jci@jcimail.com
Web site: www.juniorchamber.com

International Associations

The Customer Service Network,
P.O. Box 1196, Cheddar, BS27 3ES.
Tel: (+44) 01934 741 102.
Fax: (+44) 01934 741 113.
E-mail: info@customernet.com

British American Chamber of Commerce,
8 Staple Inn, London, WC1V 7QH.
Tel: (+44) 020 7404 6400.
Fax: (+44) 020 7404 4544.
E-mail: enquiries@bacc.co.uk
Web site: www.bacc.org

Organisations for Self-employed People

UK

OwnBase (The National Association for Home-based Working),
Birchwood, Hill Road South, Helsby, Frodsham, WA6 9PT.
E-mail: ownbase@jcoleman-smith.freeserve.co.uk

Business Opportunities Digest,
28 Charles Square, London, N1 6HT.
Tel: (+44) 0171 417 1710.

UK and International

BNI (Business Network International) Breakfast Clubs:

UK: Gate End, Northwood, Middlesex, HA6 3QG.
Tel: (+44) 01923 826 181 or 0800 018 6181.
Fax: (+44) 01923 827 813.
E-mail: bninet@aol.com

US: 199 S. Monte Vista Avenue, Suite 6, San Dinas, CA, 91773-3080.
Tel: (+1) 909 305 1818.
Fax: (+1) 909 305 1811.
Web site: www.bni-europe.com (UK and Europe)
Web site: www.bni.com (International)

Women's Networking Organisations

There are numerous women's organisations in many countries, a large number of which are for people working in particular fields; for example, journalism, the arts, finance and travel. Details of such organisations will be available in directories in your own country. Also, as mentioned in Chapter 1, many top corporations, particularly in the US, have their own networks for women. We list here some organisations which have a more general appeal.

British Association of Women Entrepreneurs (BAWE),
114 Gloucester Place, London, W1H 3DB.
Tel: (+44) 020 7935 0085
Fax: (+44) 020 7224 0582.
E-mail: president@bawe-uk.org
Web site: www.bawe-uk.org
World Association of Women Business Owners (BAWE is the UK arm of this organisation).
Web site: www.fcem.org

European Women's Management Development Network (EWMD)
Avenue Louise 149, B-1050 Brussels, Belgium.
Tel: (+32) 2 535 9771.
Fax: (+32) 2 535 7499.
E-mail: info@ewmd.org
Web site: www.ewmd.org

Network for Successful UK Women,
Perran Cottage, New Road, Swanmore, SO32 2PE.
Tel: (+44) 01489 893 910.
E-mail: netwomen@enterprise.net
Web site: www.netwomenuk.org

National Federation of Women's Institutes,
104 New Kings Road, London, SW6 4LY.
Tel: (+44) 020 7371 9300.
Fax: (+44) 020 7736 3652.
E-mail: hq@nfwi.org.uk
Web site: www.nfwi.org.uk

National Union of Townswomen Guilds,
Chamber of Commerce House, Harbourne Road, Birmingham, West
Midlands, B15 3BU.
Tel: (+44) 0121 456 3435.
Fax: (+44) 0121 452 1890.
E-mail: tghq@townswomen.org.uk
Web site: www.townswomen.org.uk

The Professional Family Women's Network,
4 Waverley Gardens, Barking, Essex, IG11 0BQ
Tel/Fax: (+44) 020 8594 2811.
E-mail: paula@pfwm.org.uk
Web site: www.pfwm.org.uk

Men's Networking Organisations

Most of the men's associations tend to be either clubs or charitable
associations and many of them can only be joined by invitation. Some
of the longest established men's associations are now also open to
women. Recent legislation also seems to be having an effect on
organisations that seek to exclude sectors of the community,
particularly on the grounds of gender. Examples of organisations
focused mainly on men are Freemasons, Lions, Round Table, Scouts.

YMCA England,
640 Forrest Road, Walthamstow, London, E17 3DZ.
Tel: (+44) 020 8520 5599.
Web site: www.ymca.org.uk

Also, mainly for men:
Rotary International in Great Britain and Ireland, Kinwarton Road,
Alcester, Warwickshire, B49 6BP.
Tel: (+44) 01789 765411.
Web: www.ribi.org
E-mail: secretary@ribi.org

NLP Associations

The Association for Neuro-Linguistic Programming (ANLP),
P.O. Box 10, Porthmadog, LL48 6ZB.
Tel: (+44) 0870 8704970.
Fax: (+44) 0870 444 0790.
E-mail: admin@anlp.org
Web site: www.anlp.org

The Business NLP Group,
66 Belgrade Road, London, N16 8DJ.
Tel: (+44) 020 7249 7472.
Fax: (+44) 020 7249 7472.
E-mail: businessmatters@geo2.poptel.org.uk

The NLP Education Network,
39 Jennings Road, St. Albans, Herts, AL1 4NX.
Tel: (+44) 01727 869782.
Fax: (+44) 01727 842 181.
E-mail: ednet@new-oceans.co.uk
Web site: www.new-oceans.co.uk/ednet

The UK NLP Health Network,
16 White Horse Road, London, E6 6DP.
Tel: (+44) 0208 475 0386.
E-mail: nlp@sherridge.freeserve.co.uk

Trainset®
Trainset House, P.O. Box 8505, London, NW6 3SS.
Tel: (+44) 020 7692 7373.
E-mail: info@trainset.org

Central London NLP Group.
E-mail: postmaster@nlpgroup.freeserve.co.uk
Web site: www.nlpgroup.freeserve.co.uk

LET (Local currency exchange) Schemes

Letslink UK
Tel: (+44) 01705 730 639

lets-link — The National LETs Magazine,
Basement Flat, 54 Campbell Road, Southsea, Hants, PO5 1RW.
Tel: (+44) 01705 730639.
Fax: (+44) 01705 730639.
E-mail: lets@letslinkuk.demon.co.uk
Web site: www.letslinkuk.demon.co.uk

Health and Fitness Associations

Society of Teachers of the Alexander Technique
Tel: (+44) 0207 351 0828.

The Professional Association of Alexander Teachers
Tel: (+44) 01642 363542.

Feldenkrais Guild UK
Tel: (+44) 07000 785 506.

North American Society of Teachers of the Alexander Technique
Tel: (+1) 612 824 5066.

Canadian Society of Teachers of the Alexander Technique
Tel: (+1) 514 522 9230.

New Zealand Feldenkrais Guild
Tel: (+64) 649 378 8091.

South African Society of Teachers of the Alexander Technique
Tel: (+27) 021 47 0436.

Australian Feldenkrais Guild
Tel: (+61) 8 8269 7783.

Australian Society of Teachers of the Alexander Technique
Tel: (+61) 008 339 571.

Carol Harris

Management Magic,
P.O. Box 47, Welshpool, Powys, Wales, SY21 7NX, UK.
E-mail: management.magic@border.org.uk
Web site: www.border.org.uk

Index

Meta Model, 139–41, 142
Meta Programmes, 169–74; *see also* motivation; Neuro-Linguistic Programming
Microsoft Outlook, 29
Milton Model, 142
mind mapping, 85–6, 203
monitoring, 8, 67, 94, 243–52; *see also* evaluation
motivation, 8, 49, 57–65, 93, 103–7, 138, 146, 180, 247
  "carrot and stick", 58–9, 170
  challenge and skill, 107
  depth of information, 62–4, 170
  levels of, 103–7
  "me or you", 59–61, 170
  "the rule book", 61–2, 170
  theories of, 103
  what do you notice?, 64–5, 170
  see also language; Neuro-Linguistic Programming
movement, 101, 112, 176, 180, 181, 182, 184–6, 190, 191–4; *see also* Action Profiling; gesture; posture
mutuality, 2, 13, 14, 26, 156

network, 16–17
  "active" and "inactive", 28, 29–30, 31–2
  analysing your, 25–6
  building your, 33–41
  business development, 223
  developmental, 229–30
  diagram, 24–5
  identifying your, 23–6, 47
  keeping in touch with your, 29–32
  managing your, 26–32; *see also* information
  profession or function, 222
  responding to contacts, 32–3
  setting up; *see under* networking
  shapes of, 16–17
  structures of, 16
  targeting your, 26
  types of, 16
  versus organisation, 17
  who could be included in your?, 23–5
networking, 1–2
  activities, 13, 49–50, 57, 72, 84–5, 89, 152
    desirable, 84–5
    essential, 84–5
    possible, 84–5
  and motivation; *see* motivation
  approaches to, 51–7, 57–65
  attitudes towards, 45–6
  benefits of, 17–20
    business applications, 18–19
    information handling, 19
    personal and social applications, 18
    skills development, 20
    social contact and support, 19
  contexts, 13–14, 33–41, 44–5, 102
  definition, 2, 13–14
  distance, *see* distance networking
  drawbacks, 21
    administration, 21
    availability, 21
    health, 21
    personal inclinations, 21
    time, 21
  elements of effective, 4–6, 73–4
  examples, 11–13, 18, 30, 35, 37, 38, 39, 40, 41, 59, 61, 62, 64, 65, 68, 72–3, 75, 76–7, 78, 79, 80, 81, 84, 88, 90, 91, 94–5, 115, 116–17, 118–19, 120, 123, 124, 125, 126, 127, 138, 149, 158–60, 164, 165, 166, 167, 170–3, 174–5, 196, 212–13, 220, 221–2, 223, 224, 226, 229, 230, 248
  experience of, 43–5, 48
  face-to-face, 9, 70, 72, 79, 129–94

states (cont'd)
  psychological, 176–7
    aggressive, 176
    assertive, 177–8
    non-assertive/submissive, 177
strategic thinking, 69–73
  commitments and
    responsibilities, 70
  needs and desires, 71–2
  personal situation and lifestyle,
    69–70
  preferences, abilities and
    experience, 70–1
  resources, 71
strategy, 7, 25, 7, 67, 69–73
  creating, 72
style and shape, 117, 119
support, 90
  groups, 223–5
SWOT analysis, 73

tactics, 7, 67, 69, 80–1
T'ai Chi, 182
team roles, 1–2
technology, 15, 214–16
telephone, 14, 30, 52, 70, 80, 82, 89,
  102, 105–6, 150, 209–13, 232
  follow-up, 211
  gatekeeping, 211
  manner, 210–11
  messages, 212
  timing, 210
Thatcher, Margaret, 119
thoughts, 3, 5, 6, 98, 99, 100–1, 163,
  165–6, 177, 193, 246–7
tidiness, 88–9
time, 21, 71, 79, 86–7, 90, 237
training courses, 39
Transactional Analysis, 176
travelling, 35–7

values, 5, 6, 155, 163, 166–7, 174–5,
  247–8
venue, 232, 238, 239
visitors and guest presenters, 240

visualisation, 51, 57, 96–7, 104–6,
  106–7, 177, 182, 247, 253
voice, 50, 94, 105–6, 112, 246
  exercises, 134–8
  warming up, 134, 137–8
  see also breathing; posture;
    speech
voluntary organisations, 233–4
Vroom, Victor, 103

waiting rooms, 41
wardrobe; *see* dress
wisdom, 27
word of mouth, 235
writing to contacts, 200
  brochures, newsletters and
    bulletins, 201–6
    content, 205–6
    grammar, punctuation,
      spelling and word use,
      203–4
    precision, 205
    sentence length, 204–5
    signposting, 202
    structuring, 202–3
    tense, 205
    writing style, 202
  business letters, 200
written/printed material, 53, 196–
  209
  design elements, 199–200, 202
    colour, 199
    format and layout, 199–200,
      202
    graphics, 200
    materials, 200
    paper type/quality, 199
    typeface, 199
  letter-writing; *see* writing to
    contacts
  types of, 196–7
  see also business stationery;
    promotional items

Yoga, 182